SOCIAL MEDIA

HOW TO ENGAGE, SHARE, AND CONNECT

SECOND EDITION

REGINA LUTTRELL

ROWMAN & LITTLEFIELD
Lanham • Boulder • New York • London

Published by Rowman & Littlefield
A wholly owned subsidary of The Rowman & Littlefield Publishing Group, Inc.
4501 Forbes Boulevard, Suite 200, Lanham, Maryland 20706
www.rowman.com

Unit A, Whitacre Mews, 26-34 Stannary Street, London SE11 4AB, United Kingdom

British Library Cataloguing in Publication Information Available

Library of Congress Cataloging-in-Publication Data
Names: Luttrell, Regina, 1975- author.
Title: Social media : how to engage, share, and connect / Regina Luttrell.
Description: Second edition. | Lanham : Rowman & Littlefield, [2016] | Includes bibliographical references and index.
Identifiers: LCCN 2016016521 (print) | LCCN 2016026055 (ebook) |
    ISBN 9781442265233 (cloth : alk. paper) | ISBN 9781442265240 (pbk. : alk. paper) |
    ISBN 9781442265257 (electronic)
Subjects: LCSH: Online social networks. | Social media. | Public relations.
Classification: LCC HM742 .L874 2016 (print) | LCC HM742 (ebook) | DDC 302.23/1—dc23
LC record available at https://lccn.loc.gov/2016016521

∞™ The paper used in this publication meets the minimum requirements of American National Standard for Information Sciences—Permanence of Paper for Printed Library Materials, ANSI/NISO Z39.48-1992.

Printed in the United States of America

Brief Contents

Contents

Part II   Formulating a Strategy   51

Part III   The Social Media Plan   187

15   The Roadmap to Success: Developing a Social Media Plan   189

Figures

Now, more than ever, this book is important to read. Social media has fundamentally changed the way businesses connect with customers. Smart businesses embrace the change and understand that consumers now have a voice and expect to be heard. The businesses that don't change are the ones getting left behind.

Think about this for a moment. Facebook has more than 1 billion users around the world. Each minute, more than three hundred hours of new videos are uploaded to YouTube. And people spend more time on social media than any other online activity, including email. The ability to share content has reached unprecedented levels.

Social media has supercharged our ability to share, and yes, sometimes we share too much. Smart brands are finding new ways through social media to interact with customers and prospects, showing that the value of social media is more than just talking about what you ate for breakfast.

In the following chapters you'll learn how to transform your business into a social organization with concrete examples of how to develop, manage, and measure social media efforts to reach business objectives.

As an invited speaker to numerous conferences around the world, I am frequently asked, "Does social media work?" That's like asking if a stick works. Depends upon your objective. A stick works for propping open a door. It obviously works less well for doing delicate eye surgery. Social media is just a tool. You have to choose—and properly use—the right tool for the right job. You'll learn in this book how to properly use social media for a variety of business objectives, including how to develop a comprehensive social media plan.

Social media plays a pivotal role in the success of the award-winning Pure Michigan tourism campaign. A few winters ago, our organization generated $17 million in public relations buzz around the world at virtually no cost by responding quickly to an obscure tweet. A tweet from the travel blog *Awesome Mitten* reacted to Travel Wisconsin's depiction of that state as a mitten. The initial tweet only received eleven retweets. Rather than ignore it, we quickly launched a website called WhoIsTheRealMittenState.com, with opportunities for visitors to vote, live tweet, and post messages.

An ensuing, good-natured social media debate was initially picked up by Michigan press outlets, then Wisconsin, then national and international news outlets, ultimately generating nearly 400 million media impressions around the world. The funniest headline, from Gawker, said, "Dumbest War Ever Erupts Online: States Fighting over Which Looks Most like a Mitten." In the end, Pure Michigan and Travel Wisconsin joined in a campaign to collect mittens for charity. The flurry of social media activity lasted three weeks and cost Pure Michigan virtually nothing except some staff time. The "mitten debate" is an example of real-time content marketing, a social media best practice. Rather than see the initial tweet as a distraction, we listened to fans and gave them more of what they wanted.

If we were not monitoring our tweets, if we were not quick to act, we would have missed the opportunity. We have opportunities like this daily to engage our fans, build advocates, and make Michigan one of the most talked about destinations on the social web. This book will teach you social media best practices like this, which can be applied to your business today.

I'm honored to call Dr. Regina "Gina" Luttrell a colleague and a friend. The first edition of this book received rave reviews and is used by numerous universities across the nation. With her deep background in corporate public relations, marketing, and social media strategy, Gina provides real-world experience in how social media fits into an overall marketing communications program. This book is a must-read for any social media practitioner, public relations professional, business owner, or executive who is looking for something easy to read, comprehend, and execute.

I've known Gina for years, and I remember that in one of our first meetings I told her how Pure Michigan ranks number one or two on more social networks than any other state tourism brand, as measured by number of followers. We're proud of that, but that's not how we measure the success of our social efforts. We look at whether we are reaching the right audience and getting them to engage with our content. When it comes to followers, why is quality better than quantity? Well, you'll have to read the book to find out.

Chad W. Wiebesick
Executive in Residence at Eastern Michigan
University's Center for Digital Engagement
VP of Integrated Marketing & Communications,
Ann Arbor Area Convention & Visitors Bureau

The profound effect that social media has had on the communications industry is arguably even more important to the field of public relations. The emergence of social media technologies inspired the development of a new marketing model—one that promotes the user as an integral part of the conversation rather than merely an onlooker.

Written in a relaxed and pragmatic tone, this book is succinct and practical in nature. The intent is for the publication to serve as a guide to better understand, create, and develop sound social media strategies. The reader can either choose to complete the book in its entirety or refer to single chapters related to a topic of interest to them. With that in mind, it is my hope that the book presents itself as a unique practical guide and a "go-to" reference related to all things social media. Each individual chapter is meant to introduce and expose the reader to a specific topic; however, when combined with topics presented within other chapters, the entirety of the book is able to guide practitioners through the process of creating successful social media campaigns.

Audience for the Text

This book is useful for both students and public relations and social media practitioners. Students are presented with an applied approach to social media that is rooted in the history of the industry and are exposed to the supporting theories. Ideally, theory should inform practice within the field. I have selected the best from social media management and also introduce students to new models, allowing further insights into processes and practice. Practitioners will gain valuable practical insights into the applications of social media and enhance their understanding and execution of social media technologies. The design of this publication is intended to help those who are, or intend to become, part of social media planning within an organization. Individuals with a background in public relations, marketing, advertising, corporate communications, or management may find themselves pulled into social media strategies at some point in their careers. The information provided within these pages should help guide these inputs and decisions on social media strategy, ultimately resulting in a more effective and robust process.

Organization of the Text

This text is broken into three sections, with part I, "The Advancement of an Industry," covering the first three chapters. Chapter 1 introduces readers to the Four Quadrants of Public Relations and how social media integrates within each area. Chapter 2 provides the historical context of social media. Readers are presented with a new social media model, the Circular Model of SoMe for Social Communication (*Sh*are, *o*ptimize, *Ma*nage, *e*ngage) and the role it plays as a central function in social media planning. Finally, chapter 3 highlights how social media and public relations work together with marketing and advertising.

Part II, "Formulating a Strategy," includes chapters 4 to 14, which focus on the various social media tools available to develop creative, engaging, and meaningful social media plans. From social networking sites to photo sharing and crisis communication strategies, these chapters are filled with nuggets of information and practical examples that every practitioner will benefit from.

Last, part III, "The Social Media Plan," contains the concluding chapter, chapter 15, which outlines the different aspects of a social media plan. Each step that contributes to the strategic planning of a social media plan is explored, including key metrics. Comprehensive case studies are also provided as learning tools and can be analyzed, deconstructed, and applied within the framework of your own organizational social media planning.

New to This Edition

This second edition includes updated case studies, international relations callout boxes, infographics throughout the text to reinforce content, and two new chapters:

"Social Media Ethics": With the constant presence of social media, professionals have unearthed many opportunities for reaching and engaging their audiences. This has become a two-way street of mutual benefit for both a company and its consumers. The freedom to select what consumers want to read and whom they want to befriend results in new ethical challenges for practitioners. Included within this new chapter are examples of ethical issues faced by companies today and a guide to making solid ethical decisions.

"'Sticky' Social Media": Consumers are exposed to hundreds of social media messages daily. But how many of those messages or images do people truly remember? For years professionals have referred to memorable campaigns as "sticky." Why? Well, because they stick with the consumer well after the person has been exposed to the message. Developing a "sticky social" campaign requires a different approach than we have ever seen. This chapter provides a set of rules for launching effective social media campaigns in a world transformed by new social rules. Readers will explore several "sticky social" examples and what made these efforts catch on and, more importantly, spread.

Unique Features of the Text

There are various "Theory into Practice" case studies scattered throughout the chapters of the text. Each case study provides the reader with real-world examples of successful campaigns related to the topics presented within the chapter. This feature is intended to help guide practitioners toward a contemporary understanding of the public relations profession as it stands today, as well as to provide a foundation to create a comprehensive social media plan based on a practical, professional basis.

Quick links are also provided in each chapter to help readers connect more deeply with the presented topics. I invite readers to join me in the conversation on Twitter (@ginaluttrell) by using #LRNSMPR to discuss the book, ask questions, or chat about the links provided.

There is an abundance of infographics to summarize chapter contents, as well as international relations callout boxes to highlight how European corporations are utilizing social media to connect with people.

Finally, a book such as this would not be complete without interviews with professionals. You will find commentary from some of the greatest minds in the industry interspersed throughout the book. A series of videos, available at http://ginaluttrellphd.com/videos, further enhance content presented within the material.

Finally, to help with course preparation, ancillary materials, including an instructor's manual with sample assignments and chapter prompts, as well as slides of infographics and illustrations included in the book, may be obtained from the publisher; email textbooks@rowman.com for details.

Acknowledgments

A project such as this could not be completed without a great deal of support from others. To the people who always believe in me, encourage me, and warm my heart, Todd, Emma, and Avery. And my little Coco Bean, for being my faithful writing companion.

Thank you once again to Rowman & Littlefield for investing in a second edition so soon after the release of the first. Much appreciation to my senior editor, Leanne Silverman, and to her assistants, Karie Simpson and Carli Hansen, for being a constant source of support. A special note of appreciation to Leah Rodriguez for working on the ancillary materials and whose youthful outlook provided much inspiration.

For this second edition, a big thank-you to all who contributed: Chad Wiebesick, Caitlyn Tuzzolino, Edelman, LEWIS Pulse, Likable Media, and Marco Seric.

To the students and professionals who will read this book, I thank you as well. I hope my passion for social media, public relations, marketing, and communications shines through. Feel free to connect with me on Twitter (@ginaluttrell). I can't wait to engage, share, and connect with you!

Introduction: "But I Already Know Social Media"

Think about this for a moment: more than half of all human beings on this planet are currently under the age of thirty.

There's also a good chance that you, reading this book, might belong to this group.

If you find yourself in this demographic, there is a high probability that you have never known life without the Internet, never held a phone in your hand that has a cord that is attached to the wall, most likely never gushed with excitement at a new set of bound encyclopedias on the bookshelf, and while you may be a fan of music, you probably listen to the majority of music on your laptop, iPod, or phone.

Much of your time is spent on Snapchat, Instagram, and Twitter. These social media platforms are almost a part of your DNA. Being connected has been the norm for about as long as you can remember. In fact,

- One-third of women aged eighteen to thirty-four say that they check Facebook when they first wake up in the morning—even before going to the bathroom![1]
- One in six marriages around the world now happen because of people who met using online social networks.[2]
- If Facebook were a country, it would be the third-most populated country in the world based on the size of its user base.[3]
- Adults who actively use Twitter rank it as the most timely source for news and events, largely surpassing "traditional" media outlets, including cable news channels.[4]

With all of this in mind, you may ask yourself, Why do I need this book? I already know social media. I live it every single day. In fact, it is safe to say, I can't live without it.

You need this book because it's different from any other textbook you've experienced. You may know how to tweet or snap an ephemeral picture message, but those experiences are personal. This book flips everything you know, or think you know, about social media around. This text examines social media through the eyes of a business.

Social media has profoundly changed the way consumers engage with brands and with one another—the effects of which the public relations world has only begun to distinguish and understand in the past several years.

As brands strive to build relationships and engage in dialog with consumers, the investment toward doing so continues to increase. In fact, 71 percent of companies plan to increase their digital marketing spending this year by an average of 27 percent.[5] Serving as facilitators for the world's content architects, these social platforms provide an unprecedented avenue for the posting and exchange of information and ideas.

As my friend Ryan Schram, chief operating officer of IZEA, so aptly put it, "Social is merely a 'teenager' in terms of how long it has been around as a concept, let alone actively in the lives of the people who participate in it."

From public relations directors to social media strategists, professionals within the industry are taking notice. Having their brands represented in the "conversations" across various social channels has become a central aspect of the planning process.

Yet so many professionals in the industry are vastly unprepared to engage.

Why? Because it is likely they only understand social media through a personalized lens.

In this book you learn how to interpret business objectives, understand when C-suite executives talk about the "bottom line," become intimately familiar with strategic approaches to social media planning and evaluating, and comprehend the connections between public relations and other areas of marketing. The focus uses a strategic approach to build and sustain brand relationships using coordinated efforts across the social sphere.

Social media make up a digitally enabled, mobile environment that embraces the real-time attributes that consumers themselves not only willingly participate in but constantly update. Over 2.8 billion people have access to the Internet, and 74 percent of online adults use social media. Taking part in social media provides businesses a multitude of opportunities to:

improve brand loyalty through storytelling and content marketing;
increase conversation rates by interacting with current and prospective customers;
leverage social media to increase brand awareness and recognition;
build credibility by increasing the amount of consumer engagement and number
of followers;
develop relationship capital through building strong and meaningful relationships
through social channels.

Practitioners will quickly realize that the strategies and concepts presented within the book can aid in the identification of many potential pitfalls that brands face and, better yet, help discover a myriad of valuable opportunities for their organizations. Readers will gain a clear understanding of how to compete and engage appropriately using social media in a competitive environment.

Social media has most certainly changed the world forever. The time is now to learn how the social sphere works.

Shall we begin?

Notes

[1] Ben Parr, "The First Thing Young Women Do in the Morning: Check Facebook [STUDY]," *Mashable*, July 6, 2010, http://mashable.com/2010/07/06/oxygen-facebook-study.

[2] Chadwick Martin Bailey, "Match.com and Chadwick Martin Bailey 2009–2010 Studies: Recent Trends: Online Dating," Match.com, last modified March 2010, accessed January 28, 2014, http://cp.match.com/cppp/media/CMB_Study.pdf.

[3] Graeme McMillan, "If Facebook Was a Country, It'd Be Larger Than China in Three Years," Digital Trends, February 6, 2013, http://www.digitaltrends.com/social-media/facebook-could-be-larger-than-china-in-three-years-time.

[4] Amy Mitchell and Dana Page, "Twitter News Consumers: Young, Mobile and Educated," Pew Research Center, last modified November 2013, accessed January 28, 2014, http://www.journalism.org/files/2013/11/Twitter-IPO-release-with-cover-page.pdf.

[5] David Moth, "71% of Businesses Plan to Increase Digital Marketing Budgets This Year: Report," Econsultancy, February 3, 2014, accessed November 30, 2015, https://econsultancy.com/blog/64248-71-of-businesses-plan-to-increase-digital-marketing-budgets-this-year-report-2.

THE ADVANCEMENT OF AN INDUSTRY

1 PART

The Four Quadrants of Public Relations

1

This chapter explores the four quadrants that public relations professionals work in—media, community, business, and government—paying particular attention to their interrelationship and how social media plays an ever-present, integral role.

The Four Quadrants of Public Relations Explained

In 1944 Rex Harlow wrote "Public Relations at the Crossroads," wherein he summarizes the duties of public relations professionals. In essence, Harlow highlights that public relations professionals contend with a myriad of relationships, including internal and external relations, personal relations, personnel relations, industrial relations, stockholder relations, board of directors' relations, customer relations, government relations, supplier-creditor relations, community relations, trade relations, opinion surveys, advertising, and publicity. Additionally, Harlow also notes that public relations responsibilities of the time generally include press, radio, motion pictures, printing, public speaking, and professional writing.[1]

Even in today's rapid-paced work environment, Harlow's insights still ring true, as those of us in the public relations profession understand that we have to be able to do it all. In fact, it is now an expectation that we serve as experts in multiple arenas within the field to be triumphant in supporting the companies and organizations that we represent.

What is implied, but not directly stated, in Harlow's summary of the profession are the Four Quadrants of Public Relations. The idea is simple. Within these four quadrants, all functions of public relations fall. To be well versed in each quadrant, while also understanding each individual element, is critical to the development of today's public relations practitioners. The Four Quadrants of Public Relations include

1. *Media*—inclusive of publicity, as well as traditional and social press
2. *Community*—inclusive of internal, external, online, employee, consumer, and personal interactions
3. *Business*—inclusive of investor relations, C-suite executive advisement, and social care (customer service)
4. *Government*—inclusive of political, lobbying, public affairs, and issues management

Public relations practitioners should think of each element as completely interrelated and strive to incorporate aspects of all four quadrants into their daily activities in order to develop a higher level of strategic implementation.

Success is realized when public relations professionals include all four quadrants in the public relations planning process. However, the supporting concepts behind the Four Quadrants of Public Relations are not new. *The novelty lies in how these quadrants are grouped and explained in an interrelated fashion.* Public relations practitioners have a defined responsibility to mediate between an organization and its public to build relationships with a variety of stakeholders by disseminating information to the public as well as seeking or collecting information. This information, or

The Four Quadrants of Public Relations. *Source*: Regina Luttrell.

feedback, often provides public relations practitioners and their organizations with insight into how the public perceives the organization and its operations. Utilizing this open, two-way, symmetrical communication, as exemplified in the Grunig-Hunt model, allows for a higher level of mutual understanding and offers a more balanced approach to consumer-company interactions.[2] Communication should ideally move between an organization and its publics effectively. The symmetrical communication model is one of the more robust models that public relations professionals practice because this model promotes a greater sense of engagement with an organization's targeted audience by listening, connecting, and facilitating through action rather than merely pushing messages out.[3] A continual, open line of communication between a public relations practitioner and the publics being served is essential in our digital age of socially driven public relations activities.

Historically speaking, the idea of open communication has always been at the cornerstone of defining public relations.[4] Going forward, it will become increasingly important to focus on sustaining an open model of communication with the public. The theory behind the Four Quadrants of Public Relations relies heavily on this type of engagement in order to interact with various publics, and since social media is also founded on the open communication concept, this communication model will take on considerable importance.

With this in mind, it is essential to understand how the four-quadrant model relies on any single segment building upon another, yet maintaining its interconnectedness with all of the other segments. Let's examine how each segment works individually and then how they work together.

Quadrant 1: Media Relations

In practice, public relations professionals work closely with the media to distribute their messages to the public. The media (specifically news sources, inclusive of online, television, print, radio, and electronic media) have long been viewed by the public as trustworthy and highly regarded.[5] It is the job of public relations professionals to build strong, mutually respectful relationships with journalists. Traditionally, public relations practitioners manage their media-relations responsibilities by sending press releases and pitch emails, arranging interviews, organizing press conferences, and responding to media inquiries.[6]

The outcomes of these efforts are easy to recognize each time we turn on the television to watch the nightly news. The information that is shared during these telecasts is carefully, tactfully, and strategically "placed" by public relations practitioners across America. To the untrained eye, the news is presented in a manner that appears as though a journalist researched the story, gathered the interviewees, and put the thirty-second TV news spot together. In truth, many of these news stories are actually the fruit of diligent public relations practitioners. It is our job as professionals to identify a newsworthy trend and capitalize on it.

For example, the American Bar Association (ABA) is frequently reported on in the news. This organization has been regularly referenced in news stories in both local and national news outlets, as well as in major print publications. Responsibilities of the media relations division within the ABA include serving as the organization's press secretary, as well as ensuring that the messages and issues of the ABA are reported accurately by providing the correct resources to journalists communicating the stories.[7]

When the ABA launched Operation Enduring LAMP, a mobilization of America's lawyers to aid those called up for active military service, the timing and focus of the news conference were developed by the public relations practitioner to ensure the best possible results for placement and coverage. Because of the practitioner's relationships with the media, the event generated national network and newspaper coverage, which in turn benefited the association by swelling its ranks with a large number of new pro bono lawyers to help in the effort.[8] The newsworthy trend here relates to services offered to active military personnel as the timing of this initiative coincided with the onset of the war in Iraq.

When Downsize Fitness, a consortium of fitness centers that exclusively caters to overweight clientele, reached out to Zapwater Communications to assist in creating a media campaign focused on increasing awareness about the fitness centers and subsequently driving an uptick in membership applications, the results turned into front-page national news. The challenge here was to differentiate Downsize Fitness from typical, run-of-the-mill fitness centers. With the focus of the media pitches being based on the owner's own struggle with weight loss, Zapwater Communications dedicated its efforts to reaching out to daily newspapers and broadcast media. The initial media win came in the form of securing a feature article in the *Chicago Tribune* by health and fitness writer Julie Deardorff. Publication of this article spurred a flurry of additional media hits, and the story was ultimately syndicated in more than 120 news outlets.[9] PBS *Nightly Business Report* ran a segment on the founder and the newest fitness trend to hit America.[10] This publicity campaign, dubbed "Downsize Fitness: Downsizing the Obesity Epidemic," won the grand prize at the 2013 Bulldog Awards for Excellence in Media Relations and Publicity.[11]

Typically, campaigns like Operation Enduring LAMP and Downsize Fitness are built on a coordinated use of varied communication techniques and tools employed by public relations practitioners and the instinct to know what stories are "pitch perfect." Pitching the right story is dependent upon a practitioner's ability to spot and capitalize on newsworthy trends occurring around the world. Practitioners work with the media to place editorials in newspapers; produce video and audio news releases; arrange radio, TV, print, and social media interviews; promote websites for their organizations; and offer easy access to additional materials that complement the news stories. By leveraging a company or organization's best assets, including subject matter experts, and seizing the news of the day, media relations can be leveraged to strategically build a favorable image, to educate the public, or to use the ensuing public opinion as a court of appeal.

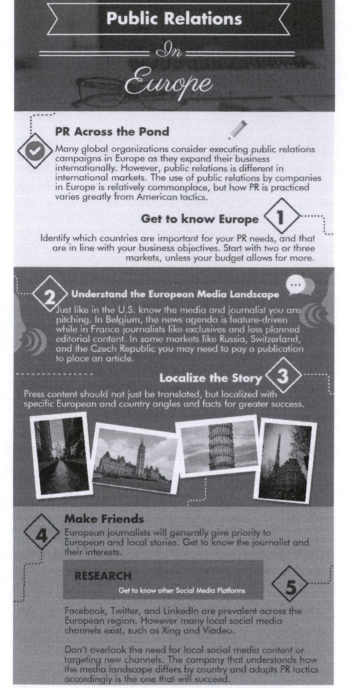

Public Relations

In

Europe

PR Across the Pond

Many global organizations consider executing public relations campaigns in Europe as they expand their business internationally. However, public relations is different in international markets. The use of public relations by companies in Europe is relatively commonplace, but how PR is practiced varies greatly from American tactics.

Get to know Europe ⟨1⟩

Identify which countries are important for your PR needs, and that are in line with your business objectives. Start with two or three markets, unless your budget allows for more.

⟨2⟩ **Understand the European Media Landscape**

Just like in the U.S. know the media and journalist you are pitching. In Belgium, the news agenda is feature-driven while in France journalists like exclusives and less planned editorial content. In some markets like Russia, Switzerland, and the Czech Republic you may need to pay a publication to place an article.

Localize the Story ⟨3⟩

Press content should not just be translated, but localized with specific European and country angles and facts for greater success.

⟨4⟩ **Make Friends**

European journalists will generally give priority to European and local stories. Get to know the journalist and their interests.

RESEARCH

Get to know other Social Media Platforms ⟨5⟩

Facebook, Twitter, and LinkedIn are prevalent across the European region. However many local social media channels exist, such as Xing and Viadeo.

Don't overlook the need for local social media content or targeting new channels. The company that understands how the media landscape differs by country and adapts PR tactics accordingly is the one that will succeed.

Sources: Boucetta, Yasmeen. 'LEWIS 360° – The Blog of Global Communications Agency, LEWIS PR.' LEWIS 360 The Blog of Global Communications Agency LEWIS PR Thinking about PR in Europe Five Considerations before You Board That Flight Comments. September 23, 2011. Accessed November 15, 2015. http://blog.lewispr.com/2011/09/european-pr.html.

Decker, Bill. "They Do Public Relations Differently in Other Countries." December 31, 2012. Accessed November 15, 2015. http://www.bizjournals.com/denver/blog/broadway_17th/2012/12/they-do-public-relations-differently.html.

It would be cliché to state that practitioners must be "out-of-the-box thinkers," but if we are to assess issues and trends successfully and identify the correct demographics within the public, then we must look beyond the typical confines previously presented.[12] The aforementioned examples highlight not only the importance of the relationship between the public relations practitioner and the media but also the varied job duties and skills required of a practitioner within his or her daily activities. It can be seen that the public relations practitioner is no longer responsible solely for delivering the message but also for creating the message, maintaining the message, and cultivating the message.

Quadrant 2: Community Relations

In addition to media playing a pivotal role in public relations, community relations also holds an equally important role in the success of public relations practitioners. The buzz surrounding corporate social responsibility (CSR) has become an integral component of community relations. With increasing frequency, companies and organizations are giving back to the communities in which they reside, which in turn require public relations practitioners representing these organizations to further cultivate the relationships between the organization and the community. The responsibility of community relations is the second of the four quadrants that we will explore.

We must remember that "community" no longer means just the physical community but also an online community. Today's public relations practitioners live with one foot in the real world and one in the virtual community. Public relations campaigns now require a great deal of effort from the public relations practitioner to support the organization's online activities, often promoted via Facebook pages, Pinterest boards, Twitter feeds with specific hashtag identifiers, videos, and photo-sharing sites (including Flickr and Instagram). Engaging the targeted audience online should now be considered a natural component of any public relations campaign planning process. A recent GAP study revealed that social media monitoring accounted for an average of 70 percent of a company's core public relations or communications budget.[13] Separately, participants of the study further indicated that overall social media activities accounted for 66 percent of an organization's public relations and communication allocations. These results illustrate that social media responsibilities have significantly increased and have emerged as a mainstream responsibility of public relations professionals.[14] Keep this idea in mind as we examine the second quadrant more closely.

As a rule, this role of "community liaison" helps develop crucial relationships within the community. Community relations practitioners are being asked to perform a multitude of tasks, including creation, implementation, and management of an organization's community awareness initiatives.[15] This means that these individuals promote community initiatives and programs inclusive of resource sharing, community education programs, workshops, events, and symposiums identified as key corporate areas for promotion. They are also the organizational resources who create strategic alliances with representatives of consumer, employee, and public interest groups; key provider practices; vendors; governmental agencies; and prominent community organizations.[16] Community relations practitioners may even participate in community activities surrounding corporate issues, including serving on committees, meeting with elected officials and politicians, sitting on various planning boards, attending and speaking at community board and similar meetings, creating timelines, attending various networking events, or performing other tasks.[17]

Corporations like General Electric, TOMS Shoes, IBM, Starbucks, Cisco, and Verizon are just a few examples of companies that are leading the way in a corporate citizenship revolution by contributing to the transformation and empowerment of the communities of which they are an integral part. This is beneficial not only for the communities but also for the corporations. It is the intention of the corporation to uphold its image and reputation within the community while also contributing in a positive way.

With this idea of corporate citizenship in mind, a variety of organizations have committed themselves to improving public education around the world. IBM, for example, is focused on preparing the next generation of leaders and workers as it supports community priorities and concerns. Through the KidSmart Early Learning Program, IBM exposes many of the world's remotely located and underprivileged students to new and exciting technologies that they would not normally have the chance to experience. Reading Companion, also part of IBM's initiatives, is an interactive software application that assists in learning to read.[18] By making this software available to the neediest populations, IBM is attempting to solve education's toughest problems with solutions that draw on advanced information technologies. To achieve its goals, IBM forms partnerships with states and school districts located in the United States, as well as in developing countries, to better research technology solutions designed to help support school reform efforts and raise student achievement.[19] Another example of a company that prides itself on giving back to the communities that it conducts business with is Cisco. The company has developed a community service campaign designated "GETideas" that establishes a global community focused on transforming trends within the educational sector. This program affords its communities a forum wherein education leaders can share resources, brainstorm ideas, and establish best practices related to evolving educational philosophies within schools.[20] GETideas.org establishes an online platform for educators to engage with and learn from one another, all the while informing and preparing the current generation more effectively than previous generations. Participants can visit the organization's website to gain valuable information, but, equally as important, visitors also have the opportunity to connect with other educators utilizing the initiative using Twitter, Pinterest, Facebook, and the organization's YouTube channel.

Kraft Foods Group also understands the importance of working with the community to achieve its goals. The company gives back to the community in various ways. Every April, Kraft Foods holds its annual company-wide celebration of volunteer service, Make an Impact. Employees from both the United States and Canada worked on more than four hundred volunteer projects that supported the company's community involvement priorities: fighting hunger and promoting healthy lifestyles.[21] In an email interview, Leah Bradford, associate director for corporate community involvement and vice president of the Kraft Foods Group Foundation, said, "Community Involvement is part of our heritage. Our employees have always had a passion for service and they share their time, talent and resources to support nonprofit organizations all year long. There are a number of issues facing our communities. We focus our efforts on areas where we can make the most impact. Hunger and obesity are serious challenges for society and our business. As a food company, we use our expertise in food and nutrition to fight hunger and promote healthy lifestyles across North America." Employees planted community gardens, sorted and packed donated items at food banks, and led activities that supported nutrition, education, and active play for children during their week of giving back. Consumers were able to interact with the company on its Facebook page not only to peruse photos of employees giving back at various locations across the United States and Canada but also to engage in conversations about the campaign. Additionally, Kraft Twitter followers participated by tweeting what they did to help out in their local communities during National Volunteer Week. For an initiative such as this, the responsibility for managing the company's social networking sites falls directly to the public relations practitioners.

These examples aim to highlight that a company's donations of capital or services, either within the actual community or online, become important contributions from a public relations standpoint. These initiatives provide a positive impact for the populations and communities that they touch and also for the organization in fostering good relationships in communities that directly impact brand and image.

Quadrant 3: Business Relations

In general, there are few successful organizations in business today that are exempt from establishing some level of a relationship with their immediate community. Organizations must strive to interact and connect with the public in a positive manner, which, in turn, affects their external image. In today's business landscape, there is an increased level of responsibility expected of the public relations practitioner to guide the CEO or other executive officials through the organization's public relations plan, reputation management, and brand management. For the past few years, the Edelman Trust Barometer survey has shown a slow recovery of credibility for CEOs. Currently, a mere 43 percent of those surveyed believe that CEOs are credible spokespeople.[22] The study revealed that more than half of the globally informed public thinks that the pace of development and change in business is too fast. Simply put, innovation is driven by greed and money rather than a desire to improve people's lives, and there is not enough government regulation of many industry sectors.[23] This perception can have obvious ramifications for a company's brand, image, bottom line, and ultimate ability to build trusting relationships with its consumers. By participating in a model of corporate citizenship, it is evident that one of the key responsibilities of a business is to be a good citizen. It is essential to understand that the function of the public relations department is to help businesses achieve a desired level of citizenship within the community. *Therefore, public relations must be a part of every department within a business.* This is an important takeaway. As a result, it is easy to see how business relations play a critical role in the daily lives of public relations practitioners.

The process of conducting daily business results in organizations performing a variety of public relations activities in order to stay involved with their publics. CEOs are being held accountable for the company's strategic plan. Public relations has always been responsible for closely monitoring its implementation, including assessing and addressing factors impeding successful execution of planned activities.

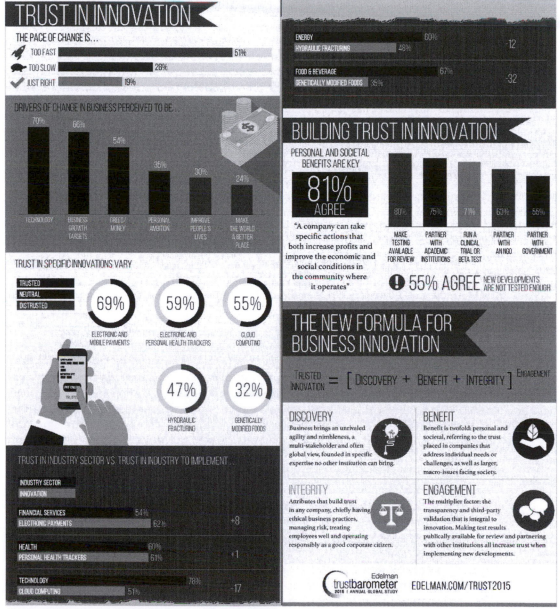

Source: Edelman Trust Barometer.

Strategic thinking should include—in addition to customary market and competitive obstacles—significant nation-state cultural, social, and political biases. To connect with consumers, companies will many times sign up as cosponsors of various events designed to advance human rights or address environmental opportunities.[24] Unfortunately, in recent years many companies have faced scandals that have tarnished their image. The messaging regarding the outcomes of these scandals also falls to the public relations practitioners to manage, but we will touch on that topic in the "crisis" chapter.

Corporate scandals have had an overwhelming impact on how the public assesses corporations, their leaders, and their securities.[25] Companies today must give back to society in order to regain public trust. Accountability and responsibility are differentiators in today's global workforce. Results from a recent Reputation Institute's Pulse Study indicate that a company's character is responsible for more than 40 percent of a company's reputation.[26] Corporate responsibility and accountability are interwoven. Public relations practitioners around the globe are being called on to help both for-profit and nonprofit businesses ensure "accountability" on all levels. As large corporations expand to new areas of the globe, the ability to conduct business successfully in other countries will be judged by how well these corporations operate in their home countries.[27]

The good news is that there has been a recent uptrend in businesses addressing these "mishandlings" of corporate citizenship scandals. This movement has been aided by the organizational onboarding of government officials or oversight entities within public relations plans. Some experts feel that having a government tie-in lends authenticity to the work the organization is trying to accomplish. This scenario may also be part of why the fourth quadrant of public relations, government relations, is on the rise.

Quadrant 4: Government Relations

Government relations have long been the foundation of the public relations industry dating back to the ancient Roman and Greek civilizations.[28] While not acknowledged as "public relations" at the time, the activities performed could unarguably be considered public relations tools and tactics. The use of persuasion within public speeches, holding of publicity events, and meeting with public officials would be interpreted as public relations activities as the role is characterized today.[29]

In the modern environment, practitioners participating in government relations are also known as public affairs officers or public affairs specialists. These practitioners frequently possess the difficult job of supporting the company's public policy initiatives as well as developing legislative and regulatory proposals on behalf of the company (while also simultaneously practicing effective public relations strategies). It is within their job responsibilities to maintain positive relationships with the legislature, since they work so closely with these elected officials. They are also accountable for lobbying the legislature in order to advocate on the behalf of legislation important to enhancing an organization in a strategic manner.

One example of note, Rock the Vote, will help clarify this concept. This public relations campaign was endorsed by politicians and political groups from both major political parties. More than twenty years ago, prior to the 1992 and 1996 presidential elections, a nationwide public relations campaign was launched focusing on the mass registration of young voters (ages eighteen to twenty-four). Resulting from the success of the inaugural 1992 Rock the Vote campaign, governmental agencies took notice and looked to achieve an even higher level of registered voter participation from this same demographic of voters in the coming election season. In 1996, Rock the Vote came to life again and has been a mainstay political initiative every election year since.

When this public relations campaign was rolled out in the early 1990s, younger voters only had the option of signing and addressing two types of post-cards pledging to vote. If we fast-forward to the current period, the emergence of social media has provided participants a myriad of convenient avenues allowing new voters to register.

Originally, in promoting the Rock the Vote initiative, public relations practitioners' utilized mass media and community events as their main avenues of distribution—specifically MTV. (Note the connection to media relations, community relations, and obviously government relations here.) The public relations agency responsible for this successful public relations campaign created various public service announcements that were aired on MTV around the clock, including nationwide radio announcements, coordinated traveling bus tours to register young voters, and famous personalities hired to endorse the importance of voting.[30] The campaign also targeted community events that younger voters would likely attend, such as concerts on college campuses.

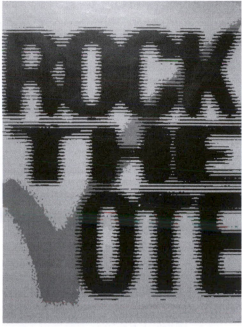

Original Rock the Vote Poster Used in the 1992 Public Relations Campaign. *Source*: Regina Luttrell.

Voter registration tables were set up at these events, allowing for convenient registration. The public relations campaign garnered phenomenal media attention and was a huge success. Efforts exhibited by the public relations practitioners during these two public relations campaigns reaped 2 million new young voters—the most new young voters in history at the time.[31] This public relations initiative ended a twenty-year cycle of declining voter participation and was decidedly considered a success, with a 20 percent increase in youth turnout compared to the previous 1988 presidential election.[32] Metrics related to success for the campaign were established by comparing the number of new voters with previously registered voters. Rock the Vote is still active today.

It should be mentioned that politicians also use public relations tactics for personal benefit as they conduct their daily activities and annual campaigns. These tactics become important in instances wherein a politician desires to raise money or attract votes. When politicians are successful at the ballot box, they use public relations to promote and defend their service in office, with an eye toward the next election. Public relations practitioners are responsible for leading the way in shaping these carefully worded messages as they coordinate speaking engagements; plan special events at nursing homes, churches, and daycare centers; write press releases; and ensure that the politician is on message each time. This is often accomplished by providing the political speaker with carefully thought-out talking points related to the key messages of interest.

Applying an Interconnected Approach

We can see that there are a large number of responsibilities and outcomes that rely on the skills of public relations practitioners. There is not a single formula for success. Specifically, let's look at media relations. This segment of public relations can be considered a free-standing, specialized function within the world of public relations,

Theory into Practice

Coca-Cola

How the Coca-Cola Company and its global initiative to fight obesity employs the Four Quadrants of Public Relations successfully.

Overview

In May 2013, the Coca-Cola Company launched a global initiative to help fight and prevent obesity. By offering lower-calorie and no-calorie beverage alternatives, providing a higher level of transparency regarding the nutritional information displayed on packaging, and ceasing to advertise to children less than twelve years of age, the company announced it would also support projects that reinforced the importance of physical activity in countries around the world where Coca-Cola conducts business. This includes the corporate headquarters located in Atlanta, Georgia.

This is an example of a public relations campaign that has utilized the Four Quadrants of Public Relations effectively.

Media

To launch the global initiative, Coca-Cola scheduled a press event wherein a pledge of $3.8 million was made on behalf of the Coca-Cola Foundation to support statewide programs that aided in promoting an active lifestyle. One such program included a local organization, Georgia SHAPE, which is spearheaded by the governor of Georgia.

Within the Coca-Cola Company's press center, information was provided to the media, including press releases related to the global initiative; partnerships with local organizations such as Georgia SHAPE; b-roll; photos of chairman and CEO of the Coca-Cola Company Muhtar Kent, Georgia governor Nathan Deal, and City of Atlanta mayor Kasim Reed; and other pertinent information ready-made for the media to use.

Community

By partnering with local organizations, the initiative promoted a number of company-coordinated public events wherein community members, families, and children participated in activities supporting physical activity. During each event, Coca-Cola provided participants with branded T-shirts and took photos and video footage that was used in its media kit, referred to as "Coming Together." The photos and videos were also used on the company website.

Business

Organizations across Georgia were awarded grants that supported Coca-Cola's global initiatives. Each business gained acknowledgment of its commitment to help foster a healthier lifestyle by being mentioned by name, as well as in the Coca-Cola Company press releases. Georgia SHAPE, supported by Governor Deal, was at the center of the press highlights and was included in the public event and on all written press releases.

Government

Georgia governor Nathan Deal took part in a press event where he publicly supported the efforts of the Coca-Cola Company. Within the company press release, Governor Deal is quoted as saying, "Working with Coca-Cola and others to strengthen programs such as Georgia SHAPE and Walk Georgia gives Georgians of all ages and abilities more opportunities to become physically active."

The governor's presence at the event, as well as the inclusion of his quote in the press release, implies to the public that the governor supports both the Coca-Cola brand and the initiatives it has launched. This partnership establishes a strong bond between the company and local government.

By taking a step back to see how this example integrates each of the Four Quadrants of Public Relations, it is easier to see how each independent quadrant contributes to a fully coordinated, successful public relations campaign executed by the Coca-Cola Company that benefits not only the local communities but also the company itself. Initiatives such as this help reinforce the Coca-Cola brand in a positive light. Additionally, partnering with a local nonprofit like Georgia SHAPE to launch an initiative of this type is a natural fit considering the new initiatives Coca-Cola supports.

Ultimately, the success of these types of initiatives is only as good as the public relations practitioner's ability to see the bigger picture. If any of the four quadrants are used independently rather than as an integrated effort, achievement of the overall goal can quickly dissipate.

View the full "Coming Together" press kit to read the official press release and to download b-roll, photos, and infographics: http://bit.ly/14nlAiq.

as could any of the Four Quadrants of Public Relations for that matter. However, in understanding each quadrant, the overlap between the quadrants, how to work within each quadrant, and incorporating a diverse range of essential skills, we can see a pattern for successful public relations planning, process, and implementation. Aspects of each of the four quadrants rely on one another to be successful.

Within media relations, practitioners must have the ability to successfully conduct outreach to the news media on behalf of an organization or company. It is essential to have the right communication skills to complete this task, along with superior writing abilities. It is also vital to understand how to reach out to the media in the appropriate way, use the appropriate channels, communicate the right message, and successfully land a news-worthy story. The skills associated with media relations should be inherent to a public relations practitioner.

When working with the community, practitioners also take on the task of enhancing an organization's participation and position within the community by initiating/establishing outreach efforts. This aspect of a public relations practitioner's role cannot be accomplished without the correct set of skills. The public relations practitioner must know how to build those relationships.

In parallel with community relations, the approach to business relations is also executed in a similar manner. Public relations practitioners ultimately build and continually foster relationships within the business community. Organizations today want to make sure the actions they take are interpreted as "good citizenship." It is the job of the public relations practitioner to have the appropriate skills to accomplish this aspect of developing these relationships.

Finally, public relations practitioners have also assumed the role of involving their respective organizations in the development of public policy and government

#LRNSMPR

Learn More: The Four Quadrants of Public Relations in Action

- Dunkin' Donuts: http://bit.ly/1851sUK
- AKA Central Park: http://bit.ly/13qM3tx
- Macaroni Grill: http://bit.ly/110VaPK
- Starbucks "Community Service": http://bit.ly/YNyUMO
- GE Sustainability: http://invent.ge/17Ch04I
- Zappos "Higher Purpose: The Community": http://bit.ly/1088l67
- "IBM's KidSmart Early Learning Program 2011": http://bit.ly/1OU9kZ0
- "2015 Edelman Trust Barometer": http://bit.ly/1hlsVLp
- "How to Build a Corporate Culture of Trust": http://bit.ly/1Gspfhz
- "How Brands Build Trust in a Digital World": http://huge.is/1LbS82p
- "Public Affairs and Government Issues Management": http://bit.ly/1MUodPX
- "Government Public Relations: Public Diplomacy or Propaganda?": http://bit.ly/1VBpmyc

relations. Being able to represent an organization's interests to governing bodies and regulatory agencies with the expectation of mutual understanding is also a key responsibility of a public relations practitioner, or, as we mentioned previously, a public affairs professional. Knowledge of public speaking and governmental and effective communication are essential when working in government relations.

The profession of public relations aids an organization in establishing mutually adapted relationships with external entities—be that with the media, the community, other businesses, or the government. It is the role of the public relations practitioner to foster these relationships within each quadrant of public relations. Being able to interconnect and apply the required skill sets from each quadrant in order to gain an increased understanding of the organization's "big picture" is equally important. As evidence, public relations practitioners must have a variety of expertise to accomplish their job duties, with each skill supporting one of the Four Quadrants of Public Relations: media, community, business, and government.

Notes

1 R. Harlow, "Public Relations at the Crossroads," *Public Opinion Quarterly* (1944): 551–56.
2 D. Wilcox et al., *THINK Public Relations* (Upper Saddle River, NJ: Pearson Education, 2013).
3 D. Moss and B. DeSanto, "What Do Communications Managers Do?," *J&MC Quarterly* (2005): 873–90; L. Wernet-Foreman and B. Devin, "Listening to Learn: 'Inactive' Publics of the Arts as Exemplar," *Communication World* (2006): 287–94.
4 F. Seitel, *The Practice of Public Relations* (Upper Saddle River, NJ: Pearson, 2014); Wilcox et al., *THINK Public Relations*.
5 Wilcox et al., *THINK Public Relations*.
6 Wilcox et al., *THINK Public Relations*; Seitel, *The Practice of Public Relations*.
7 R. Stein, "Our Media Pros," *ABA Journal*, no. 12 (2003).
8 Stein, "Our Media Pros."
9 T. Sinkinson, "Lessons in Landing Front Page Placement: Zapwater Communications Downsizes the Obesity Epidemic for Downsize Fitness," *Bulldog Reporter*, 2013, accessed May 20, 2013, http://www.bulldogreporter.com/dailydog/article/lessons-in-landing-front-page-placement-zapwater-communications-downsizes-the-obesi.
10 Sinkinson, "Lessons in Landing Front Page Placement."
11 Sinkinson, "Lessons in Landing Front Page Placement."
12 D. Anderson, "Identifying and Responding to Activist Publics: A Case Study," *Public Relations Research*, no. 1 (1992): 151–65.
13 "GAP VII: Seventh Communication and Public Relations Generally Accepted Practices Study (Q4 2011 data)," University of Southern California (USC) Annenberg, Strategic Communication and Public Relations Center, 2011, http://ascjweb.org/gapstudy/corporations.
14 "GAP VII: Seventh Communication and Public Relations Generally Accepted Practices Study (Q4 2011 Data)."
15 K. Keller, *Best Practice Cases in Branding* (Upper Saddle River, NJ: Pearson, 2007).
16 Wilcox et al., *THINK Public Relations*.
17 Seitel, *The Practice of Public Relations*; Keller, *Best Practice Cases in Branding*.
18 "Citizenship Initiatives: Focused on Issues Where We Can Apply IBM's Technology and Talent," IBM, accessed May 20, 2013, http://www.ibm.com/ibm/responsibility/initiatives/citizenship.shtml.
19 Keller, *Best Practice Cases in Branding*.
20 "Corporate Social Responsibility," Cisco, accessed May 20, 2013, http://csr.cisco.com/casestudy/getideas.
21 "Kraft Launches First Celebration of Community Service," Kraft, accessed May 20, 2013, http://files.shareholder.com/downloads/ABEA-3QV6OO/2459222506x0x653268/a734c1e6-1ade-4df0-943c-642060d36fac/Make_an_Impact_2013_release_FINAL_4.12.13_.pdf.
22 "Global Results: 2015 Edelman Trust Barometer," Edelman, accessed October 5, 2015, http://www.edelman.com/insights/intellectual-property/2015-edelman-trust-barometer/trust-and-innovation-edelman-trust-barometer.
23 "Global Results: 2015 Edelman Trust Barometer."
24 J. Budd, "Opinion . . . Foreign Policy Acumen Needed by Global CEOs," *Public Relations Review* (2000): 123–34.

25 "Citizenship Initiatives."

26 "Pulse Study," Reputation Institute, accessed May 20, 2013, http://www.reputationinstitute.com/advisory-services/reptrak-in-country.php.

27 Keller, *Best Practice Cases in Branding.*

28 Wilcox et al., *THINK Public Relations.*

29 Seitel, *The Practice of Public Relations.*

30 Keller, *Best Practice Cases in Branding.*

31 D. Burgess et al., "Rocking the Vote: Using Personalized Messages to Motivate Voting among Young Adults," *Public Relations Quarterly* (2000): 29–52.

32 Keller, *Best Practice Cases in Branding.*

The Evolution of Social Media 2

This chapter discusses the evolution of social media and situates social media within today's global environment.

What Is Social Media?

Why ask, What is social media? when everybody already knows?

We're asking because organizations are failing at social media every day for numerous reasons, the most common being that they simply do not understand the premise behind social media. Another reason is that they are trying to fit marketing or advertising principles into social media since they don't understand the fundamental ideals behind social media. As a result, many organizations tend to seek outside assistance in this area and hire one of the many self-proclaimed "gurus" to manage their social strategies—but often the so-called guru isn't really an expert at all. Most organizations tend to overlook how smart their consumers really are and need to evolve beyond using the same old marketing techniques and tactics to spam consumers. Consumers know the difference between true engagements with a company or brand versus simply being sold to.

To gain a deeper level of understanding of social media so that you don't repeat this common mistake, let us break down the two words separately and explore their meanings as they relate to social media.

Social: so-cial *adjective* \'sō-shəl\[1]
marked by or passed in pleasant companionship with friends or associates
of or relating to human society, the interaction of the individual and the group,
     or the welfare of human beings as members of society
tending to form cooperative and interdependent relationships with others.

As you can see, "social" relates to the need that we, as human beings, have to connect with others through companionship via relationships with others in society, either individually or in groups. Think about your own relationships. We want to be around people who make us most comfortable and have similar interests, ideas, ideals, and experiences.[2] This premise also holds true for consumers who desire to interact with companies that they relate to, connect with, and feel comfortable aligning themselves with.

Media: me-di-a *noun* \mee-dee-uh\[3]
Communication channels through which news, entertainment, education, data, or promotional messages are disseminated. Media includes every broadcasting and narrowcasting medium such as newspapers, magazines, TV, radio, billboards, direct mail, telephone, fax, and Internet. *Media* is the plural of *medium* and can take a plural or singular verb, depending on the sense intended.

The word "media" relates to the channels through which we make connections with others. The sampling provided in the definition is narrow in scope. Today, we connect through pictures, email, texting, websites, and a myriad of mobile and handheld devices.

In bringing the two words together, we can begin to understand how this book applies the term "social media" and how you should interpret the term going forward. A commonly accepted definition of the term "social media" holds that it refers to the "activities, practices, and behavior among communities of people who gather online to share information, knowledge and opinions using conversational media. Conversational media are web-based applications that make it possible to create and easily transmit content in the form of words, pictures, video, and audio."[4] Social platforms, including Facebook, Twitter, Instagram, Pinterest, WordPress, and LinkedIn, among others, are forms of social media. They represent conversational media since each application allows users to gather online and easily exchange photos, videos, audio files, and content while building and cultivating relationships. Social media competence should be viewed as how a company or brand effectively utilizes each of the aforementioned platforms to connect, interact, and cultivate trusting relationships with people.

As we begin to situate social media in a historical context, we must also understand the innate connection between social media and social networks. Social networks comprise a complex system of web-based services that allow for the self-organization of individuals to construct a public or semipublic profile with a set of users with whom they share a connection.[5] This connection is important in understanding not only the relationship between the two but also their principal differences and how they are commonly interpreted as being the same.

Social Media's Rise

We can no longer argue that social media is on the rise or that it is in the early phases of adoption. Social media is here, and it is growing by leaps and bounds. At this point in the social revolution, social media is in the refinement stage wherein best practices and case studies are being shared. People are finding new ways to engage with the brands, events, and people that matter most to them. Think about the interesting statistics shown on the opposite page.[6]

If we simply look at the numbers involved, now more than ever, public relations practitioners must understand how to create, cultivate, maintain, and grow successful social strategies by building strong social relationships.

In its current form, social media can still be considered relatively new. However, the roots of social media surprisingly began in 550 BCE with the introduction of the postal service. Historically speaking, much of what we currently define as social media occurred during the twenty-first century. To build a greater understanding of social media, it is essential to examine the early forms of social networking and how it has evolved into its current form.

Prehistory: Ancient Persia, 600–490 BCE to 1800s

The post, as referred to during this period, was the first form of communication between people allowing correspondences beyond the confines of their villages. It is argued that the original credible claim for the development of a true postal system has its roots in ancient Persia, attributing the invention of the postal system to King Cyrus the Great.[7] With the establishment of a postal system, people could converse with one another over larger geographical areas. However, these early forms of communication were not without problems. Letters could take hours, days, or even months to arrive at their final destinations.

It wasn't until 1792 that Claude Chappe, a French inventor, developed the first practical telecommunications system of the industrial era. He became a

facebook

There are nearly 1.4 billion Facebook users

47% of all internet users are on Facebook

 4.5 billion likes are generated daily

 Nearly 75% of Facebook's revenue comes from mobile advertising

 Facebook messenger has 500 million users

 Direct uploads of user videos to Facebook now exceed YouTube

Google+

Google+ cost over half a billion to design and develop

363 million users

+1 The +1 button is hit 5 billion times per day

twitter

 Twitter has 284 million active users at last count

   88% of Twitter users are on mobile

 500 million tweets per day

YouTube

 More than 1 billion unique visitors per month

 300 hours of video are uploaded to YouTube every minute

 Half of YouTube views are on mobile devices

 Mobile revenue on YouTube is up over 100% y/y

Influential Global Social Media Channels

- China's Qzone possesses 639 million users
- Wechat is close behind with 468 million users throughout China
- Russia's "VKontake" has 100 million users
- Orkut, popular in India and Brazil, boasts 100m users

Instagram

 Instagram has **300 million users**

- 70 million photos and videos are sent daily
- 53% of INTERNET users aged 18-29 use Instagram

Pinterest

 80% of Internet users on Pinterest are female

70 Million users are on Pinterest

88% purchase a product they pinned

Linked in

 LinkedIn has 347 million registered members

Total revenue at the end of 2014 was $643 million

 There are over 39 million students and recent college graduates on LinkedIn

Mobile

- In India mobile devices account for 72% of all website traffic
- There are 1.65 billion active mobile social accounts globally
- 561 million active mobile social accounts are located in East Asia

Snapchat

Snapchat has been valued at close to $20 billion at the last valuation

 Snapchat has 100 million monthly users

- Social networks will earn $8.3 billion from advertising in 2015

Sources:
YouTube, 33 Social Media Facts and Statistics You Should Know in 2015, Growing social media, Pewinternet.org, Linkedin.com

Source: Regina Luttrell.

telecommunications mogul through what has been called the "mechanical internet."[8] The telegraph transmitted messages instantaneously, altering communication thereafter. The electronic telegraph was the first form of communication that transmitted and received messages over long distances. Rightfully so, the telegraph has earned its place in the historical landscape of social media.

1890s

The year 1890 brought the telephone, and in 1891 society was introduced to the radio.[9] The telephone and radio both brought about a sense of community. People were connected across long distances in a more intimate way. Information moved between and among people, from big cities to small, rural communities.

1960s

The 1960s were rich with introductory technologies that have since become an integral part of our daily lives. In 1966, a crude form of email first came about. It was not the typical email as we understand it today. Early email was similar to a file directory. Users were able to place a message in another user's directory, where he or she would retrieve it upon logging into the system. The first email system of this type was MAILBOX, used by the Massachusetts Institute of Technology.[10] The Advanced Research Projects Agency Network (ARPANET), launched in 1969 along with CompuServe, served as the first major commercial online service in the United States.[11]

1970s

The year 1978 brought about two very important contributions to the history of social media. Multi-user Dungeon (MUD), created by Roy Trubshaw, is the first and oldest virtual community in existence.[12] Additionally, BBS, a computer system, was also introduced, allowing users to log in to a central location where they could connect with other users. Once logged in, users were able to exchange messages with others, upload or download software and data, read news, and even direct chat.[13]

1980s

In 1985, The WELL (Whole Earth 'Lectronic Link) was introduced; it is one of the oldest virtual communities that has been in continuous operation since its inception.[14] By 1988 Internet Relay Chat (IRC) was used for file sharing, link sharing, and keeping in touch.[15]

It was around this time that a real technological breakthrough was about to be introduced that would change how virtual communities formed and interacted going forward. Web 1.0 was initiated during the 1990s. This period of growth ushered in the introduction of the uniform resource locator (URL) and the basic search functions. Internet technologies became accessible to the public on a larger scale. Web 2.0 was the platform on which new, innovative applications could be built. The web became easier to navigate and offered a more dynamic user experience. The result was a generation of tech-savvy individuals who were able to navigate the ever-growing Internet. This initial foundation positioned technology where it is today.

1990s

The year 1997 marked the first introduction of what we now have come to understand as a social networking site. Coined SixDegrees, the site offered users the ability to create personal profiles, set up friend lists, and search friend lists belonging to other users within their networks. They could send messages to one another, affiliate themselves with networks, and invite family and friends to become members. This quickly became popular due to its level of interactivity.[16] In 2000, SixDegrees was purchased for $125 million. One year later it was shut down. These options may not seem impressive by today's standards; however, in 1997 no other site offered a combination of these features.[17] The concept was well ahead of its time. Additionally, LiveJournal was one of the Internet's most popular early blogging and online communities built around the use of personal journals. This community was started by Brad Fitzpatrick in April 1999.[18] During 1998 and 1999 other well-known social sites were introduced, including MoveOn, Asian Avenue, BlackPlanet, Napster, Third Voice, Epinions, and Blogger.[19]

2000s

The twenty-first century has generated many of the most popular social networking sites, many of which are still in use today. In the early 2000s, some of the largest growth experienced by social networking sites occurred. In 2001 Wikipedia was first launched, 2002 brought about Friendster to the Internet, and in 2003 we were introduced to both Myspace and LinkedIn.[20] Myspace was the first social networking site to allow users to completely customize their pages and upload music and video. LinkedIn was the first social networking site dedicated to business users. Other popular social networking sites that came onto the scene in 2003 included last.fm, Photobucket, Second Life, and Delicious.[21] In 2004, Digg, a website wherein users share links and vote as to whether they "digg" the article or want to "bury" it, came into existence. Flickr popped onto the scene in 2004 as well, and now it boasts 92 million users who share approximately 1 million photos daily.[22] Ning, Orkut, mixi, Piczo, Hyves, Care2, Multiply, and Harvard Facebook were established in 2004. YouTube, the first massive video-sharing site, launched in 2005, along with high school Facebook, Bebo, Yahoo! 360, and reddit. In 2006 Twitter and Facebook emerged and gained use and popularity quickly. Twitter's status sprang out of use at the South by Southwest (SXSW) conference.[23] Tweets increased from twenty thousand per day to sixty thousand per day. Today, more than 500 million tweets are sent daily. When Facebook originally launched, users signed up at an unprecedented rate. Currently, Facebook is the most visited social networking site in the United States, with a user base that would independently rank as the third-largest country in the world.[24] In 2007 Tumblr and FriendFeed materialized. In 2008, we were introduced to Spotify, Ping, Groupon, and Kontain, and in 2009, the ever-popular location-based social networking service Foursquare launched with great popularity. More recently, the photo-sharing site Instagram rose to mass appeal in 2010, along with Google Buzz and Pinterest. Continuing with this trend, in 2011 Google introduced Google+, and Pheed was unveiled in 2012, a unified platform whereby users can share photos and videos, text, create voice notes, and live broadcast. Finally, this brings us to 2013, in which Vine was launched by Twitter.[25] Vine is a mobile service that allows users to capture and share short looping videos. Similar to tweets, videos on Vine are brief, lasting six seconds or less.[26]

Through this chronological history of the advancement of social media, encompassing both social networking sites and social media tools, we have seen brilliant developers, coders, gamers, idea generators, and early adopters. None of the technological achievements seen in the social media community would have been possible without forward-thinking pioneers who developed the principles, values, ideals, and standards behind the social media movement.

Stewart Brand, Howard Rheingold, Kevin Kelly, Esther Dyson, and John Perry Barlow were early visionaries of the Internet and the emerging digital world in which we live today.[27] Rick Levine, Christopher Locke, Doc Searls, and David Weinberger developed the first set standards for social media engagement that we have come to utilize today.

Let's meet these pioneers who made history by taking social media and making it an everyday occurrence, both personally and within a business environment.

Pioneers of Social Media

Stewart Brand (1938–) @longnow

Writer Carole Cadwalladr characterized Stewart Brand as "the heart of 60s counterculture" and a widely revered "tech visionary whose book anticipated the web."[28] Brand published *The Whole Earth Catalog*, which was described by Steve Jobs as "Google only on paper" in his Stanford commencement address. The catalog contained information on everything from deerskin jackets to the latest technological advances, including ideas about cybernetics from Norbert Wiener.[29] *New York Times* writer John Markoff said the catalog was "the Internet before the Internet. It was the book of the future. It was a web in newsprint."[30]

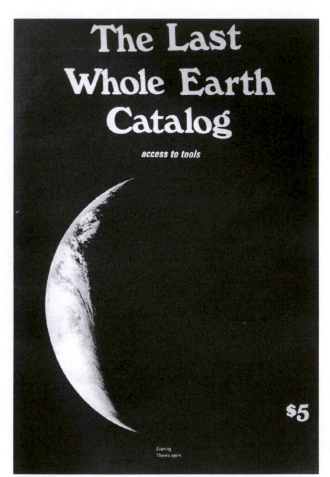

Thinking the *Whole Earth Catalog* legacy was coming to an end, Stewart Brand issued the *Last Whole Earth Catalog* in 1971. *Source*: Regina Luttrell.

Brand is credited with putting the two words "personal" and "computer" together, thus introducing the concept of owning your own *personal computer* to the world. He was a man before his time and "understood before almost anyone else . . . that cyberspace was some sort of fourth dimension and the possibilities were both empowering and limitless."[31] He helped shape the public's understanding of computing. This revelation led to many early Internet technologies, virtual communities, and ideals. He led the way in cofounding The WELL and later the Global Business Network, *CoEvolution Quarterly*, the Hackers Conference, and Long Now Foundation. All of these were based on the concept of a social presence among users.

Howard Rheingold (1947–) @hrheingold

At a time when the idea of an online community could not yet be rationalized and an emerging interest in the cultural and social implications of modern media was merely a thought, Howard Rheingold was building a foundation for these interactions. He was another pioneer who was ahead of his time. Described as a critic, writer, teacher, artist, designer, theorist, and community builder, Rheingold is "one of the driving minds behind our net-enabled, open, collaborative life-style today" and is considered a founding father of social media.[32]

Early in his career, Rheingold wrote about the history of the individuals behind the personal computer, which in turn fueled later research and ultimately his book *Tools for Thought*. In 1985 he began writing for The WELL, wherein he became an influential contributor on life inside virtual communities and the implication of this newly formed communications medium. It was during this experience that he coined the term "virtual community," a term synonymous with social media today.[33] He became editor of the *Whole Earth* review in 1985 and then shortly thereafter editor in chief of the *Millennium Whole Earth Catalog*. By 1994 he founded and became the executive editor of HotWired, one of the first commercial content websites published by *WIRED* magazine.[34] After leaving HotWired, he founded Electric Minds in 1996, where he chronicled the growth of online communities. In 1998, he created Brainstorms, a private web conferencing virtual community that caters to those who want to have conversations about "technology, the future, life online, culture, society, family, history, books, health, home, mind, phun, money, spirituality, media, and academiaville."[35]

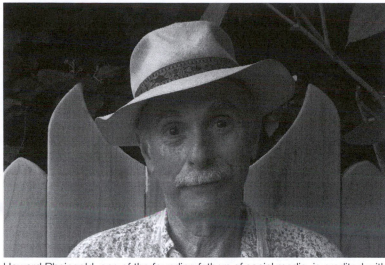

Howard Rheingold, one of the founding fathers of social media, is credited with coining the term "virtual community." *Source*: Howard Rheingold.

An Interview with Howard Rheingold

During my PhD studies, I was fortunate enough to have Howard Rheingold as a professor; he has since filled the role of mentor as well. His writings, insights, and teachings have inspired and challenged me to think critically about the Internet and social media and how I currently view and understand them. Howard was gracious enough to chat with me on a number of topics related to this book and also to share some thoughts on his time at The WELL, the beginnings of social media, where social media is today, and the future of social media.

In the book, you are featured as one of the pioneers of social media. Can you tell me what social media was like before we, meaning society, even knew what it was? When you were part of "The WELL," it was a groundbreaking time which many of us were not part of.

Howard: Well, you know, I think that you have to go back about three prehistoric eras to talk

about that. There have been an awful lot of people who think it started with Facebook. I had a company called Electric Minds in 1996 in which I talked about the social web—about the web becoming a social medium. So that was 1996. To, I think, a lot of people that was pretty prehistoric. The article I wrote—well, let's see, the book, *The Virtual Community*, was 1993. That was the year of the famous *New Yorker* cartoon on the

Internet 'Nobody Knows You Are a Dog.' That was when the Internet sort of broke into the public consciousness for the early adopters. My article that coined the term "Virtual Community" was 1987, and so that came from "The WELL," which I joined in 1985. And we felt—we being the people on "The WELL" at that point—felt that this was going to be big. We didn't really have an idea of what the shape of the web would turn out to be but we knew that people would want to communicate in this way in the future. When I set out to write *The Virtual Community*, it was very clear that there was a much longer history than that. There were the BBSs. At one point in the US there were about 50,000 BBSs around the time of The WELL. And these were mostly inexpensive PCs with a modem and usually a teenage boy's bedroom and like only one person could log on at a time. There was also Usenet, which started in 1980, which was worldwide and pretty large. There were, I would say, tens of thousands of people, if not hundreds of thousands of people, on Usenet. Most of them, what we would now call "geeks," but weren't called geeks then, you know electrical engineers, people, computer science professors, researchers, and before that it, of course, was the ARPANET, and that went back to 1969–1970. And before that even was Plato, the system that controlled data, created in Minneapolis. So for some, you know it's the old William Gibson quote, "The future is already here. It's not evenly distributed." There were people online in the 1960s, 1970s, and 1980s. It really took off with the web. If you think about it, it's a little bit strange that the Internet was worthy of a *New Yorker* cartoon in 1993. The web really didn't exist yet. It was all text, and you had to give arcane commands on your keyboard. It was mostly email that attracted people. So there's a long, long history here that most people don't really know about.

I agree with you. I don't think that people realized where social media was going to go at that time, but I believe technology was on the brink of something "big." Did you expect people to use the technology the way that we are using it now?

Howard: Well, there were things called MUDS then—Multi-user Dungeons—where people had fantasy worlds that were totally based on text. And the pretty widespread fantasy among MUDDERS was that someday we would have graphical MUDS. You would have kind of cartoony computer graphics worlds. The idea that people would be

streaming video to each other from their phones in their pockets was totally out of the question. Nobody even imagined that. I participated in some of the first experiments with video. There was something called See-You-See-Me that the Mac had way back in the late 1980s. And the frame—well, it was black and white. It was postage stamp sized. The frame rate was very, very low, so it was kind of jerky. That we would do what we are doing right now for free, full color, real time, pretty good detail video—that was not really something that people foresaw. But we did—you know, I think the social affordances were foreseen. The fact that you could communicate with someone you had never met, on the other side of the world, but you shared a particular interest, I think was very important. Again, the social side of it—connecting with people around shared interests, even if you did not know them, that was—that is, radical.

I suppose that's what many businesses mistake. Businesses use social media to connect with their audiences, but they fail to understand the notion that people are on the other side of this network. I find that to be very interesting.

Howard: Well, let me say a couple of things about that. First of all, when I was out talking about Electric Minds in 1996, I pointed out that social communication had driven the growth of the Internet from the very beginning, and as soon as the tools were there, it was going to drive the web as well. And I think that that is essential. I think that people wanting to communicate with people has not been something that has been added on recently. It has been a driving force.

We have seen how Twitter has changed the landscape for companies, reporters, and civil uprisings. In your opinion, what is the most important quality or impact social media possesses? For example, when the tsunamis hit, there were donations that came from all over.

Howard: Well, it is an instantaneous, global way for ordinary citizens to participate in everything from news gathering to disaster relief to political organizing. That is a radical change. The police and the army have always been able to communicate with each other wherever they were. An illustration of many-to-many communications. That has never existed before. You have the alphabet and the printing press broadly expanding the number of people who are able to receive broadcast communication—read the newspaper, tune in on the radio, watch the television. Of course there were only a small number of people who were able to create the content—to tell them what the news was. Now, anybody with a smartphone with a camera is a reporter. You see these massive demonstrations; the difference between the massive demonstrations today and the massive demonstrations of the past is that everybody there knows where their friends are. They are talking on the phone, they are tweeting, and they are sending SMS messages. The ability to organize collective actions—whether that is political demonstrations or organizing disaster relief or fact checking a news report; the ability to organize with people you were not able to organize with before in places and at speeds that you were not able to organize before. Now that is radical. It's not only many to many; it's everywhere now because of mobile communications.

To build off of that answer, do you think that our communication or content is going to become more abbreviated? For example, today, we have Vine, which is six-second videos, and Instagram and Pinterest and all of these other sites that compress communication. Blogs allow us to expand upon our thoughts and link out to other places, but some of the newer technologies are quite short.

Howard: You know, I just think that there is a rich ecology of communication media and cannot imagine that there are going to be too many people that are going to communicate in tiny bursts. But I think that all of us are adding that to our vocabulary.

What do you think the future of social media looks like?

Howard: The future of social media. Well, you know I wrote a book called *Net Smarts*, and the premise behind that book is that we have all of this power at our finger tips but the critical uncertainty about whether the web is going to end up being any good for us in the long run. Because there is a lot of bad stuff, I am not an unpredictable enthusiast. There is a lot of spam and porn and porn-spam and bad information, misinformation, deceptive information, bad people, crimes—will it

just descend into a mass of garbage? I think the answer is that it depends on how many of the people that have access to the media also have some know-how about it. So I wrote about attention and training attention—a huge distraction issue. I don't think that distraction issue means that your smart phone or laptop is going to magnetically suck your attention away; I think that it means that you need to exercise some control over your attention. Which nobody has time and you have not practiced. The next one is "crap" detection. You know, if you are talking about Googling your symptoms, or you are talking about rumors about political figures, bad information has real consequences. And we live in a world where you can now ask any question, any questions, and get an answer, get a lot of answers, anywhere in the world within a second. It is up to you to determine whether the answers are accurate or inaccurate. That's a big, big change. People need to learn how to do that. It is not rocket science—certainly at the elementary level. And [we need to learn] how to participate. Unless we want Facebook and Google and Apple to dictate how we communicate online, we need to continue to blog and create new media like Twitter. Individuals need to put up websites and link to others. Don't leave it to the big guys. Collaboration [is also important]. [There are] so many different genres of collaboration. Virtual communities, smart mobs, crowdsourcing, collective intelligence, social production. If you know how to do it, you can wield a lot of power with others collaboratively. And then finally, some network literacy. Understanding how things work in a networked world. So, again, I wrote *Net Smart* to try to do something about it. There are some strong critiques of social media, and those are important. But a critique can only tell you that something is broken. It does not tell you how to fix it. I think how to fix it is education and more people learning how to use these media productively, effectively, mindfully.

I certainly appreciate your time and consideration for this interview. Do you have any closing thoughts that you would like to share with us?

Howard: Technology is moving faster than our social institutions. If we are going to do this kind of learning that is going to improve the commons, we have to teach each other.

Still an ever-present voice in the social community, Rheingold presents at conferences throughout the world, writes, researches, and teaches. A nonresident fellow of the Annenberg School for Communication at Stanford University, he now personally teaches students about the virtual community and social media. UC Berkeley students study digital journalism. In 2008, he won the MacArthur Foundation's Digital Media and Learning Competition. With this award, he developed and created Social Media Classroom and Collaboratory (http://socialmediaclassroom.com). Spreading the idea of open education, he founded Rheingold University (http://www.rheingold.com/university), a completely online learning community where participants can take courses in everything from "Introduction to Mind Amplifiers" to "Social Media for Educators."

Kevin Kelly (1952–) @kevin2kelly

For more than twenty years, innovator, writer, and technology guru Kevin Kelly has been viewed as one of the most significant information technology revolutionists of our time. As a member of Brand's original group of visionary technologists, Kelly acted as publisher and editor from 1984 to 1990 of the *Millennium Whole Earth Catalog*, where he authored articles on topics that leveraged power to individuals. He took an active role in helping to launch The WELL, and he cofounded the ongoing Hackers Conference.[36] In 1993 he launched *WIRED* magazine and served as executive editor for six years, during which time the magazine was the recipient of the National Magazine Award for General Excellence twice.[37]

Today he holds the title of senior maverick at *WIRED* and is publisher and editor of the Cool Tools website. His most recent book, *What Technology Wants*, builds upon his book *Out of Control: The New Biology of Machines, Social Systems, and the Economic World*. In this book Kelly included an in-depth look at the connections between computer science, biology, systems theory, cybernetics, and artificial intelligence. Kelly introduced us to "vivisystems," or lifelike, complex, engineered systems capable of growing in complexity. He wrote about a new era in which the machines and systems that drive our economy are so complex and autonomous as to be indistinguishable from living entities.[38] *What Technology Wants* takes Kelly's initial theories and expands upon them, arguing that technology is alive, much like each of us, and has evolved in the same way human beings have evolved.[39]

John Perry Barlow (1947–) @JPBarlow

WIRED magazine contributor John Perry Barlow's manifesto, "A Declaration of the Independence of Cyberspace," could be considered his most influential early paper. In a response to the U.S. government's passing of the Telecommunications Act of 1996, Barlow wrote that the United States did not have the right to apply laws to the Internet because it was outside any country's borders. Barlow suggested that the Internet could develop its own social contracts to determine how to deal with its problems based on the Golden Rule, "Do unto others as you'd have done to you."[40] This was the first time in U.S. history that laws governing the Internet were enacted.

Barlow founded the Electronic Frontier Foundation (EFF), an international nonprofit digital rights group protecting free speech, fair use, privacy, and international rights as they pertain to the Internet and addressing transparency problems that threaten digital freedoms.[41]

Esther Dyson (1951–) @edyson

One of the world's preeminent visionaries of the digital age, Esther Dyson has written about how the Internet affects an individual's life. She was the first individual to expand upon the notion of the "humanization" of the Internet and to introduce this concept to a wide audience. "Everything that happens on the Net will happen to human beings. . . . [T]he Net is not going to push us into some antiseptic digital landscape."[42] Her predictions from 1998 have become today's reality. Social media allows for us to extend our emotional and intellectual selves through the use of social networking sites. We develop relationships, conduct business, share ideas, and even connect globally. Her publications on technology include *Release 1.0*, her monthly technology-industry newsletter; her 1998 book *Release 2.0: A Design for Living in the Digital Age*, about how the Internet affects us individual beings; *Release 3.0*, a bimonthly column for the *New York Times*; and *Release 4.0*, her blog.[43]

The Forward-Thinking Four

Rick Levine (@ricklevine), Christopher Locke (@clockerb), Doc Searls (@dsearls), and David Weinberger (@dweinberger) teamed up to write *The Cluetrain Manifesto: The End of Business as Usual*. The book revolutionized concepts and perceptions of how business is conducted under the impact of the Internet. Through a series of ninety-five theses, they explain that businesses are fundamentally human: "Markets consist of human beings, not demographic sectors. Conversations among human beings sound human. They are conducted in a human voice. Whether delivering information, opinions, perspectives, dissenting arguments or humorous asides, the human voice is typically open, natural, uncontrived."[44] The central message of the book is that the marketplace is a conversation and that the web gives people a voice. Locke, Levine, Searls, and Weinberger agree that too often conversations by individuals are ignored by large corporations because these corporations see the Internet as another vehicle to broadcast marketing messages. Consumers, employees, and stakeholders yearn for genuine dialogue on the Internet.

For the first time, the ideals and basis of all interaction via social media was summarized in *Cluetrain*. The fundamentals of this new marketplace and how to converse effectively are illustrated through three simple decrees as outlined in the book:

Be authentic to stakeholders: Talk like people and eliminate buzz words and overly technical terms.

Have fun and laugh: People drive the Internet; they drive interactions, so be real with them and cultivate authentic conversations.

Above all, listen: The marketplace is where conversations are happening. Without careful attention, businesses can miss out on important exchanges.

I had the opportunity to ask David Weinberger about the inspiration behind *Cluetrain*. He responded with the following:

Cluetrain grew out of a set of conversations among the four of us about just how wrong the media and most businesses were about the Web. They were viewing the Web primarily as a business opportunity, whereas we thought it was obvious to the people on the Web that we were there because we finally got to talk about what mattered to us with the people we wanted to talk with, and to do so in our own voice. That is, the Web was and is social more than anything else.

The forward-thinking four: Rick Levine, Christopher Locke, David "Doc" Searls, and David Weinberger. *Source*: Rick Levine, Creative Commons License.

Modern visionaries like Brian Solis (@briansolis), Deirdre Breakenridge (@dbreakenridge), Guy Kawasaki (@GuyKawasaki), Philip Sheldrake (@sheldrake), Scott Monty (@ScottMonty), Becky McMichael (@bmcmichael), Stuart Bruce (@stuartbruce), Adam Parker (@AdParker), Rachel Miller (@AllthingsIC), and Don Tapscott (@dtapscott) understand that "authenticity, honesty, and personal voice underlie much of what's successful on the Web."[45]

Global Perspectives

Social media can be viewed as a catalyst for global transformation. The world is changing before our eyes, day by day, minute by minute. With every change begins a metamorphosis. Philip Slater's *The Chrysalis Effect* outlines the process of change that the world is experiencing and compares these shifts to a caterpillar's metamorphosis into a butterfly.[46] Our global world, through social media, is in the midst of one of the largest transformations we have ever seen.

As a result, we are connecting with one another through social networking sites, online and virtual communities, chat rooms, instant messaging platforms, newsgroups, multiplayer games, wikis, blogs, microblogs, and video-sharing sites. People are establishing and maintaining social relationships and even organizing collective action. In recent years, we have started to see a shift toward a more inclusive global community. The Internet, cyberspace, and virtual and online communities are part of this global evolution. The "Internet has created a generation of people accustomed to finding their own answers, creating their own systems, forming their own new communities."[47] The impact that social networking sites have on society has only just begun to surface.

When people took to the streets to protest fraudulent conduct of the presidential election in Iran in June 2009, they had a new tool at their disposal: Twitter. Massive street protests in Egypt spread virally as the tech-savvy demonstrators used TwitPic, Facebook, and YouTube to disseminate videos and photographs. An earthquake in the United Kingdom, the Boston Marathon bombings, the US Airways plane crash into the Hudson River, the Mumbai massacre, and, yes, even Michael Jackson's death are all examples of breaking news via social networking sites. Haiti, a small country located in the Caribbean, was struck by a massive catastrophic earthquake in 2010 with a magnitude of 7.0 and at least fifty-two aftershocks measuring 4.5 or greater on the Richter scale. An estimated 3 million people were affected by the earthquake, and the Haitian government reported that roughly 230,000 people had been killed, 300,000 injured, and 1 million made homeless. Experts also estimated that at least 250,000 homes and 30,000 commercial business buildings had collapsed or were severely damaged. The global social community came together to support a country in need through the new-age communication tools making up social media. U.S. mobile users donated more than $8 million just a day after the earthquake struck via the Haiti earthquake relief text message appeal.[48] The donations were pledged in $10 increments to the Red Cross for Haiti disaster relief, by far the largest outpouring of support via mobile devices in history.[49]

The widespread enthusiasm generated by status updates on Facebook raised $100,000 and unprecedented awareness. Even more impressive, the donations to the American Red Cross exceeded the total amounts "received in the first 48 hours of both Hurricane Katrina and the 2004 Indian Ocean Tsunami."[50] Today, through the use of Facebook, Twitter, and text messaging, organizations that want to have an effect globally can accomplish this very efficiently. Through "retweeting" and "liking" of information on Twitter and Facebook, organizations are able to get the word out and drive people to their websites. Instances of global catastrophes can now be supported by any organization simply by posting a series of short videos on a website and setting up an electronic donation system. These steps allow an organization's consumer base to easily contribute to and support the cause at hand. All told, the heart of social media employs an integrative global culture.

The F5 tornado that struck Moore, Oklahoma, in May 2013 is another example of how much social media has become integrated within society. An outpouring of support for all who were affected via Twitter came in the form of hashtag identifiers that included "#Oklahoma," "#OKC," and "#PrayforOklahoma."[51] Facebook communities were set up that provided weather alerts, information about resources, and options for the global community to donate time and money. Google helped confirm the safety of tornado survivors, while the Oklahoma Humane Society and reddit users worked together to inform the public of the whereabouts of missing pets.[52] Entire communities of people within the social sphere, ranging from everyday citizens to news anchors, shared powerful images of the catastrophic damage on Instagram.

More recently, the Boko Haram organization abducted 276 schoolgirls in the northern Nigerian village of Chibok. This event not only outraged the Nigerian people but moved the world to act. While Nigerians demanded action at home, globally the social media community rallied around a call to #BringBackOurGirls. Even the First Lady of the United States, Michelle Obama, posted a photo to Facebook and Twitter of her holding a sign with the hashtag #BringBackOurGirls.[53] In less than three weeks the hashtag was shared over 1 million times by everyone from celebrities to common citizens.

These are only a few examples that illustrate just how important these new communication channels between communities have become. The acceptance of social media as a primary mode of communication is significant because it speaks to the extensive integration of social media into everyday communication. This phenomenon is even apparent from outer space—or, for you social media junkies, Google Earth—for all 6.8 billion people who inhabit the Earth share one world. The convergence of the Internet allows us to become a single, global community by putting everyone online. Our ability to unite together universally has exploded. We work in partnership with people all over the world, from big cities to small villages, from startup companies to large corporations—everyone doing his or her part to enact change. Social media technologies offer a way to direct this massive interconnectivity of networks into real, sound solutions for a number of global concerns, including feasible drinking water, improved sanitation, food production, public health, energy challenges, and nearly every other area of need. Whether we are trying to bring an end to racism, educate others on the hazards occurring to the environment, protect our children, or give selflessly amid devastation from an act of nature, the power of social media is greater than all of us.

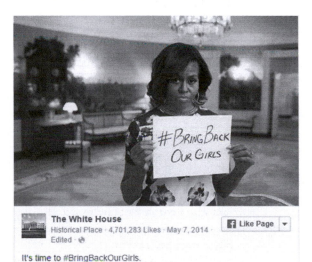

The White House
Historical Place · 4,701,283 Likes · May 7, 2014 · Edited · 👁

It's time to #BringBackOurGirls.

Read about how the U.S. is helping Nigeria in the search for those who were kidnapped → http://go.wh.gov/MCNAK7

60,549 Likes · 7,473 Comments · 25,039 Shares

👍 Like   💬 Comment   ➤ Share

First Lady Michelle Obama tweeted a photo that shows her holding a sign reading, "#BringBackOurGirls," in reference to the missing Nigerian schoolgirls.

International Relations

Global Social Channels

VK, originally VKontakte, is the largest European social network. Available in several languages, it is especially popular among Russian-speaking users. Similar to most social networks, VK allows users to message each other publicly or privately; create groups, public pages, and events; share and tag images, audio, and video; and play browser-based games.[1] VK boasts approximately 280 million active users, is ranked twenty-second among Alexa's global Top 500 sites, and is the second-most visited website in Russia, after Yandex.[2,3] According to eBizMBA Rank, VK is the eighth most popular social networking site in the world, with an average of 71 million daily users.[4]

WeChat, a popular service in China, provides text messaging, hold-to-talk voice messaging, one-to-many messaging, video conferencing, gaming, video and photo sharing, and even location services. It is one of the largest standalone messaging services, with 600 million active users, 70 million of them outside China.[5]

Qzone, another Chinese social networking website, allows users to write blogs, keep diaries, send photos, listen to music, and watch videos.[6]

---

1. "Social Gaming: Revenue in Russia, 2010–2013," Statista.com, accessed November 15, 2015, http://www.statista.com/statistics/205549/social-gaming-revenue-forecast-in-russia.
2. "vk.com Site Info," Alexa Internet, accessed November 15, 2015.
3. "Top 15 Most Popular Social Networking Sites," eBizMBA, accessed November 15, 2015, http://www.ebizmba.com/articles/social-networking-websites.
4. "Top 15 Most Popular Social Networking Sites."
5. S. Millward, "It's Time for Messaging Apps to Quit the Bullshit Numbers and Tell Us How Many Users Are Active," Techinasia.com, accessed November 15, 2015, https://www.techinasia.com/messaging-apps-should-reveal-monthly-active-users.
6. "Basic Help 基础帮助 (2008)," Tencent, accessed November 15, 2015, http://qzone.qq.com/helpcenter/index.html.

People connect, and technology facilitates these relationships. With these two concepts in mind, we can now look at the numerous tools that populate the social media landscape.

Components of Social Media

As you will learn in part III of this book, understanding the primary role of the various avenues of communication via the social web is critical when evaluating when, where, and how to communicate with your consumers.

The landscape of social media is a complex bio-network of overlapping platforms that vary in use and support communication through networking sites, publishing applications, discussion boards, and mobile applications. In *The Social Media Bible*, Lon Safko introduces the idea that the social web has been organized into fifteen categories.[54] Brian Solis pegs this number at twenty-eight, which he represents in his graphic pictorial "The Conversation Prism."[55] Both present a thorough explanation of the various tools, communities, and social sites that a company can use to interact with consumers.

Commonalities exist between the categories presented by Safko and Solis. Although it may not seem obvious, a social media model can be extracted from these categories, allowing for the development of an organizational social strategy. I would like to introduce such a model for social media planning: the Circular Model of SoMe for Social Communication (*S*hare, *o*ptimize, *M*anage, *e*ngage). Up to this point, there has yet to be a widely accepted model for social media planning. In keeping with a more simplistic approach to understanding the application of social media planning, the Circular Model of SoMe for Social Communication is based on

The Circular Model of SoMe for Social Communication (Share, optimize, Manage, engage). *Source*: Regina Luttrell.

the fundamentals supporting *The Cluetrain Manifesto* and James Grunig's two-way symmetrical model of communication.

Share

Social media through social networks help people connect with others who share similar interests, passions, and beliefs. Organizations that use specific networking strategies wherein their consumers are participating in conversations are able to socialize online together with their targeted populations. A degree of trust is formed between users within each of these networking sites. These are the users who can become consumer influencers.[56] With 53 percent of the people on Twitter recommending companies or products in their tweets and 48 percent of people delivering on their intention to buy the product, sharing the right information within the right category of the social web is extremely important.[57] Astonishingly, 90 percent of online consumers trust recommendations from people they know, and a whopping 70 percent trust the opinions of unknown users.[58] Why would a company *not* want to get to know its consumers and influencers?

A sampling of social networking sites considered "sharing" sites include

Facebook
Instagram
Pinterest
Snapchat
LinkedIn
YouTube
Vimeo
Flickr
Orkut
Kaboodle
Bebo
hi5

This is certainly not intended to be a comprehensive list of all sharing sites on the social web but rather to provide an understanding of the types of sites that would be categorized under "share." This list could be further broken into subcategories such as business networking (LinkedIn), photo sharing (Instagram), video (YouTube), or even collaborative consumption (Kaboodle).

Optimize

To optimize its message, an organization must listen to what is being said and learn from the conversations being shared. Your stakeholders will talk about your brand with or without you. However, the conversations that they have will be much richer if you, as a practitioner, are part of them. Public relations practitioners operate in a new world where people have come to expect transparent communication. It is our job to give them that. Meaningful exchanges filled with substance lead to mutual fulfillment. Tools such as Social Mention allow organizations to track and measure in real time the conversations that are being had about you, your company, the products that you offer, and just about any topic being discussed across the web's social media landscape. Social Mention monitors more than one hundred social media sites directly, including Twitter, Facebook, FriendFeed, YouTube, Digg, and Google. There are numerous listening and targeting tools available that allow organizations to collect important metrics: Sprout Social, Meltwater, Sysomos, Radian6, Linkfluence, Spiral16, Klout, and Collective Intellect are a few examples. By simply being informed about what is being said about your organization and on what social networks the conversations are taking place, it will be easier to participate in authentic exchanges between your consumers and your business.

Manage

Conversations occurring on social sites happen quickly, in a matter of seconds in fact. Consumers have come to expect quick responses and answers from public relations practitioners and social media strategists who manage online presence. Surprisingly, many companies are not prepared for the quick response consumers have come to expect. Responses to consumers are limited by availability of time on any given day, other job responsibilities, and simply the ability to manage the volume of interactions that emanate from a company's various social streams. Many times it is the case that a company simply may not have the resources to monitor and manage its social presence. All of these factors contribute to slowed responses to consumers.

In 2008, we saw for the first time the term "attention dashboard." This is described as a tool that pulls content from various sources across multiple networks into one place in an effort to monitor and manage what is being mentioned on the social web.[59] Today these are better known as "social media dashboards." TweetDeck and HootSuite are among the most popular and widely used social media monitoring systems on the market. By incorporating these tools within its communications arsenal, a company can stay current with conversations, respond to consumers in real time, send private messages, share links to company news and recently published blog posts, and monitor trending conversations. Tools such as these allow a company to easily engage with consumers, stakeholders, and influencers.

Engage

Engaging in conversations with your consumers and influencers is the most critical component of a social strategy. The more challenging question to answer might be "Where to engage?"

I equate social strategies to the rush to create websites in the late 1990s. During this period of advancement, nearly every manager approached his or her public relations practitioner and laid down the decree "Build us a website!" Naturally, our response as public relations practitioners was to ask, "What is the purpose of the website? What shall we have on it?" Not surprisingly, without a blink of an eye, this nebulous manager would spout back, "I don't know! But everyone else is getting one, so we need one too!"

This is happening again today as it relates to social strategies. In today's workplace, public relations practitioners hear, "Everyone is on Facebook, so go create us a Facebook page!" We have learned that this response simply is not the answer. An organization needs to be where its consumers are. If your consumers are not on Facebook, it does not make sense to waste precious resources targeting an area that will yield very little. With that in mind, it should be obvious that no two social strategies will look the same. Social strategies are unique to each company and each brand. Coca-Cola, for example, does not employ the same strategies and tactics for Coke that it uses for Sprite. The social strategies that work for Panera Bread will not necessarily work for Gerber.

An important takeaway here is that conducting research analysis allows you to understand how to properly measure your company's current presence within the social sphere. These results will make it easier to determine the level of effort put forth and the dialogue being discussed regarding your organization or brand on social media platforms. Are your consumers on Twitter? Is Instagram or Pinterest a place where you see your influencers engaging in activity? Does the demographic of your stakeholder base sway toward sites like LinkedIn or Plaxo? Only a thorough analysis will reveal the direction your company should be headed. A social audit may be the place to start.

There are many tools that assist companies in conducting a social media audit. Public relations professionals can use the *CMO's Guide to the Social Landscape* to help break down some of the available social media channels and their impact on specific areas. The document uses a color-coded scale ranking of "good," "OK," and "bad" to assess the effectiveness of customer engagement, search engine optimization (SEO), brand exposure, and web traffic.[60] The *CMO's Guide* focuses on Facebook, Google+, Twitter, Pinterest, LinkedIn, YouTube, and Snapchat. The most recent version includes a more comprehensive breakdown of available social networking sites that can be used to conduct a complete social media audit. The Social Marketing Compass is also useful in helping companies identify where to engage.[61] To use the Social Marketing Compass, a company must imagine the brand is at the center, and from there all layers radiate outward. The model presents multiple options and

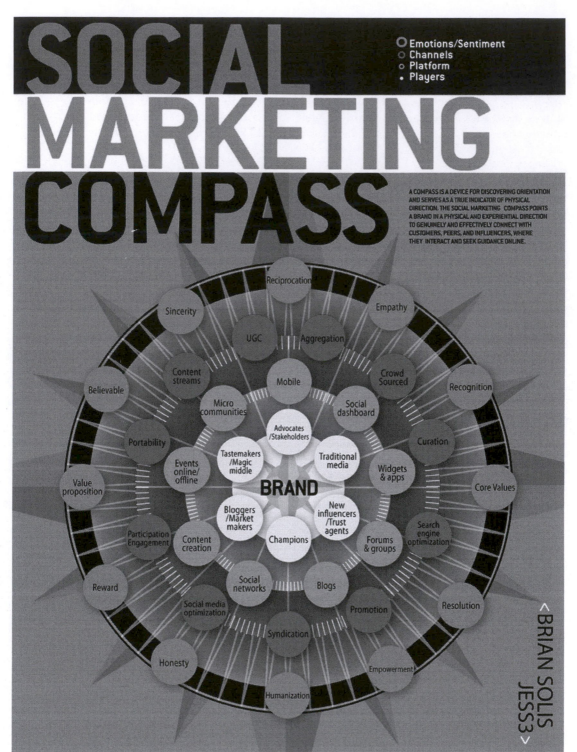

SOCIAL MARKETING COMPASS

○ Emotions/Sentiment
○ Channels
○ Platform
• Players

A COMPASS IS A DEVICE FOR DISCOVERING ORIENTATION AND SERVES AS A TRUE INDICATOR OF PHYSICAL DIRECTION. THE SOCIAL MARKETING COMPASS POINTS A BRAND IN A PHYSICAL AND EXPERIENTIAL DIRECTION TO GENUINELY AND EFFECTIVELY CONNECT WITH CUSTOMERS, PEERS, AND INFLUENCERS, WHERE THEY INTERACT AND SEEK GUIDANCE ONLINE.

< BRIAN SOLIS JESS3 >

The Social Marketing Compass. *Source*: Courtesy of Brian Solis and JESS3.

Theory into Practice

The truth Campaign[1]

As you read this case study, here are some questions to keep in mind:

Can you identify the Circular Model of SoMe for Social Communication?

Can you further identify the tactics of SoMe within this campaign?

Are there specific social media tools that are used in the truth Campaign that could be beneficial to use in your own organization? How might you best identify which tools would work best?

Can you recommend a strategy that the truth Campaign could follow to better understand the user-based metrics for this campaign?

The truth Campaign, an antismoking campaign dedicated to decreasing the use of any tobacco products by young adults and children, is active in all forms of social media as well as the Internet. Tactics include a presence on Twitter, Myspace, Xanga, hi5, and Bebo. The truth Campaign website incorporates interactive elements wherein teens can play games, download screensavers and desktop themes, view mini-sites and television advertisements, and access fact-based messaging on tobacco use, health hazards, and the prevention of smoking.[2] All of the information provided on these sites is intended to be shared. The organization is creating a global community for youth to feel connected. The utilization of these social networking sites allow teens to access and spread the campaign's messages quickly, thus coming together to take a stand against smoking and tobacco. According to its website, these social networking sites receive a combined total of around sixty thousand visits each week.[3]

The truth Campaign has also successfully integrated Facebook as an additional approach to reaching its target audience. Facebook seems the most comprehensive of all the social networking sites used in this campaign. Visitors to the truth Facebook page have access to numerous features, including original television ads, musical remixes of songs from truth commercials, facts regarding tobacco-related issues, and the ability to post comments on the "wall"—a comment space provided by the site. Visitors are also able to view the truth Campaign's pictures, participate in polls about tobacco issues, access links and other truth-specific Facebook pages and sites, and view a list of upcoming truth events and appearances. Additionally, Facebook users can illustrate their support for truth by adding it as a "cause" on their individual Facebook profiles in the form of a "Twibbon." The truth Facebook application also includes a "Truth or Dare" application loosely based on the party game of the same name. This application allows truth Facebook users to challenge their friends to either answer a question about themselves or work some slight mischief on the social networking site.[4] Each challenge completed carries with it a wager amount, giving users the chance to earn points and move up on the "Truth or Dare" leaderboard. This feature tracks scores among the users' friends in any social networks that they are a part of, including all Facebook users.

---

1 "FAQ," truth, last modified 2013, accessed June 4, 2013, http://www.thetruth.com/faq.
2 Solis, Engage.
3 Solis, Engage.
4 Solis, Engage.

---

directions to help guide companies when assessing brand, players, platform, channels, and emotions.

Where Do We Go from Here?

From the humble beginning of a simple email to our robust bio-network of social platforms, social media have caused a revolution and altered modern public relations. Today, organizations are beginning to understand that on the other side of the web, behind that personal computer, there are *real people*, and they can gain insights into the thoughts, views, and opinions of these people in real time simply by listening intently, engaging authentically, and having fun.

#LRNSMPR

Learn More: The History of Social Media

- "What The WELL's Rise and Fall Tell Us about Online Community": http://bit.ly/ZodVjU
- Passages from *The Cluetrain Manifesto*: http://bit.ly/10NVeYb
- "A Declaration of the Independence of Cyberspace": http://bit.ly/14sH0co
- "History of the Internet": http://bit.ly/16HpgBm
- The Conversation Prism: http://bit.ly/11YNF26
- "The Big Brand Theory: Nissan Builds a Car and Its Social Community": http://bit.ly/14HGURS

Notes

[1] Merriam-Webster, *Merriam-Webster's Collegiate Dictionary*, 11th ed., 2013.

[2] L. Safko, *The Social Media Bible: Tactics, Tools and Strategies for Business Success* (New York: Wiley, 2010); J. Wood, *Interpersonal Communication: Everyday Encounters*, 7th ed. (Boston: Wadsworth Cengage Learning, 2013).

[3] Merriam-Webster, *Merriam-Webster's Collegiate Dictionary*.

[4] Safko, *The Social Media Bible*.

[5] D. Boyd and N. Ellison, "Social Network Sites: Definition, History, and Scholarship," *Journal of Computer-Mediated Communication*, no. 13 (2008): 210–30, doi:10.1111/j.1083-6101.2007.00393.x (accessed May 30, 2013); J. Scott and P. Carrington, *The SAGE Handbook of Social Network Analysis* (Thousand Oaks, CA: Sage, 2011).

[6] Jeff Bullass, "33 Social Media Facts and Statistics You Should Know in 2015," Jeffbullass.com, April 7, 2015, accessed October 5, 2015, http://www.jeffbullas.com/2015/04/08/33-social-media-facts-and-statistics-you-should-know-in-2015; Jacqueline Till, "2015 Social Media Infographic: Helpful Statistics and Fun Facts—Growing Social Media," Growing Social Media, February 17, 2015, accessed October 5, 2015, http://growingsocialmedia.com/2015-social-media-infographic-helpful-statistics; Maeve Duggan et al., "Demographics of Key Social Networking Platforms," Pew Research Center Internet Science Tech RSS, January 9, 2015, accessed October 5, 2015, http://www.pewinternet.org/2015/01/09/demographics-of-key-social-networking-platforms-2; "About Us," LinkedIn, https://press.linkedin.com/about-linkedin; "Statistics," YouTube, https://www.youtube.com/yt/press/en-GB/statistics.html.

[7] "History of Iran: Cyrus the Great," Iran Chamber Society, accessed May 30, 2013, http://www.iranchamber.com/history/cyrus/cyrus.php; D. Mink, "The Complete History of Social Media," Avalaunch Media, April 15, 2013, accessed May 31, 2013, http://avalaunchmedia.com/infographics/the-complete-history-of-social-media.

[8] R. Beyer, *The Greatest Stories Never Told: 100 Tales from History to Astonish, Bewilder, and Stupefy* (New York: HarperCollins, 2003).

[9] M. Bellis, "The Invention of Radio," About.com, last modified 2013, accessed May 30, 2013, http://inventors.about.com/od/rstartinventions/a/radio.htm; M. Bellis, "The History of the Telephone," About.com, last modified 2013, accessed May 30, 2013, http://inventors.about.com/od/bstartinventors/a/telephone.htm.

[10] I. Peter, "The History of Email," NetHistory, last modified 2004, accessed May 30, 2013, http://www.nethistory.info/History of the Internet/email.html.

[11] Eric Qualman, "Social Media Video 2013 | Did You Know 2013," YouTube, 2012, accessed April 22, 2016, https://www.youtube.com/watch?v=PB99MjUz7YQ.

[12] K. Kelly and H. Rheingold, "The Dragon Ate My Homework," *WIRED 1*(3).

[13] M. Sippey, "Vine: A New Way to Share Video," Official Twitter Blog, January 24, 2013, accessed May 31, 2013, https://blog.twitter.com/2013/vine-new-way-share-video.

14 H. Rheingold, "Howard Rheingold's Story," Rheingold.com, last modified 2012, accessed June 3, 2013, http://www.rheingold.com/howard.

15 M. Lucas, A. Singh, and C. Cantrell, "Defining a Firewall," in *Firewall Policies and VPN Configurations*, ed. Anne Henmi (Rockland, MA: Syngress Publishing, 2006).

16 Wood, *Interpersonal Communication*.

17 Qualman, "Social Media Video 2013"; L. Prall, "Sixdegrees.com—Social Networking in Its Infancy," Afridesignad, September 15, 2010, accessed May 31, 2013, http://blog.afridesign.com/2010/09/sixdegrees-com-social-networking-in-its-infancy.

18 "Our Heritage," LiveJournal, last modified 2012, accessed May 30, 2013, http://www.livejournalinc.com/aboutus.php.

19 Qualman, "Social Media Video 2013."

20 Qualman, "Social Media Video 2013."

21 Qualman, "Social Media Video 2013."

22 Darrell Etherington, "Flickr at 10: 1M Photos Shared per Day, 170% Increase since Making 1TB Free," TechCrunch, 2014, http://techcrunch.com/2014/02/10/flickr-at-10-1m-photos-shared-per-day-170-increase-since-making-1tb-free.

23 Qualman, "Social Media Video 2013."

24 Bullass, "33 Social Media Facts and Statistics You Should Know in 2015."

25 Qualman, "Social Media Video 2013."

26 Sippey, "Vine."

27 F. Turner, *From Counterculture to Cyberculture: Stewart Brand, the Whole Earth Network, and the Rise of Digital Utopianism* (Chicago: University of Chicago Press, 2006).

28 C. Cadwalladr, "Stewart Brand's Whole Earth Catalog, the Book That Changed the World," *Guardian*, last modified May 4, 2013, accessed June 4, 2013, http://www.guardian.co.uk/books/2013/may/05/stewart-brand-whole-earth-catalog.

29 Prall, "Sixdegrees.com—Social Networking in Its Infancy."

30 "Our Heritage."

31 "Our Heritage."

32 "Howard Rheingold: Digital Community Builder," TED: Ideas Worth Spreading, accessed June 3, 2013, https://www.ted.com/speakers/howard_rheingold.html.

33 Kelly and Rheingold, "The Dragon Ate My Homework."

34 Kelly and Rheingold, "The Dragon Ate My Homework."

35 S. Lee, "An Overview of BBS Programs," BBSDocumentary.com, last modified 2002, accessed June 6, 2013.

36 K. Kelly, "Biography," KK*, accessed June 4, 2013, http://www.kk.org/biography.php.

37 Cadwalladr, "Stewart Brand's Whole Earth Catalog."

38 R. Luttrell, "Reflections on What Technology Wants" (manuscript, California Institute of Integral Studies, 2010).

39 TED, "Howard Rheingold: Digital Community Builder."

40 J. P. Barlow, "A Declaration of the Independence of Cyberspace," Electronic Frontier Foundation, last modified 1996, accessed June 4, 2013, https://projects.eff.org/~barlow/Declaration-Final.html; "Media," Business Dictionary, accessed May 23, 2013, http://www.businessdictionary.com/definition/media.html.

41 Barlow, "A Declaration of the Independence of Cyberspace."

42 "Esther Dyson," Edge, accessed June 4, 2013, http://www.edge.org/memberbio/esther_dyson; "EFF in the News," Electronic Frontier Foundation, last modified 2013, accessed June 4, 2013, https://www.eff.org/press/mentions.

43 Kelly, "Biography."

44 Rick Levine et al., *The Cluetrain Manifesto: The End of Business as Usual* (New York: Basic Books, 2009).

45 Luttrell, "Reflections on What Technology Wants."

46 Philip Slater, *The Chrysalis Effect: The Metamorphosis of Global Culture* (Eastbourne: Sussex Academic Press, 2009).

47 Barlow, "A Declaration of the Independence of Cyberspace."

48 "Haiti Text Donations to Red Cross Exceed $8 Million," Fox News, last modified January 15, 2010, accessed June 4, 2013, http://www.foxnews.com/us/2010/01/15/haiti-text-donations-red-cross-exceed-million.

49 "Haiti Text Donations to Red Cross Exceed $8 million," Associated Press, January 15, 2010, http://www.foxnews.com/us/2010/01/15/haiti-text-donations-red-cross-exceed-million; "Media"; "Haiti Earthquake Aid Gets Big on Facebook," Inside Facebook, last modified January 13, 2010, accessed June 4, 2013, http://www.insideFacebook.com/2010/01/13/haiti-earthquake-aid-gets-big-on-Facebook.

[50] "Esther Dyson."

[51] P. Gloviczki, "Social Media's Uses Expanding, as Seen after Oklahoma Tornado," *MinnPost*, last modified May 13, 2013, accessed June 10, 2013, http://www.minnpost.com/community-voices/2013/05/social-medias-uses-expanding-seen-after-oklahoma-tornado.

[52] R. Golijan, "Oklahoma Tornado: How to Find People, Pets," *U.S. News*, last modified May 21, 2013, accessed June 10, 2013, http://usnews.nbcnews.com/_news/2013/05/21/18400373-oklahoma-tornado-how-to-find-people-pets?lite.

[53] Brian Reis, "Michelle Obama: It's Time to Bring Back Our Girls," *Mashable*, May 7, 2014.

[54] Safko, *The Social Media Bible*.

[55] B. Solis, *Engage: The Complete Guide for Brands and Businesses to Build, Cultivate, and Measure Success in the New Web* (New York: Wiley, 2011).

[56] Safko, *The Social Media Bible*.

[57] "Twitter Statistics."

[58] "Twitter Statistics."

[59] "Haiti Earthquake Aid Gets Big on Facebook."

[60] Social Media Audit, http://bit.ly/1cl8uJR.

[61] "Haiti Earthquake Aid Gets Big on Facebook."

Status 3
"It's Complicated"

The relationships between public relations, marketing, and advertising have changed dramatically over the past five years and are becoming increasingly more complicated as the fields converge. This chapter examines the present-day public relations industry and focuses on the relationship between public relations and social media, as well as on how social media operates with advertising and marketing departments.

The Field of Public Relations Today

The field of public relations is experiencing its most dramatic paradigm shift to date. Mainstream Internet acceptance has ushered in virtual communities and, with that, the vision of a global village with unprecedented expectations for public relations practitioners to service a new, global audience.[1] As we now know, public relations practitioners in today's digital environment possess a multitude of skills.

The mounting convergence of traditional media platforms, in conjunction with new media technologies, has created a rich mixed-media environment, promoting communication and even collaboration with an audience through the web.[2] As professionals, we cannot deny that this emerging and evolving form of communication and promotion is advantageous for professional communicators as well as the consumers we serve.

The roles and relationships between public relations, social media, advertising, and marketing are evolving.

Public relations + SoMe = harmony

The Courtship of Social Media

The field of public relations and the idea of fostering meaningful relationships with stakeholders are synonymous. In fact, the Public Relations Society of America (PRSA) defines public relations as follows: "Public relations is a strategic communication process that builds mutually beneficial relationships between organizations and their publics."[3] Social media is built upon the premise of creating authentic relationships. It is no wonder that the two disciplines integrate so well and are harmonious in nature.

With this in mind, we need to work to better understand why companies are failing at social media. There are certainly various reasons for this, but one major contributor to such failure focuses on when an organization attempts to mock or rush the process of developing relationships. Too often the offenders are the advertising and marketing departments. The primary function of advertising is to sell goods and services, while the goal of marketing is to achieve the organizational economic objectives using promotion, sales, and the distribution of products or services.[4] It should be clear that neither of these disciplines is independently designed to foster authentic relationships with customers.

For example, imagine it is your first day at a new job. You have been shown to your office, completed the initial "walk-around," and been introduced to your coworkers. You have even attended the Monday Mojo meeting, and now it is lunchtime. One of your new coworkers, Jamie, invites you to join her and others from your department to go off-site for lunch. It is close to the Fourth of July holiday, and everyone is talking about their plans for the long weekend. Jamie begins to talk about the barbeque that she is hosting with family and friends at her home. All of a sudden, you speak up and say, "That sounds like so much fun, Jamie. Do you mind if my family and I come too? I'm happy to bring a side dish."

Placing etiquette aside, can you identify what is wrong with what you just said?

Everything! To begin with, you just met Jamie earlier in the morning. It might even be a stretch to say that you have known Jamie for a total of four hours, and yet you just invited yourself to her holiday picnic. Socially speaking, this would be considered unacceptable. You have not yet had the time to develop any kind of relationship with Jamie or gained her trust enough to be a part of her barbeque. Additionally, Jamie has not invited you (or your family, for that matter) to the barbeque.

This example parallels the same type of mistakes that various companies make by rolling out poorly thought-out social strategies. It is easy to identify why their social media campaigns fail miserably. The organization is essentially barging in on someone's picnic and inviting its family to the table, when nobody has even thought of including them.

Users of social media *invite* you into their lives once they feel they have been courted. When a company wishes to connect with its customer base, it should consider the connection as a personal invitation into each individual's life. Remember, your customers are human beings. Their reach is greater than your grasp. Listening and conversing over time is how meaningful relationships are built and trust is earned.

It's All about "Me, Me, Me" in This Relationship

Listening does not mean talking about you all the time. Companies must abandon the "me, me, me" and "I, I, I" philosophy of chatter for a more balanced "you-we" approach. Too often, a company will create a Facebook page or Twitter account to broadcast information about itself and any relevant achievements. There are countless feeds on social networking sites related to new hires, products or services, employee promotions, and long, drawn-out bios on the C-suite executives. This type of information equates to being on a date with a person who is guilty of never listening and continually boasts about his or her life and accomplishments. With this in mind, we would all do well to learn a lesson from Red Bull. This company consistently connects with its stakeholders in unique ways. With more than 36 million fans on Facebook alone, Red Bull understands the value of establishing a connection. The company's main Facebook page typically posts new material once or twice daily; yet you would be hard pressed to find any posts that include an image of its product. Rather, Red Bull's Facebook page focuses on images and videos of extreme sport athletes that it sponsors.

To take steps toward becoming more successful on a social level, organizations must break the habit of self-promotion. Although this sounds simple, this task can be quite difficult to execute correctly. This is due in part to the fact that many executives are eager to promote all of the great successes happening within the company. Naturally, these same executives view the company's social networking platforms as the place to announce such content to its customer base. This is only partially the case. Company social networking sites are established to engage with consumers, not bombard them with how great the company is. If your consumers have followed your business on Twitter, liked the company Facebook page, commented on your blog, or posted photos of themselves interacting in some way with your brand, they already know how great the company is. It is your job to keep them there by contributing to meaningful conversations. It is the job of the public relations professional and social strategist to understand the role that social media plays and to educate executives about how to engage with consumers using social sites. Public relations has traditionally been considered a function of management, with practitioners advising on strategies and coaching in tactics. This perception should also be applied to social media.

Mindful Listening in Social Media

Within the social media arena, the basic principles of interpersonal communication are a necessity. As humans, we "communicate to develop identities, establish and build relationships, coordinate efforts with others, have impact on issues that matter to us, and work out problems and possibilities."[5] Conversing, engaging, and developing online relationships with consumers through a company social site highlights some of the roles that practitioners assume, as well as the channels through which a company or brand can connect with its intended audience.

The concept of listening to stakeholders has been deeply rooted within the public relations industry for years.[6] Practicing mindful listening, public relations practitioners build formidable relationships with external stakeholders. To be successful today, we need to continue to listen to these stakeholders for a variety of reasons, all the while mastering the many available assorted tools to collect distinct information.

SoMe Drives Engagement

The Circular Model of SoMe for Social Communication is a concept that promotes listening. Companies benefit from real-time insights from consumers because they establish a window into their thoughts, views, feelings, and reactions regarding a given brand. Gathering these unaltered opinions that transpire via social networking sites would have been nearly impossible prior to the mainstreaming of social media. Because consumers feel comfortable enough to praise or prosecute brands on social networking sites, their opinions can be interpreted as pure. Contributing to the conversation is how a company becomes part of its community. The moment a company embarks on a social strategy, it is no longer a logo or a tagline or a nebulous presence—it has become human. Users of social media expect genuine, authentic connections; therefore, the responsibility shifts to the brand to deliver.

It is also important to note that social media strategies should not be implemented in seclusion. Social media must be ingrained throughout an organization on every level and deep within every department. This is a key point in that one can see that it makes sense that the marketing and advertising departments need to be part of the social strategy planning process.

Dave Senay, FleishmanHillard president and CEO

Many years ago, we recognized the changing communications environment and increasingly heard client demands for integrated solutions.

Can't We All Just Get Along? Integrating Public Relations, Social Media, Marketing, and Advertising

Companies are investing time, money, and energy in their social media strategies and are beginning to see the value—therefore, everyone wants to "own" the strategy. The marketing team believes it should lead the strategy, while advertising considers itself the proper proprietor. Neither is correct. Today, the public relations department should drive social media strategies, aligning synergies between the three. Because of the inherent connection that public relations and social media share, it makes sense for public relations departments to lead the social strategy. We, as public relations professionals, are the ones developing the relationships with the consumer base. One might argue that in the not-so-distant future, social media will be a department unto itself, working harmoniously with public relations, marketing, *and* advertising. Until then, the bulk of the responsibility for social media strategies should fall to public relations.

Distinct differences between public relations, social media, marketing, and advertising have been defined. However, the need to integrate and send a single, clear message via various channels is evident. The 1990s gave rise to terms like "integrated marketing communications," "convergent communications," and "integrated communications."[7] More recently, we have seen integrated marketing public relations, which includes social media strategies and tactics.[8] The idea of integration creates a consistent message. Success can be seen when each function recognizes that they complement one another. Each discipline has strengths, and together these strengths complement and reinforce a comprehensive strategic plan.[9] Choosing the best attributes from each function based on its strengths and weaknesses will result in a synergy

---

Theory into Practice

Integrating Efforts

In May 2013, Dave Senay, president and CEO of FleishmanHillard, unveiled a newly refreshed corporate brand. The company press release noted,

> The new branding reflects the evolution of the leading public relations firm into a fully integrated communications company that provides clients with the world's most complete communications solutions. FleishmanHillard has redefined the boundaries of traditional public relations by becoming channel agnostic, able to solve client business problems by working across paid, earned, shared and owned (PESO) media channels.

Richard Edelman, of Edelman Public Relations, responded to the announcement by commenting,

> I agree with Senay's assessment of the convergence of media. I also agree with his recruitment of non-traditional talent. Where we part company is his strategy for becoming a one-stop shop that is as much an ad agency as PR firm. At Edelman, we are going to evolve and expand the remit of the

public relations business. The world is moving in our direction. We are not selling to an audience; we are trying to build relationships across the community of stakeholders.

Use the links below to read the full articles, and then assess whether you agree with the views held by FleishmanHillard or Edelman Public Relations.

Is the communications industry moving toward a "one-stop shop"?

Should agencies focus on targeted efforts within a specific field?

How does a company integrate efforts and yet maintain the strengths of each field?

What are the pros and cons of each approach?

FleishmanHillard: "FleishmanHillard Unveils Newly Refreshed Brand": http://bit.ly/19kEZUs

Edelman Public Relations: "The New Look of Public Relations—a Dissenting View": http://bit.ly/14kl9Ep

throughout the campaign. When the individual pieces work together, the whole becomes greater than the sum.

Market without Selling and Still Be Profitable

By applying integrated efforts, a brand can successfully build an online presence that can resonate with the intended consumers. However, this can be tricky to execute, since the social web is made up of people, and a very large group at that, many of whom don't want to be sold to. Companies can use social media marketing strategies or content marketing to help strike a balance between the human social networks, while also remembering that they are running businesses intended to be profitable. Social media marketing and content marketing are two successful methods being used today.

When a social media marketing strategy is being implemented, the individual campaigns are managed directly within the social networking sites. Whether Twitter, Pinterest, Snapchat, Facebook, Google+, or another social networking site is right for a given consumer base, these sites produce content about the brand and execute the campaigns there.[10] Content marketing occurs directly on a brand website or a microsite created by the company itself.[11] Social media marketing and content marketing can be implemented simultaneously; however, the outcomes of the campaigns can be quite different based on the specific goals and objectives.

It is important to remember that the key principle within both of these strategies is not to sell. According to "State of Social Media: The Social Media Report 2012," nearly one-third of social media users find ads on social networking sites more annoying than other types of Internet advertisements.[12] Businesses tend to use spokespeople or feature their products and services on their websites or social networking sites to drive sales. This type of old-school, outdated advertising-marketing mix does not resonate with the social user.[13] Products and services come second to sharing information, connecting with your online community, and telling your story through genuine interactions with consumers. Creating content that is not about your brand but rather relates to topics your audience is interested in is the quintessential idea inherent in successful social media marketing and content marketing campaigns. Social media marketing strategies give you the opportunity to "genuinely connect with people in ways and in places where their attention is focused and impressionable, using a human voice."[14]

The Content Marketing Institute compiled more than one hundred successful social media marketing campaigns that resonate with consumers. A sampling of some creative campaigns, including some favorites, are highlighted below.

American Express: http://on.fb.me/1VJLoUR

American Express[15] has successfully used images to drive more engagement than text does. Accumulating almost 6 million "likes" on its Facebook page, the company utilizes images or videos in the majority of its posts. None of the posts ask consumers to sign up for a credit card or push sales copy; rather they illustrate through photos what is possible with an American Express card. At times they even share things such as where to find sweet treats when traveling.

Procter & Gamble: http://bit.ly/12UzI5K

BeingGirl.com,[16] a microsite developed by Procter & Gamble (P&G), delivers targeted content to its preteen and teen female audience. Using a colorful and engaging

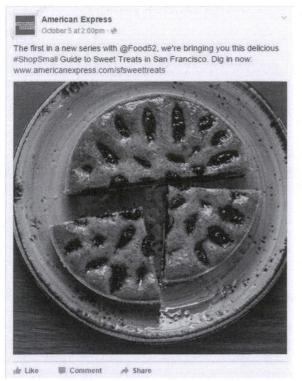

Source: American Express Facebook Page (https://www.facebook.com/AmericanExpressUS?brand_redir=259459370846061).

microsite, girls learn what it is like to be a girl and are provided with a platform for asking questions of experts on any number of topics, from premenstrual syndrome to beauty to their changing bodies. The site even addresses serious topics like confidence and self-esteem, substance abuse, cybersafety, sex and intimacy, and eating disorders. In addition to the microsite, P&G has a fan page on Facebook where community users can interact in a more public forum if they wish. But on both the microsite and the Facebook fan page, you will be hard-pressed to find any overt ads. The conversations may indeed discuss products that P&G sells, but not in the traditional marketing or advertising manner. In a study performed by Forrester Research, P&G found that a microsite like BeingGirl.com was four times more effective than a traditional marketing campaign.[17]

General Mills: http://bit.ly/1aCEois

The Tablespoon Cooking Community[18] is an interactive website for people passionate about food and entertaining. The site itself gathers first-class content on topics that matter most to its audience and delivers it straight to them, including topics related to "Quick Dishes," "Taste for Adventure," and "Rock UR Party." These categories help community members find

Source: BeingGirl.com (http://www.beinggirl.com).

content effortlessly in a much more innovative way than traditional websites allow. Community members can subscribe to the newsletter and even participate in "Table Talk"—a forum that brings members together with General Mills to connect, share recipes and ideas, and learn about the latest trends within the food industry.

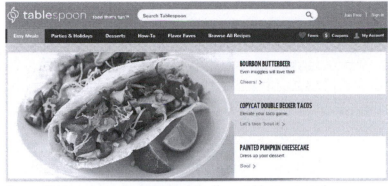

Source: Tablespoon by General Mills (http://www.tablespoon.com).

The Tablespoon Cooking Community also has a presence on Facebook, Pinterest, YouTube, and Twitter to connect in more ways.

In each of these examples, none of the parent companies directly sells its products through these forums. You do not see blatant product pitches, demonstrations, or spokespeople spewing claims. However, what you do see are brands establishing

International Relations

WATERisLIFE Hijacks #FirstWorldProblems

WATERisLIFE, an organization with a mission to provide clean water, sanitation, and hygiene programs, recently teamed up with advertising agency DDB New York to create and subsequently launch the "hashtag killer" campaign. This dynamic relationship conceived a bold idea to hijack the #FirstWorldProblems hashtag in order to promote awareness of the global water crisis and put trivial First World problems into perspective.[1] The hashtag, a perpetual presence on Twitter, pokes fun at people who have more than the basics of life covered and yet grumble when, say, a neighbor blocks their Wi-Fi access.[2]

In the video "First World Problems Anthem" (http://bit.ly/1m7JEol), a man outside a dilapidated tin-roof house says, "I hate it when my house is so big, I need two wireless routers."[3] A young girl near a stream where women are washing clothes adds, "When I leave my clothes in the washer so long, they start to smell." Additional jabs are spread throughout the video. Text at the end of the video reads, "#FirstWorldProblems Are Not Problems. Donate to help bring clean water to those in need."[4]

Not surprisingly, this campaign was embraced and promoted by celebrities, influencers, and news outlets alike, increasing awareness of the crisis. As the "hashtag killer" campaign continued to grow

throughout the social sphere, WATERisLIFE was able to change the conversation. Rather than complaining about insignificant occurrences, people began to use the hashtag to spread the message of the crisis and encourage donations supporting the greater cause.

The video garnered more than 6.97 million hits in less than a month, with donations pouring in from a worldwide audience. The campaign also won three awards at the Cannes Lions 2014 Awards: one gold and two bronze.[5]

1 Jeff Bullass, "5 Clever Social Media Marketing Campaigns That Went Viral," Jeffbullas.com, July 14, 2014, accessed November 15, 2015, http://www.jeffbullas.com/2014/07/15/5-clever-social-media-marketing-campaigns-that-went-viral.
2 Ed Payne and Chandler Friedman, "Viral Ad Campaign Hits #FirstWorldProblems," CNN.com, October 12, 2012, accessed November 15, 2015, http://www.cnn.com/2012/10/23/tech/ad-campaign-twist.
3 Payne and Friedman, "Viral Ad Campaign Hits #FirstWorldProblems."
4 Payne and Friedman, "Viral Ad Campaign Hits #FirstWorldProblems."
5 "Social Media Marketing: How #FirstWorldProblems Was Hijacked by WATERisLIFE," Digital Marketing Case Study, 2015, accessed November 15, 2015, http://www.digitaltrainingacademy.com/casestudies/2015/03/social_media_marketing_how_firstworldproblems_was_hijacked_by_waterislife.php.

themselves as trusted, friendly resources that are available and accessible via a variety of avenues.

Why "Or"? Why Not "And"?

The lines of responsibility in the public relations, marketing, and advertising departments across the country have most certainly blurred over the last decade. Social media has thrown a wrench into the neatly assembled silos that the communications industry had developed over time. Research has shown us that, generally speaking, in addition to traditional public relations activities, public relations departments oversee blogging, podcast recording, video creation, social networking site management, mobile marketing, and website development, while marketing departments tend to supervise direct mail marketing, email marketing, advertising efforts, and SEO optimization.[19]

James Collins and Jerry Porras, authors of *Built to Last: Successful Habits of Visionary Companies,* proposed that rather than using an either/or philosophy, companies should adopt a both/and approach: "A truly visionary company embraces both ends of a continuum: continuity *and* change, conservatism *and* progressiveness, stability *and* revolution, predictability *and* chaos, heritage *and* renewal, fundamentals *and* craziness. *And, and, and.*"[20]

Using the logic behind Collins and Porras's philosophy, a company may ask itself, Why not have both the public relations department and the marketing department blog? Each department has a great deal of knowledge to share with the social community. Why must a company choose either the public relations department or the marketing department? They simply do not have to, and that is the point. Sharing resources, coordinating efforts, and offering a consistent and effective message can result in a smoother, more highly integrated effort spanning multiple departments.

I cannot claim that these departments will instantly embrace the ideas presented here; nor can I assert a synchronized effort all the time. But I can say that public relations, social media, marketing, and advertising have begun to see the benefits of working together on a single message to achieve corporate objectives.

#LRNSMPR

Learn More: Social Media Campaigns

Major car companies seem to understand the idea of integrating public relations and social media efforts, resulting in successful communication strategies. Watch the following videos and read the trailing article highlighting separate campaigns from Ford, Mercedes, and Nissan.

- "How Mercedes Benz Successfully Uses Social Media to Engage": http://bit.ly/10Alsiy
- "Ford's Jim Farley on the Importance of Putting Your Brand in the Hands of Customers": http://bit.ly/19UTlrY
- "The Big Brand Theory: Nissan Builds a Car and Its Social Community": http://bit.ly/14HGURS

1. What is common among the three examples?
2. Utilizing the Circular Model of SoMe for Social Communication (Share, *optimize, Manage,* engage), identify each stage from the examples provided.
3. Explain how success was achieved as highlighted within each example.

Notes

1. H. Rheingold, *Smart Mobs: The Next Social Revolution* (Cambridge, MA: Basic Books, 2002); S. Fitzgerald and N. Spagnolia, "Four Predictions for PR Practitioners in the New Millennium," *Public Relations Quarterly*, no. 3 (1999): 12–14.

2. J. Pavlik, "Mapping the Consequences of Technology on Public Relations," *Institute of Public Relations* (2009): 2–17; C. A. Platt, "Writing in Public: Pedagogical Uses of Blogging in the Communication Course," *Electronic Journal of Communication*, no. 1 (2010): 1–16.

3. "What Is Public Relations? PRSA's Widely Accepted Definition," Public Relations Society of America, last modified April 11, 2012, accessed June 19, 2013, http://www.prsa.org/AboutPRSA/PublicRelationsDefined.

4. D. Wilcox et al., *THINK Public Relations* (Upper Saddle River, NJ: Pearson Education, 2013).

5. J. Wood, *Interpersonal Communication: Everyday Encounters*, 7th ed. (Boston: Wadsworth Cengage Learning, 2013).

6. Wilcox et al., *THINK Public Relations*; F. Seitel, *The Practice of Public Relations* (Upper Saddle River, NJ: Pearson Education, 2014).

7. Wilcox et al., *THINK Public Relations*.

8. G. Giannini, *Marketing Public Relations: A Marketer's Approach to Public Relations and Social Media* (Upper Saddle River, NJ: Prentice Hall, 2009).

9. Wilcox et al., *THINK Public Relations*.

10. T. Murdock, "Content Marketing vs. Social Media Marketing: What's the Difference?," Content Marketing Institute, last modified February 27, 2012, accessed June 22, 2013, http://contentmarketinginstitute.com/2012/02/content-marketing-vs-social-media-marketing.

11. Murdock, "Content Marketing vs. Social Media Marketing."

12. "State of Social Media: The Social Media Report 2012," Nielsen, accessed May 28, 2013, http://www.nielsen.com/us/en/reports/2012/state-of-the-media-the-social-media-report-2012.html.

13. B. Solis, *Engage: The Complete Guide for Brands and Businesses to Build, Cultivate, and Measure Success in the New Web* (New York: Wiley, 2011).

14. Solis, *Engage*.

15. "Facebook Logo," American Express, 2015, accessed October 9, 2015, https://www.facebook.com/AmericanExpressUS?brand_redir=259459370846061.

16. See the BeingGirl website at http://beinggirl.com.

17. Joe Pulizzi, "How to Develop a Microsite: 5 Examples to Get You Started," Content Marketing Institute, December 31, 2010, http://contentmarketinginstitute.com/2010/12/microsite-samples.

18. "Quick Recipes and Easy Recipe Ideas—Tablespoon," Quick Recipes and Easy Recipe Ideas, 2015, accessed October 9, 2015; see the Tablespoon website at http://www.tablespoon.com.

19. D. Guth and C. Marsh, *Public Relations: A Values Driven Approach*, 5th ed. (Boston, MA: Pearson Education, 2012).

20. J. Collins and J. Porras, *Built to Last: Successful Habits of Visionary Companies* (New York: HarperCollins, 2004).

FORMULATING A STRATEGY
Social Media Tools Used by Public Relations Practitioners

2 PART

Social Press 4

Today's practitioner moves in a fast-paced, real-time environment, but that doesn't mean that "getting ink" isn't important anymore. Now, more than ever, it is vital to gain the attention of journalists between all the media-rich messages they receive on a daily basis. This chapter explores how to break through the clutter and get your message heard by today's journalists, bloggers, and online influencers.

Ushering in a Wave of New(s) Consumers

Gone are the days when the paperboy diligently delivered the morning newspaper before sunup, and we eagerly read it page by page. No longer do we gather at five in the evening to watch the day's top news stories or turn on the radio to catch a noteworthy broadcast. In today's media-rich environment, there is a multitude of outlets for Americans to obtain their daily news fix. Online platforms play a pivotal role in how we consume news.

Research indicates that 36 percent of Americans turn to the Internet as a regular source for news. When we include social networking sites, email, mobile devices, and tablets, the number increases to 44 percent.[1] Even more staggering is the recent increase from 9 to 19 percent in the number of Americans reporting that they only consume news via social networking sites.[2] Traditional media platforms, including television, radio, and print, have been edging downward over the past decade; however, these media avenues cannot be altogether discounted.[3] This is an important point of distinction. Despite all the talk about the death of journalism, we do see that journalism is not dying at all. Publishers and journalists are evolving in the same way that public relations professionals are. News outlets are striving to ensure that the content they produce is relevant to today's audiences.[4] Americans are integrating technology into how they consume news, using both digital and traditional sources at a much faster pace than first imagined.[5]

The methods by which Americans interact with news have also changed. There is a large number of Internet users with whom we engage in conversations and talk about events that are happening around us. A two-minute advertisement posted by the *Guardian*,[6] a British newspaper, illustrates just how much of an active role viewers and periodical readers play in responding to news coverage or, as some may argue, even contribute to the news. The video ad "reimagines the Three Little Pigs as a modern news story, beginning with the Big Bad Wolf's death in a boiling pot and a SWAT team descending on the home of the porcine suspects. *Throughout the video*, reporters follow every twist and turn with help from readers across social media."[7] The commercial brilliantly illustrates the intimate relationship consumers have with news and with those who report the news.

Practitioners should also learn to recognize that anyone can be a publisher or editor. When blogs initially began popping up on the Internet, they changed everything and signaled a paradigm shift. Anyone with access to the Internet could have a voice—and today, millions of people effectively use this platform. Readers regularly publish comments on journalists' articles, tweet views and opinions, and debate one another (and journalists alike) about the coverage, facts, and details of a story. Social media essentially utilize word-of-mouth strategies at broadband speeds with instantaneous diffusion.

Reporters today must have the capacity to write, be on the air, and shoot and edit video while interacting and maintaining an online presence. The new reporter, along with consumer-generated news and online influencers, has altered the landscape of media relations. There was a time when public relations practitioners knew—and I mean *really knew*—the reporter who covered their beat; they knew they could count on a truth-seeking editor and understood that an honest, unbiased story would run.[8] Americans could rely on three television networks and a handful of dependable, honorable newspapers to deliver the top stories.[9] Today, conglomerates, fragmented media, breaking news in a twenty-four/seven cycle, and the ever-present online platforms dominate media relations protocol.

This unparalleled shift in news reporting, including how Americans obtain news, has had a direct impact on media relations and given rise to what has come to be

International Relations

Practicing PR in Spain

Is the business function of public relations really practiced all that differently in other countries around the world? Well, to some degree, yes. There are certainly a number of differences between the United States and Europe that should be accounted for. One must not only take into account any cultural differences but also consider the work environment and the ways in which professionals communicate with clients.

Marina Ferrer explains some of the distinct differences between practicing public relations in the United States versus practicing public relations in Spain:

1. Face-to-face interaction is extremely important. Although the use of new technologies is helpful to complete tasks like scheduling meetings and sharing documents, simply taking five minutes to chat over coffee will often get you better results than sending countless emails or scheduling multiple Outlook meetings. First impressions—appearance and relatability—are always important when meeting with contacts and potential clients.

2. The idea of time management is different. Tight schedules and strict deadlines usually do not work very well in Spain. Typically, few people are in the office before 9:00 a.m. That said, working on projects well past 9:00 p.m. or later is common. It is true that Spaniards' work

philosophy is not as structured as that of their American counterparts, but PR practitioners in Spain still manage to resolve problems under pressure and come up with creative solutions.

3. Getting straight to the point is not the best tactic. In Spain people like to socialize and value becoming closer with colleagues and clients. Beginning a meeting by jumping straight into the agenda is an approach that is generally not well received, as your coworkers and clients may consider this approach cold or rude. When meeting with a client or trying to accomplish tasks externally, start with more informal conversation. Spend more time talking about irrelevant things because if you connect with the people that you work with, the level of commitment from them will be higher over the long term.

4. No, people in Spain don't do "siesta" during the day. This is the biggest Spanish stereotype. Spaniards use longer breaks for brainstorming sessions, internal meetings, or client meetings. In Spain, this is a way of continuing with our work but also taking some time to refresh our minds.

Source: Marina Ferrer, "Spain PR vs. US PR: 4 Things You Need to Know," Weber Shandwick Seattle Public Relations and Digital Marketing, June 14, 2012, accessed November 16, 2015, http://www.webershandwickseattle.com/2012/06/4-differences-to-know-between-seattle-and-spain-in-pr-and-communications.

known as "social press." Traditional media relations and social press have become standard job duties for today's public relations practitioner. To penetrate news outlets and reach our audiences, we must now build relationships with traditional journalists as well as bloggers, online reporters, administrators, citizen journalists, and new influencers. By following the Circular Model of SoMe for Social Communication (*S*hare, *o*ptimize, *M*anage, *e*ngage), today's public relations practitioner can thrive in a world inundated with new influencers.

Community of New Influencers

In today's modernized societies, public relations practitioners are engaging with a different type of media professional. In addition to traditional journalists, practitioners are building formidable and fruitful relationships online at the same time. Not that long ago, public relations pros asked journalists for a "desk-side" meeting or networked at an after-hours gathering. Today, professionals have the opportunity to instantly engage with a wealth of online influencers using media like Twitter, Facebook, LinkedIn, and other powerful blogs and forums. Social networking sites are seen as a way to complement traditional media relations by bringing the relationship between public relations professionals and their contacts to life online.

Influencer Relations

Public relations professionals have been criticized over the years for attempting to apply traditional media relations tactics to online relations. Simply put, these tactics are different. A new set of tools is required in an online world above and beyond the previously accepted conventional tactics and press releases. When we correctly share, optimize, monitor, and engage with an online influencer such as a blogger, a contact on Twitter, or a forum administrator, we are opening the door to building a successful relationship in the social press world.

Blogger Relations

A predominant opinion in the online community is that the blogosphere is fueled by *people*—people who are part of the human network of connections we make on a regular basis.[10] These individuals could be journalists, analysts, experts, or simply writers who are passionate about sharing their views. As with pitching traditional journalists, it is critical to get to know bloggers as well. It is essential to understand the blogger's focus and point of view, writing style, length of time blogging, audience, and even his or her preferred way to be contacted. These questions are not unlike the ones that you might already utilize when getting to know a journalist. To send a press release to everyone in the newsroom is inappropriate. The same rule of logic is implied in blogger relations: don't spam bloggers with irrelevant information that has little or nothing to do with their area of expertise.

In 2007, Chris Anderson, editor of *Wired Blog Network* and *The Long Tail*, wrote a blog post that sent shockwaves throughout the public relations profession, so much so that it still resonates today.[11] He published hundreds of public relations professionals' email addresses after one too many "lazy flacks" bombarded his inbox with irrelevant news. You read that correctly: *he published their email addresses for the world to read*. His post came out of frustration. Bloggers want public relations professionals to tell a story that is engaging and relevant to their readers, just like journalists. Engaging genuinely and effectively takes a good deal of practice. Effective blogger relations can be boiled down to two simple rules: Rule No. 1: follow, listen, and interact. Rule No. 2: be a good storyteller.

Rule No. 1: Follow, Listen, and Interact

According to Nielsen, bloggers are active across many social media platforms. These individuals are two times more likely to post and comment on consumer-generated video sites like YouTube and nearly three times more likely to post on message boards and in forums.[12] Finding the right blogger will become critical to a company's overall plan to gain social press, earned media, and awareness. As a rule, big does not always mean better in the blogosphere. Search for blogs that are relevant to your company or area of expertise. Find out where your customers are on the web, whom they read, and who influences them. If you do not know where to begin searching for this information, consider using tools like Technorati, Alltop, or Gorkana and search their databases.[13]

Once you identify a list of bloggers who are influential within your company's sector, become knowledgeable, transparent, and trustworthy to them. In essence, begin establishing a relationship with them. This is done through careful exploration of their blogrolls.[14] Public relations practitioners should read the blog frequently and comment regularly. The only way to form a solid relationship with a blogger is by understanding him or her. Make sure you link to the blog, even tag the blog in your own company blog, tweet important articles that the blogger writes, and participate in the blogger's community without the anticipation of being covered.[15] Ultimately, you want to immerse yourself within his or her blog world. This takes time and patience, but the rewards are bountiful.

Rule No. 2: Be a Good Storyteller

You must first establish a solid relationship with a blogger before you can tell your story.[16] Public relations professionals have always been storytellers. To effectively tell your story to a blogger, you need to make sure that it is interesting and compelling. Creating videos and offering ebooks, interviews, podcasts, images, or a Pinterest board can help tell your story and grab the blogger's attention.[17] Your content should be genuinely useful and exciting. A "one-size-fits-all" approach will not work with bloggers.

The Perfect Pitch

Once you have established yourself and your company as part of the blogger's community, pitching your news to him or her will become easier and easier. Keep in mind, just as in traditional media relations, there are rules. In fact, the rules are similar.

Personalization: When pitching to bloggers, address them by name and demonstrate that you've read their blog by injecting a reference to it in your opening sentence.[18] This illustrates that you are interested in what they are writing about and take part in their community because you know them, understand them, value their likes and dislikes, and have a keen appreciation for what types of articles their readers want to hear more about.

Creating an impact—softly and with value: Bloggers aren't into press releases that include quotes from CEOs; nor are they inclined to respond when asked to write a blog post or for a retweet of a recently published article.[19] What a blogger wants is a compelling story that is truly interesting and connects back to the purpose of the blog.[20] *A story is not worth covering simply because the company we work for thinks it is.* This is a valuable takeaway.

Brevity: A whopping 6.7 million people publish blogs on blogging websites, and another 12 million write blogs using their social networks.[21] On average,

What Do Journalists Want?

Meeting Reporter's Needs
Understanding the challenges and goals of today's reporters is paramount!

Breaking News	Photos	Interesting	Facts
77%	73%	60%	70%
Linking company news to the breaking news of the day is likely to elevate the success of your pitch. By integrating your PR campaign with timely, relevant information, you can differentiate your brand's story from other pitches and press releases that reporters receive.	Reporters indicate that photos are their most favorite asset that PR professionals provide. Attention grabbing, photos, graphics, infographics, and videos not only help the media outlet, but also tell a brand's story in their own voice.	The next press release you write should not only focus on the breaking news that you are sharing, but include facts, angles, quotes and other assets to increase the value to reporters.	Journalists often describe the essence of their work as finding and presenting "the facts." Give them what they want. Include quotes, statistics, and numbers that help tell the story.

0 10 20 30 40 50 60 70 80 90 100

Company Website 92%
Company's Online Newsroom 77%
Social Media 42%   Spokespeople 42%
Trade Publications 41%   Blogs 34%
Wikipedia 32%

Where Do Reporters Conduct Their Research?

Daily Dose of SM	Email Rules	You Had Me at Hello
67% of journalists spend up to two hours a day on social.	83% of reporter's prefer being pitched via email.	79% of journalists said the subject line impacts their interest in reading a press release.

Sources:
Business Wire http://bit.ly/21L7ir6
Cision: bit.ly/1VJyVuW

More than half of journalists surveyed in a recent Social Journalism Study believe that they would not be able to carry out their work without turning to their social media accounts for help. Yet, when being pitched a story idea by PR practitioners, 83 percent prefer an email over a tweet. *Source:* Infographic design: Regina Luttrell; source content: Cisison (http://bit.ly/1VJyVuW).

bloggers write between three to five blog posts each week. Their time is precious, and so the better written and honed your pitch is, the better your chances for a response.

Online influencers permeate the Internet. Twitter, Facebook, and niche forums have become havens of influence within the media world—both online and behind the desk.

Twitter Relations

Public relations professionals should get in the habit of using Twitter to engage with online influencers rather than simply using it as a network to connect with peers.[22] More than half of all journalists worldwide use Twitter to follow trusted sources and find stories.[23] Twitter has come to play a vital role in how journalists gather and break news, as well as how they locate credible sources that become critical contacts as they are putting a story together. Prior to the social media revolution, journalists relied on wire services to gather important information. Today, they examine their Twitter feeds daily or organize their feeds using tools like HootSuite, allowing an individual to create lists according to topics or individuals that they follow.[24] With the creation and availability of HootSuite (or similar platforms), journalists can essentially create their own newswire services.

Journalists are also turning to the service Twitterfall because it highlights the most popular topics being discussed at any given moment.[25] One of the most famous tweets in the United States came from Keith Urbahn, a former chief of staff to Defense Secretary Donald Rumsfeld, when he tweeted, "So I am told by a reputable person they have killed Osama bin Laden. Hot damn." Simply due to the fact that Urbahn is a credible source in this instance, this tweet went viral quickly.[26]

At the end of the day, as public relations practitioners, we need to better understand how to leverage services like Twitter in shaping our news sources and information channels. By referencing the Circular Model of SoMe for Social Communication, identifying influencers can become much more straightforward and simplified than first thought.

Share: Become part of the Twitterverse. Being active in conversations with journalists, bloggers, online influencers, and editors can help you discover who is most relevant in your personal learning network (PLN).

Optimize: Use your time wisely and refer to your existing media contacts. Look through your media lists, contacts, and stacks of business cards. Then take those names and find those professionals on Twitter and other social networking platforms.

Manage: To locate new influencers, use tools like Social Mention or Twitter Search to find influencers who are relevant to you. You can also use lists like those found on Listorious or PeerIndex to help as well.

Engage: Once you have identified influencers who are pertinent to you or your business, build your relationship beyond Twitter. Refer to their blogs, newspapers, or media that they work for and take part in discussion forums, offer up items you see that may be of interest to them, and connect them with sources. Since a pitch is not generally going to happen over Twitter but rather through more conventional avenues like email, it is important that you gain their attention. Just because you follow them does not mean they will follow you, so you need to put in twice the effort to make them notice you and become a trusted resource.

Forum Administrator Relations

Forums, which are also referred to as message boards, are fertile with audiences that provide quality insights and engagement in conversations specific to that niche group. They are intended to be a location for discussions relevant to a specific topic or industry. These focused conversations are central to the success of an organization's online media relations initiatives and should not be overlooked. As with all types of outreach via the Internet, blogosphere, or Twitterverse, persistent engagement within targeted forums is essential prior to a public relations professional's pitching an administrator.[27]

Developing a strong online presence with influencers will carry over into traditional media relations. The two are a bridge to one another and are not mutually exclusive. Media relations are still considered a top skill that all public relations practitioners must possess, hone, and cultivate.[28]

Progressive Media Relations

The role of public relations practitioners is to regularly manage the relationship between their organization and the media, regardless of the medium.[29] The evolution of media communicated through the Internet has led to a compression in publication timing and a greater focus on breaking news, neither of which diminishes the job of the reporter or the public relations professional. Each profession still has distinct roles and responsibilities.

(Insights on working with professionals in today's media environment can be seen in interviews available at http://ginaluttrellphd.com/videos.)

Reporters' Job

Reporters are tasked with a relatively short list of duties compared with those of public relations professionals. They *must*

generate reader interest;
objectively tell *all* sides of the story, *not just your company's*;
gather information from multiple sources: customers, competitors, analysts;
obtain timely, useful information;
work under deadline pressure (twenty-four/seven news cycle and second-to-second tweets);
report on a variety of news, which may or may not include your area of expertise, industry, or company.

Public Relations Practitioners' Job

The responsibility of a public relations practitioner is a bit more complex, but the fruits of building a healthy relationship with journalists, bloggers, and online influencers are most often realized through news coverage, fair reporting, and an enhanced receptivity to pitched stories. You are the middleman, the connector between an organization and the public. Once you establish yourself and your area of expertise, you can become a valuable resource for journalists.

Try to keep the following principles in mind when working with traditional media or hybrid media (indicative of media in their original medium—newspaper, radio, TV), as well as online media formats, including websites, blogs, and social networking sites:

• Establish credibility
  • Get as much information as possible prior to meeting or pitching to journalists.
    • Understand the journalist's interests and, yes, even biases.

Theory into Practice

Pitching Journalists via Social Media

Eight tips for successfully using social media in pitching journalists, from Airfoil Group

Social networks provide a valuable avenue for pitching journalists, and those who master social techniques often can engage with reporters earlier and more deeply. The communications professionals of Airfoil, based in Detroit and Silicon Valley, have been exceptionally successful in establishing such relationships with journalists and offer their own personal recommendations for ways to incorporate social media into the pitching matrix:

Do your homework. Never pitch to a reporter on Twitter unless you are 100 percent sure they would be interested in the story. No public relations professional wants to risk being called out on Twitter for pitching something irrelevant or being annoying.

Use social media as a way to easily see whether reporters are writing about topics similar to the one you're pitching. Then offer a fresh perspective or source for a story: "Saw you're into robots, this might be up your alley: Sphero, robotic ball controlled with a swipe #kidsloveit."

If you're pitching a reporter via email or phone, mention that you follow them on Twitter, Instagram, or other channels and comment on something they recently posted. Encourage reporters to follow you as well by putting your social channels (as appropriate) in your signature and business cards.

Because Twitter can be personal, check to see how the reporter uses it. Most often, reporters are tweeting with the world, but it's good to check on whether they write something like "Personal Twitter" in their bio. Tweet directly to them, rather than using direct messages, because you can only direct message (DM) people who follow you back.

Use Twitter sparingly to avoid looking like a spammer. Recommended use is two or three times monthly for pitches, usually only after a reporter is unresponsive via phone or email.

Keep pitches short and to the point. For example, "Hey (@reporter)—Have new national consumer survey results on social media behavior/trends + infographic. Interested in an advance?" If they respond that they are interested and provide an email address, email them with the full pitch and a subject line of "Per Twitter" or "Per our Twitter Convo" to better stand out in their inbox. Afterward, respond to their tweet with something like "Great—just sent you an email" to remind them to look.

When you already have a relationship with a reporter through email or phone, use social media as a way to maintain and grow your relationship. Talk about anything other than your clients, so the relationship becomes increasingly authentic; this also builds trust. That way, when it comes time to pitch them via social media, it's not so nerve-wracking and doesn't across as transactional.

It's a good idea to follow reporters on Twitter for a number of reasons. Reporters tweet a lot about pitches they receive, so it's just useful to see their feedback. They may also call for sources via Twitter. Additionally, Twitter is a good source for discovering what reporters care about in their own lives. Finally, always retweet or tweet about a story that you've worked on with a reporter.

Airfoil maintains offices in Silicon Valley, Detroit, London, and Hong Kong. It is an independent firm specializing in marketing communications and public relations for both emerging and leading technology companies. Connect with Airfoil at www.airfoilgroup.com; Twitter, @airfoilpr; YouTube, http://www.youtube.com/user/airfoilpr; Facebook, https://www.facebook.com/AirfoilPR; and LinkedIn, http://www.linkedin.com/company/20238?trk=tyah.

- Become familiar with the journalist's knowledge of the industry. So often, journalists have multiple beats to report on. Your industry may be one of three or four that the journalist covers, and so understanding the depth to which he or she is familiar with your topic will be important as you build up your relationship with this person.
- Distinguish the media outlet and its audience.
  - Tailor your message to the audience and the journalist. This means you need to do your homework and know the readership and the reporting style of the person you are pitching.
  - Time your message to publication or the journalist's deadlines.
  - Initiate contact if and when appropriate.
  - Distinguish pitches between online influencers and traditional media.
  - Know and respect the journalist's deadline.
- Determine your agenda.
  - Analyze your audience.
  - Identify your objectives.
  - Identify the key points or messages that you want to promote.
- Do not wing it!
  - Set time aside prior to meeting any reporter or taking part in an interview to relax and collect your thoughts.
  - Rehearse your key messages. Be sure to support your points with colorful anecdotes and compelling statistics. Keep your responses as jargon free as possible. Your company may have an acronym for every day of the week, but it does not mean that anyone outside your company understands the meaning. For example, in the telecommunications industry a frequent acronym used is "COW." To the average person, this is an animal, but to a well-versed telecomm person it is a "cell-site on wheels." See how easily one could misinterpret the meaning?
  - Do not forget to provide the most important information first!
- Tell the truth: Do not lie, because the truth will eventually reveal itself.[30] You risk ruining the credibility and relationship that you have worked so hard to foster. Public relations practitioners should never withhold bad or negative-leaning information because it can turn into a damaging, negative story quite easily.
- Do not pick a fight: Journalists are neither friends nor enemies; they are professional colleagues. They never forget how to work with public relations professionals, but if you make an interview difficult,

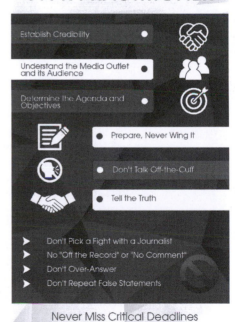

Source: Regina Luttrell.

they will remember you and may opt not to call on your expertise.[31] You need them just as much as they need you.

- Fatal flaws—do not succumb!
  - *Commenting "off the record":* There is no such thing! Public relations practitioners and journalists develop healthy, professional relationships over time, but make no mistake—regardless of how friendly you become with the journalist, anything that you say is fair game and can be reported in a story. Take it from Barbara Morgan, the communications director for New York City mayoral candidate Anthony Weiner. Her comments to a reporter landed her in hot water all over the news and social sphere when she called intern Olivia Nuzzi a myriad of less-than-flattering adjectives. (Read the full article: http://nydn.us/16k56uq.)
  - *Answering "no comment":* This makes it look as if the company has something to hide.
  - *Speaking "off the cuff":* When you speak from the hip, you risk committing an outrageous verbal faux pas. People who work with the media must remember that they "are" the company. Regardless of personal feelings, such a person represents the company at all times. Speaking "off the cuff" can get your media representative in quite a bit of trouble and possibly damage the organization's image and brand. It is a good idea to develop a media relations policy for working with the media to ensure that all representatives understand the company's etiquette.[32]
  - *Repeating false statements:* Don't do it. Each spoken word during an interview is a sound bite or quote. If the reporter phrases a question negatively or uses undesirable language, and you then repeat the negative wording when responding, your overall message could be interpreted adversely.
  - *Sticking to the facts:* It is okay if you don't have an answer, but get back to the journalist as soon as possible with the information. It is quite common to respond with something like "I don't have those numbers in front of me, but let me find out and I'll get back to you."
  - *Overanswering:* Once you have made your point, stop talking. Too often, we are afraid of silence. Avoid filling the silence. Overanswering can lead to "off the cuff" responses, and we all know where those can lead!
  - *Missing deadlines:* The news cycle moves quickly. It is our job to help journalists meet their deadlines. Your company can easily be overlooked when a journalist is on deadline and cannot reach you for a comment. More often than not, this is becoming common practice in our digital-driven news cycle.
- Devour news! Whether you get your information online, in print, over the airwaves, or on the run via mobile devices, you must always be informed as to what is going on in the world, what stories are trending, and which stories journalists in your industry are reporting on.[33]
- Say thank you! Too often, public relations professionals neglect to send a quick note of appreciation for the reporter's time and the ensuing article.

New Tools of the Trade

Connecting with reporters has never been easier. In addition to social networking sites, there are online tools that public relations professionals have available to help connect them directly with journalists, bloggers, and online influencers.

As an example, HARO (Help a Reporter Out)[34] is a free service that connects reporters looking for sources on articles they are developing. Individuals who sign up for the service receive three emails a day that include queries from independent writers, freelancers, bloggers, and big media outlets, including the *New York Times* and ABC News. In addition to simply responding to inquiries, the emails can also be used to observe and jump on stories that are currently trending. For example, when gas prices began to rise and people across the United States were seeing $3 to $4 per gallon prices for the first time, nearly every query on HARO was seeking experts to comment. I viewed this trend as an opportunity to pitch my local Associated Press (AP) reporter. At the time this was occurring, I was working in the home-care industry as a public relations manager. Home-care workers were quitting their jobs in droves because their pay did not cover the rising cost of gas. The higher cost of gas was specifically impacting their ability to complete their multiple daily client visits. The impact was certainly not exclusive to my area, and so I pitched the AP reporter with the angle that this was an issue affecting the broader home-care industry. Upon follow-up, the reporter loved the pitch and ran with it. The story appeared in almost every major newspaper across the United States. What was even more astonishing was that from this single AP article, the story catapulted to a featured segment on *The CBS Evening News* with Katie Couric. Every public relations professional should have an account with HARO.

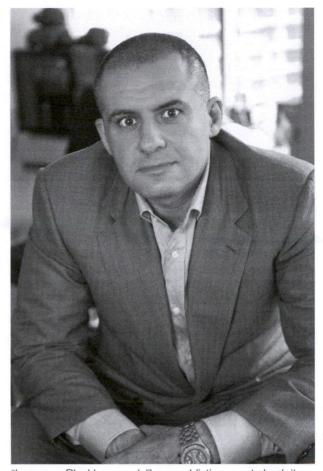

"I carry my Blackberry and, like an addiction, must check it every few minutes; not to do so can mean missed media opportunities, or worse, a newswire quote which reads, 'couldn't be reached for comment'—which occurred recently when I didn't call a reporter back within an hour. The journalist also expected instant gratification, and when I finally did call back, it had already appeared on more than 80 websites. Is this indeed life today?" *Source*: Ronn Torossian, CEO, 5W Public Relations, in *Bulldog Reporter.*

Equally as effective, Muck Rack is another tool that can help connect public relations professionals directly with journalists.[35] However, this service does have a cost associated with it. Muck Rack is quite popular with journalists and bloggers because the pitches that they receive are short and concise—only three hundred characters long, relevant, and specific to the reporter's interest and beat.[36] Public relations professionals also go to this website because they can use it to monitor, pitch, and further develop relationships with journalists and bloggers. Muck Rack does allow users to search by topic, publication, and beat. Additionally, by allowing users to personalize their accounts with a set of keywords, the website allows alerts to be set up based on when a story runs regarding its company, industry, and even its competitors.

Where Do We Go from Here?

In today's fast-moving business environment wherein breaking news is often tweeted before major news outlets can even broadcast the story, many of the key conversations that we participate in happen in our online communities. It is

Gas Prices Pitch

Subject Line: High Gas Prices Compromise Health Care for Elderly

Mr. Stevens,
I think I may have a story idea with wide appeal that I want to share with you. Everyone is feeling the crunch at the gas station—that's not news. However, fuel prices are having a severe impact on providing home-care services to the elderly, disabled, and chronically ill.

The rising cost of fuel is greatly impacting services provided by home-care agencies. We have found that agencies are having a difficult time recruiting and retaining workers due to the cost of fuel. To alleviate some of this pressure, a few agencies lease cars, some provide a set reimbursement, some give gas cards or bus passes, but it's not enough to make up for the cost of fuel. Some agencies have received calls from aides that they are stuck on the side of the road—out of gas!

In addition, agencies providing Medicaid took a 35 percent cut in this year's state budget, while fuel prices have increased 100 percent in the past couple of years.
Simply put, high fuel prices are affecting access to cost-efficient and patient-preferred home care. Plus, agencies have a difficult time finding aides for referrals in rural areas.
While we are a local association, home-care providers across the nation are experiencing the same problems, which is why I feel this story has such wide appeal.

I will be following up in the next day, but please feel free to contact me should you have questions before then.

Sincerely,
Regina Luttrell
Assistant Director, Public Relations and Marketing

---

here that our media influencers reside and where their messages carry an elevated level of importance. For this reason, public relations practitioners must make every effort to ensure they have identified and cultivated a relationship with the correct media influencers in support of their organizational business strategies and objectives. Employers of public relations professionals have already come to expect that they have hired individuals who are bringing substantial knowledge and relationship management skills, as well as a mastery of the available online tools, in order to effectively communicate and engage with established online communities.

Those public relations professionals who follow the influencer relations guidelines for cultivating relationships will become invaluable, interactive additions to their organizations and open new possibilities and communication channels that were previously unavailable. By choosing not to participate in these conversations, an organization misses out on opportunities to broaden its exposure and promote its brand.

#LRNSMPR

Learn More: Social Press

- "Effective Blogger Relations": http://bit.ly/13YJhlZ
- "Samsung's Blogger Relations Failure": http://bit.ly/19dlRKK
- "Nine Tips for Awesome Blogger Relations": http://bit.ly/1370blN
- "Pitching the Perfect Pitch to Bloggers": http://bit.ly/1bgXi1i
- "Using HARO to Create Fresh, Compelling Content": http://bit.ly/15fJ8rr

Notes

1. T. Rosenstiel, ed., "Ideological News Sources: Who Watches and Why. Americans Spending More Time Following the News," Pew Research Center, 2010, accessed July 22, 2013, http://www.people-press.org/files/legacy-pdf/652.pdf; K. Hampton et al., eds., "Social Networking Sites and Our Lives: How People's Trust, Personal Relationships, and Civic and Political Involvement Are Connected to Their Use of Social Networking Sites and Other Technologies," Pew Research Center, 2012, accessed July 22, 2013, http://www.pewinternet.org/files/old-media/Files/Reports/2011/PIP%20-%20Social%20networking%20sites%20and%20our%20lives.pdf.

2. Hampton et al., "Social Networking Sites and Our Lives."

3. Rosenstiel, "Ideological News Sources"; Hampton et al., "Social Networking Sites and Our Lives."

4. J. Romo, *Share This: The Social Media Handbook for PR Professionals* (West Sussex, UK: Wiley, 2012), chap. 16.

5. Rosenstiel, "Ideological News Sources"; Hampton et al., "Social Networking Sites and Our Lives."

6. "Cannes Lion Award-Winning 'Three Little Pigs Advert,'" *Guardian*, February 29, 2012, https://www.youtube.com/watch?v=vDGrfhJH1P4.

7. T. Nudd, "The 10 Best Commercials of 2012," *Adweek*, November 26, 2012, accessed July 14, 2013, http://www.adweek.com/news/advertising-branding/10-best-commercials-2012-145324?page=1.

8. F. Seitel, *The Practice of Public Relations* (Upper Saddle River, NJ: Pearson Education, 2014).

9. Seitel, *The Practice of Public Relations.*

10. B. Solis, *Engage: The Complete Guide for Brands and Businesses to Build, Cultivate, and Measure Success in the New Web* (New York: Wiley, 2011).

11. C. Anderson, "Sorry PR People: You're Blocked," *Long Tail*, October 29, 2007, http://bit.ly/1bRpBRy.

12. "Buzz in the Blogosphere: Millions More Bloggers and Blog Readers," Nielsen, last modified March 8, 2010, accessed July 26, 2013, http://bit.ly/16i9ZC1.

13. Romo, *Share This.*

14. Solis, *Engage.*

15. Solis, *Engage.*

16. A. Parker, *Share This: The Social Media Handbook for PR Professionals* (West Sussex: Wiley, 2012), chap. 15.

17. Solis, *Engage.*

18. R. Johnson, "Pitching the Perfect Pitch to Bloggers," *Hoosier PRSA Blog*, July 12, 2010, http://bit.ly/1bgXi1i.

19. G. Livingston, "Anatomy of a Great PR Pitch," *Geoff Livingston*, September 9, 2010, http://bit.ly/1aDVpYM.

20. Livingston, "Anatomy of a Great PR Pitch"; Johnson, "Pitching the Perfect Pitch to Bloggers"; H. Whaling, "Effective Blogger Relations," prTini, September 15, 2010, http://bit.ly/13YJhlZ.

21. "Buzz in the Blogosphere."

22. Parker, *Share This.*

23. G. Macmillan, "How Twitter Won the Social Media Battle for Journalism," *WallBlog*, March 5, 2013, http://wallblog.co.uk/2013/03/05/how-twitter-won-the-social-media-battle-for-journalism.

24. H. Hahn, ed., "What Is Good Twitter? The Value of Social Media to Public Service Journalism," Eurovision, 2013, accessed July 26, 2013, http://bit.ly/15kr5An.

25. See Twitterfall at http://www.twitterfall.com.

26. Hahn, "What Is Good Twitter?"; N. Newman, ed., "Mainstream Media and the Distribution of News in the Age of Social Discovery," Reuters Institute for the Study of

Journalism, accessed July 26, 2013, http://reutersinstitute.politics.ox.ac.uk/publication/ mainstream-media-and-distribution-news-age-social-discovery.

[27] Romo, *Share This*.

[28] Seitel, *The Practice of Public Relations*; D. Wilcox et al., *THINK Public Relations* (Upper Saddle River, NJ: Pearson Education, 2013).

[29] Seitel, *The Practice of Public Relations*.

[30] Seitel, *The Practice of Public Relations*.

[31] Seitel, *The Practice of Public Relations*.

[32] Seitel, *The Practice of Public Relations*.

[33] Seitel, *The Practice of Public Relations*.

[34] See the Help a Reporter Out website at http://www.helpareporter.com.

[35] See the Muck Rack website at http://www.muckrack.com.

[36] See the Twitterfall website at http://www.twitterfall.com.

Sharing Expertise 5

Corporations create and curate their own content using multiple media platforms. Doing this takes time; doing it effectively takes knowledge, skill, and the right tools. In this chapter, you will learn how to successfully use self-publishing tools to connect with consumers and disseminate your company's message, while concurrently selecting and organizing content.

Content Reigns Supreme

Journal articles, trade magazines, conferences, and blogs all repeatedly preach the mantra "Content is king, content is king, and content is king." Bill Gates was the first to introduce this premise to readers in his aptly titled article "Content Is King." Gates discussed the impact that the Internet would have on the creation and curation of content and wrote, "One of the exciting things about the Internet is that anyone with a PC and a modem can publish whatever content they can create."[1] This statement foreshadowed the world that we live in today: the Internet ushered in a revolution of self-publishing tools and leveled the playing field.

Keep in mind that every good tool is only as valuable as its supporting tactics. Social media strategies have become integral to social development because they provide channels that connect audiences with similar interests, thus enabling dialogue where meaningful relationships can be forged. Information is the key to holding any customer's attention. By developing a solid social strategy and focusing efforts on superior content creation, a business can

- build long-lasting relationships;
- increase a company's social influence;
- improve SEO efforts.

Blogs

The general population uses blogs more frequently than any other self-publishing tool. Around the globe, a new blog is created every one-half second. If we do some quick math, this accounts for an average of 172,800 blog posts that are added to the Internet on a daily basis.[2] Worldwide, 6.7 million people maintain over 181 million blogs. WordPress, Blogger, and Typepad are the most popular blogging platforms because they have easy-to-use, easy-to-understand interfaces that facilitate growth from novice blogger to pro blogger.[3] Blogs tend to focus on a single area of interest, an industry, or a particular topic. The blogosphere contains everything from "foodie" blogs to "techie" blogs. Maintenance of a blog is generally the responsibility of an individual, group of individuals, or corporation. The intent of a blog is to encourage communication by establishing conversations within a community of like-minded people. Interactive in nature, blogs incorporate text with photos, links, and videos, allowing the author to paint a complete picture of the topic of interest.[4] Public relations professionals can utilize blogs as a platform to create branded content.

Corporate Blogging

Corporate blogs can be a blessing and a curse.[5] As with other forms of communication via the social web, corporate blogs provide information about a company using open, two-way communication. They establish a channel that can demonstrate expertise, communicate insights, listen, engage and respond to customers, and promote meaningful conversations about the company and its principles, values, and vision.[6] Oftentimes, corporate bloggers become industry experts on the subjects that they support regarding a particular company's services and products. By positioning the blog content properly, corporate bloggers can provide valuable information to all interested parties on a consistent basis. Companies that possess blogs or participate in blogging communities effectively deal with a myriad of issues, including crisis situations, often in the very medium where these topics are first discussed. By participating in these conversations, corporate blogs allow a company to react quickly. If properly executed, blogs are a platform where a company can determine the direction of content.

However, corporate blogs often miss the mark. Only 16 percent of online consumers who read corporate blogs indicate that they trust them.[7] This statistic does not mean that companies should throw in the towel and give up on corporate blogging; rather, it highlights the fact that corporate blogs need to evolve and rethink their strategy.[8] One challenge for a large number of corporate blogs is that, frequently, the content is better suited for a marketing piece. Blogs should place minimal focus on a company's products, CEO highlights, or accomplishments. Generally speaking, corporate blogs that resonate stick to the eighty/twenty rule.[9] That is, they contain content that is relevant to their audience at least 80 percent of the time to increase engagement. The remaining 20 percent is dedicated to content about the company or company products. Blogs that establish a purpose and encompass the larger online community make sense.[10] With that in mind, some disadvantages of corporate blogs do exist and pertain directly to the messenger, messages, and content. A number of discussions focus on who, within the organization, should hold the responsibility for blogging.[11] Initially, corporate blogs acted as personal journals. This, in theory, would empower executives to become effective bloggers by allowing their voices to benefit from personalization.[12] If a company chooses a poor corporate blogger, it could have a negative effect on the blog. That is why there are so few examples of good corporate blogs. Notwithstanding, Southwest Airlines and Dell are two companies that consistently maintain excellent corporate blogs.[13]

Nuts about Southwest, the corporate blog maintained by Southwest Airlines, is successful because it has everything to do with its customers and nothing to do with the marketing of the company.[14] The blog is separate from the company website and is maintained by a myriad of bloggers—thirty in all—including employees, customers, and partners. This variety is exactly what makes it unique and effective. The blog embraces the "FunLUVing" attitude of the company and connects Southwest employees with its community of flyers in a fun, engaging way.[15] Nuts about Southwest provides information ranging from blog posts to videos, social updates, photos, Pinterest boards, and podcasts—all with the user in mind. This simple-to-use platform also incorporates the use of tags that allow users to quickly find the content they want to read or see.

Direct2Dell, the official Dell corporate blog, was launched in 2006 and is one of the oldest business blogs that thrives in its market segment.[16] The intent of the blog is to open the lines of communication between the customers and the company—*to participate in the conversation*. With regular updates, the blog provides a balance of commentary on new products, product releases, consumer services, customer tips, and issues that are relevant to customers. If we apply the eighty/twenty rule to this blog, it is easy to see why the Direct2Dell blog is effective in promoting conversations with the company's customer base.

Additional examples of effective corporate blogs include those of

Starbucks: This company embraces the true concepts behind social media, and its blog only tangentially relates to coffee. Rather, Starbucks uses its blog as a worldwide think tank. Customers can submit ideas for new drinks, different food items, and product packaging though the blog. The company then blogs about the proposals put forth by Starbucks customers and allows the readers to grow them through comments and ratings. Some of your favorite items may have come from this consumer-generated blog.

Fiskars: Yes, Fiskars scissors has one of the most engaging and loyal blogging communities on the social web. In 2005 the company examined how to connect and communicate with the crafters who use its products. A four-city casting call was issued for crafters possessing big personalities and a passion for crafting. From this search, four outstanding ladies—Stephenie Hamen, Holly Harris, Cheryl Waters, and May Flaum—now lead the corporate blog and are genuine craft ambassadors both online and off. Today they are known as "The Fiskateers." The blog encourages its participants to share crafting ideas and, of course, to use Fiskars products.[17]

General Electric: General Electric's corporate blog, GE Reports, is a place where community users can immerse themselves in viewing beautiful photography, poetic storytelling, videos, and graphics, all of which illustrate a point. The company describes its blog as a "no-frills way of communicating what's happening" at GE, with the goal of becoming a resource for people who are interested in learning more about the company. Of all the corporate blogs, GE Reports will not only surprise you but possibly educate you as well.[18]

There are many attributes, features, and elements that contribute to the success of corporate blogs. Because blogs provide an opportunity for organizations to talk directly to more than 180 million people at any given moment, ensuring proper maintenance of a company blog is paramount.[19]

Getting Started

The decision to initiate a corporate blog should not be taken lightly. It is a long-term communication strategy. It takes time and resources to start a blog, develop the voice of the blog, and build an active community.[20] Many companies are thrilled to launch a blog, but after the initial excitement fades, the corporate blogs often die off. The

Five Helpful Blogging Tips

1. Keep blog posts to between 250 and 600 words.
2. Brevity counts! Short headlines are key. This allows others to retweet important posts. Plus, titles with eight words received a 21 percent higher click-through rate as compared to the average.
3. Take part and encourage conversations. Negative comments can be an opportunity to develop good customer relations.
4. Become part of the blogging community by participating on other blogs.
5. Be authentic. Your online community will see through marketing strategies.

standard life cycle of a blog is quite dim to begin with. It takes off in the initial week with a flurry of two or three posts, which then decrease to once a week, and then to once a month, before being abandoned altogether.[21] When a company decides to embark upon blogging, there are ten simple steps that it needs to first consider:

1. *Determine the blog team:* A blog cannot be sustained by one person alone. It requires a team of people to support the efforts of the blog.[22]
2. *Determine the blog's purpose:* Blogs can be used in a variety of ways, but a company should focus on a short list of purposes for the blog; otherwise the intent can be diminished or confusing. Decide what messages you would like readers to take away from your blog. These messages can help build brand awareness, expand reach, encourage loyalty, foster customer satisfaction, increase sales, assist in times of crisis, and cultivate thought leadership.[23]
3. *Determine the blog's target audience:* The blog's overarching goal will help you establish the target audience. Research the habits of the target audience. Do its members comment and participate in the online community, or are they lurkers?[24]
4. *Determine the persona and voice of the blog:* Every blog has a persona and voice. Blogs are not traditional marketing pieces. They are less formal in nature, project a personality, have a distinct point of view, and contain no corporate-speak. Blogs need to be well written. The best blogs engage us and make us want to participate in them. It may take time to find a company persona and voice. When starting a blog, ask multiple people at the company to try their hands—human resources, engineers, customer service, product development, customers, and vendors. The individuals who are good bloggers will gravitate to the top, while the others should cease blogging for the company. Every now and then, try to incorporate blog posts from C-suite executives. Their voices should round out the corporate blog.[25]
5. *Develop the meaning for the blog:* Determine the type of content the blog will contain.[26] Create categories that will be covered on a consistent basis. For example, NYC PR Girls has eleven categories that it routinely blogs about, including PRofiles, events, public relations, and life in New York City.[27] How-tos, narratives, lists, and video posts are also often found in successful blogs.
6. *Develop an editorial calendar for the blog:* Develop an editorial calendar to keep the blog on track and maintain consistency within the blog.[28] As a rule of thumb, new blogs should post two to three times per week. Adhering to this schedule is partially why many corporate blogs are abandoned. Know what is coming up over the next week, month, and year to help bloggers stay on top of their posts. Michele Linn has created a great tip sheet for establishing editorial calendars (http://bit.ly/13frm4H).
7. *Develop a publication schedule for the blog:* Editorial calendars are useless without publication schedules. Publication schedules clearly assign deadlines for the final publication date.[29] Monday and Tuesday are the best days for a company to share content. The average blog post will receive the most traffic around 11:00 a.m. Eastern Standard Time. A good strategy is to publish on Monday or Tuesday and then promote the piece again over the weekend.
8. *Develop the rules for the blog:* All blogs should have rules.[30] These outline the social media guidelines, the types of acceptable posts, and the consequences for rule breakers. Provide prospective bloggers with clear guidelines from the outset. This will help eliminate confusion for your bloggers and your blog community.
9. *Develop a content curation plan for your blog:* "Content curation" is one of the hottest buzz phrases in the industry.[31] Beth Kanter defines it best as "the process

of sorting through the vast amounts of content on the web and presenting it in a meaningful and organized way around a specific theme."[32] A curator's duties include determining the best content and selecting the most relevant content to share with the online community.

10. *Develop a promotional plan for your blog:* Once you click "post," only the people on your team actually know that there is new content available. To grow your blog, you will need to promote it.[33] Keyword searches, RSS feeds, URL shorteners, and status updates on other company social networking sites are some of the most common elements in a promotional plan. Additionally, you can promote your new posts in your email signature or send them out directly to your customer list.

Blogging is an easy channel of communication with your customers, prospects, employees, and general stakeholders, and creation of a blog account is free and simple. Blogs are one of the few platforms whereby you own, create, and curate company and product-related content. The goal of a blog is the creation of a conversation between the writer and the intended audience via comments. With this in mind, setting aside twenty to thirty minutes each week to promote these conversations is not asking much.[34] Marko Saric, a blogger and curator for HowToMakeMyBlog, suggests that bloggers should develop a postdistribution routine to ensure consistency. Approximately 50 percent of a blogger's time should be devoted to the creation of content, with the remaining 50 percent reserved for active promotion. Keep in mind that companies can grow their presence on the social web over time through *interaction* and *engagement* with their larger community.

CONTENT MARKETING ROUTINE
after publishing your post

Promotional efforts start after you've published your post. If this work is not done, your post will most probably go unnoticed no matter how good it is. Visitors will not come automatically - follow this routine to drive traffic to your content.

 Tweet out the headline and the link to make your Twitter followers aware of the new post. Include an image for more attention!

Post the link with the image attached on your Facebook page. Displaying the image on your wall instead of the link thumbnail works best in terms of reach and engagement.

Follow the same process on your Google+ profile. You should also join relevant Google+ communities, be active in them by sharing your knowledge, and then post your link once in a while as well.

Publish the post on your LinkedIn profile as well.

Submit the post image to relevant Pinterest boards. Make sure to include a headline in all the images that you put on your site.

Stumbleupon is still a nice source of traffic and you should aim to stumble all the posts that you publish in hopes of getting some visitors from there.

Keep an active Tumblr account with the main objective being for it to be a traffic driver to your site.

Some of the articles might do well in certain subreddits on Reddit. Reddit has the potential to drive thousands of visitors to you!

 Send personal tweets and emails to certain influencers that you think the post might be interesting to in hope of getting them to sharte it with their networks.

 Link to your new post from other relevant posts in your archive!

 Comment on the most recent posts of relevant sites that have good traffic numbers. Leave valuable comments only!

 You can even write and submit guest posts to relevant and popular sites in which you would include the link to my new post.

 Depending on the niche you are in, there will be several community sites that allow you to submit content. Sites like Hacker News. There's a Hacker News type site out there for every niche.

REVIEW & REPEAT

    After several hours, take a look at the results, feedback, and data on initial push. It is useful to know before proceeding! Aim to repeat the process on selected profiles several times over the next few days!

For more blogging inspiration, visit howtomakemyblog.com

Drive traffic to your company's content by cross promoting on multiple platforms. *Source:* Infographic courtesy of Marko Saric (http://howtomakemyblog.com).

Evaluate Your Company Blog

Is your company blog effective? You can assess this by taking the time to evaluate it.

Answer the questions below *before* participating in your online community. Save your initial answers to refer to after you have completed your analysis.

Then, objectively observe and participate in your own company blog for one full week to determine its effectiveness and purpose.

Use the following criteria:[1]

- What is the blog's title and purpose? Is this clear to an outside audience? It may be clear to insiders but may not be obvious to community members.
- Who are the bloggers? What are their credentials? Are bios of the bloggers evident? Since many company blogs have several bloggers, it is important that the readers know who is writing the blog posts. For example, when Starbucks posts on its blog, the byline reads "Starbucks." However, when the vast majority of bloggers post, readers tend to see something like "Posted by Paige D.—Digital Community Manager."
- Is there an email or contact section? Community members may want to contact the blog host. Is this clearly visible?
- How often is the blog updated? What is the regularity of updates?

- Are comments from the blogging community answered? If so, how quickly? If not, why not? This may be an area to address.
- How well is the blog organized? Is the template effective?
- Are the blog's policies clearly stated? Are they easy to find? Are they followed?
- How effective are some of the blogs features? (e.g., RSS feed, podcasts, external links, photos, videos, social networking sites).
- Is the language used in the blog appropriate for the forum?
- Does an easily retrievable archive section exist?
- Is the content accurate and appropriate for the blog?

Now that you've examined your own company blog, how did it perform? Compare your original answers with the answers you now have after your week of participation. You may see that changes need to be made, areas enhanced, and issues addressed. This simple task should be performed at least three to four times per year. This will help keep the company blog on task and on message.

---

1 K. McGrath and R. Luttrell, "Blog Analysis" (lecture, College of Saint Rose and Eastern Michigan University, 2013).

Podcasting

Companies tend to forget the versatility of podcasts when planning their overall social strategy. Similar to blogs, podcasts are based on content that you own. This means that you have complete control over what you create and share. As with blogs, users should create podcasts with the audience in mind and steer clear of direct marketing of their products. Podcasts allow companies to record seminars and conferences, spotlight customer success anecdotes, invite cohosts, create a monthly talk show, MC roundtable discussions, or feature a panel of subject-matter experts.[35] With podcasts, the content options are limitless, with creativity as the main driver of valuable content.

To create, edit, and publish podcasts is a straightforward and simple endeavor. The infrastructure necessary to record a podcast is a computer or tablet, a microphone, and great content. Today's computers are preassembled with the necessary tools that make creation of a podcast very easy. Podcasts are versatile in format (.m4a, .mp3, .mp4, .mov, .wav), which means that anyone can listen anywhere. The potential reach of a podcast is vast.[36] Your audience can listen to a podcast at the gym, walking the dog, or driving to work. The key to this social channel is that it provides

Podcasting Statistics

- More than half of podcast consumers use social networks nearly every day.
- Forty percent of podcast consumers have a household income of at least $75,000 annually.
- Sixty-three percent of podcast downloads are requested from mobile devices—up from 43 percent in 2012. Mobile devices are increasingly the preferred way to listen to podcasts.

- Approximately one in six Americans listen to podcasts regularly.[1]

_____

1 T. Webster, "The Podcast Consumer 2012," T. Edison Research, last modified May 29, 2012, accessed August 7, 2013, http://www.edisonresearch.com/home/archives/2012/05/the-podcast-consumer-2012.php; Nancy Vogt, "Podcasting: Fact Sheet," Pew Research Centers Journalism Project RSS, April 28, 2015, accessed November 2, 2015, http://www.journalism.org/2015/04/29/podcasting-fact-sheet.

a platform for uninterrupted, quality time with your listeners. As a bonus, subscribing listeners are notified each time you post new content.[37] Since each podcast has its own distinct RSS feed, many are connected to podcatchers. The intent of podcatchers is to read the RSS feeds and automatically download media files for users to review at their convenience.[38] Podcatchers can download audio files in MP3 format, videos, newsfeeds, text, and photos. Some podcatchers even move the files to a user's MP3 player automatically, while others download each file to a separate folder. Either way, the delivery of messaging and material directly to individual listeners is a huge benefit of podcasts.

By developing a voice for your company, podcasts can help further cultivate relationships with your customer base. The key to all social media is the ability to be authentic. The audible word has a much stronger connection with people than the written word. Podcasts allow for audiences to hear speakers' emotions and connect with their personalities.[39] Genuine connections build loyalty. The host must engage the audience and entice listeners to return. Diction, sincerity, and attitude play a significant role in the creation of a podcast.[40]

Additionally, take time to reward and acknowledge loyal listeners. Often listeners email the host or post their opinions in comment sections. It is important to incorporate these insights into your podcasts on a regular basis. By doing so, trust will be established with the online community and positively affect the company's social presence.[41] Listeners feel a heightened sense of validation when they believe that their contributions matter.

The ability to share a podcast has also never been easier. Their format is embeddable and easy to share within websites and blogs and can be incorporated across all social platforms that the company utilizes.[42] Also, do not forget to upload all completed podcasts onto iTunes. Millions of people search iTunes daily, seeking new content, so it is important that your podcast is available to be searched for by the larger audience.[43]

Public Relations and Social Media Podcasts That Resonate

For Immediate Release (FIR),[44] hosted by Neville Hobson and Shel Holtz, is a series of podcasts that focus on topics in communication and public relations. Subscribers can listen to the biweekly podcast The Hobson and Holtz Report and learn about the current happenings in the online communication and public relations circles. Hobson and Holtz also interview experts in the technology and organizational communication arenas, review popular books on public relations and communication, and offer podcasts from public relations meetings and conferences.

The Public Relations Society of America (PRSA) broadcasts Voices of Public Relations, a series of podcasts from guest bloggers. Podcast topics include advocacy, media relations, "On the Record . . . Online," and even some case studies. The intent of the PRSA podcast format is to connect public relations professionals with experts in the field.[45]

Business Wire broadcasts the All Things Press Release podcast.[46] This is a series of three-minute-or-less podcasts that address FAQs posed to Business Wire editors and account staff. Tips, how-tos, and guidance based on industry experience are discussed courtesy of the Business Wire staff and outside counsel. Many popular podcasts include "How to Write a Good Headline," "Getting Your Press Release into Google News," and "When's the Best Time to Send a Press Release."

The Social Media Marketing podcast, with Social Media Examiner's Michael Stelzner, targets marketers and business owners.[47] Each episode reveals effective uses of social media marketing. Example podcasts contain Stelzner's interview with Mari Smith on the latest features Facebook has to offer, as well as an interview with author Jonah Berger on his latest book, *Contagious: Why Things Catch On.*

The Social Pros Podcast: Real People Doing Real Work in Social Media,[48] with creators and hosts Jay Baer, Jeffrey Rohrs, and guest contributor Zena Weist, broadcasts thirty- to sixty-minute podcasts that highlight various preeminent social media strategists, FAQ sessions, and specialized "four your information" segments, wherein guests share their insights and thoughts on four questions asked by the host.

The connection that makes these five podcasts unique is that, while the hosts are all experts in their fields, they also all own businesses. Take notice—none of these hosts hawk their wares to their listeners. Through genuine conversations, they produce interesting messages whereby listeners can learn and share with others.

Podcasting in Europe

European counterparts are also paying attention to the value of podcasts. Once regarded as a niche medium with minimal appeal, podcasting is now seen as a way to connect with consumers. According to Mike Russel from New Media Europe, "Almost everyone has a podcast these days, including some high-profile celebrities who are typically associated with mainstream media. Over the past decade, podcasting has grown beyond its humble roots and evolved into one of the most popular broadcasting techniques."

There are thousands of podcasts available on the web, with more being added daily. With tools like Oculus Rift coming to market, we can expect to see podcasts taken to the next level as they become increasingly immersive and interactive.[49]

Internet Radio

Companies can also use an alternate social channel, Internet radio, to promote their brands and reach audiences with original content. BlogTalkRadio is one such platform that fuses telephones with the Internet.[50] This web-based utility allows users to host live call-in shows similar to traditional radio shows. The only difference is that everything is online. Like most social networking services, Internet radio is free. Users do not require special equipment, and hosting a show is simple. Users access the radio show by logging on to a web portal using a given password. The host reserves a time for the show to air, and via any telephone—land based or mobile—a listener calls a BlogTalkRadio assigned telephone number.[51] Once the show is "live,"

Theory into Practice

Role Mommy

Meet Beth Feldman from RoleMommy.com

Role Mommy is an online community established to inspire, entertain, and inform today's busy moms. Beth Feldman, president and role mommy herself, has built her online community from the idea that women do not have to give up their hopes and dreams simply because they decide to have children.

About Role Mommy

Beth oversees all of the online content—from movie, television, and book reviews to witty articles and podcasts. She even produces events that feature women who are raising a family while continuing their careers at the top of their fields—from entrepreneurs to authors to fitness gurus and television anchors.

Social Channels

Beth maintains a full spectrum of social networking sites, including Twitter (@rolemommy), Facebook (https://www.facebook.com/Role-Mommy-20767216696/), and YouTube (*https://www.youtube.com/user/Rolemommy/videos*), which allows her to connect with her audience in meaningful and engaging ways. She complements her communications strategy by incorporating both BlogTalkRadio and a blog that she maintains on her website.

BlogTalkRadio (*http://www.blogtalkradio.com/rolemommy*): Beth's talk radio show provides listeners with the most up-to-date, significant information on popular and effective parenting strategies that one should consider in today's often hectic world. She employs many successful strategies that resonate with her listeners when utilizing a social platform such as this. For example, experts join her on her radio show on a regular basis to discuss topics that interest her listeners, including healthy eating, parenting techniques, and being a mommy on the go. Her listeners also get a peek into the lives of some very famous role mommies, like Sandra Lee from the Food Network. Every so often she invites listeners to catch up with her by asking questions and becoming more involved in the Role Mommy community. She keeps the format focused, which keeps her listeners coming back.

Blog (www.rolemommy.com): Beth's blog also balances the needs of her audience by addressing many of the topics important to parents. This allows for a well-rounded experience for the online community. By incorporating multiple social channels within her repertoire, Beth also recognizes that she does not have to do it all by herself. Role Mommy also features four talented contributors to the blog, Alma Schneider, Susan Hirshman, Lorraine Brock, and Danielle Feigenbaum. Alma addresses healthy habits in the kitchen, Susan focuses on money-related topics, Lorraine teaches other role mommies how to get organized, and Danielle is editor of Role Mommy's deals and giveaway sections.

Individuals who sign up for Beth's social community can do so through an RSS feed, allowing them to receive the most recent blog posts and radio shows. This technique empowers her audience to stay connected to her topics even when they are on the go.

Source: B. Feldman, "About Role Mommy," Role Mommy, last modified 2013, accessed August 1, 2013, http://www.rolemommy.com/about.php.

---

the listeners' phone numbers populate the computer screen, and the host fields the calls with just a click of a mouse.[52] Listeners may also download a podcast version of the show if they are not able to join the live session.

In a business sense, BlogTalkRadio is a tool to connect with customers by answering their questions or seeking their advice in a live format. For example, if you own a cleaning service business, it could benefit the company to produce a weekly live call-in show wherein consumers can have their toughest questions answered. Topics might range from guidance on cleaning to questions to ask when interviewing and hiring a cleaning service. Companies can use the live call-in format as an opportunity for customers to directly connect with the CEO or other C-suite executives. A format such as this provides customers the opportunity to associate more intimately with your brand, thereby further solidifying their relationship with the company. Moreover, a BlogTalkRadio show should complement other social media channels, including the corporate blog. A series of blogs on ethics in public relations would lend itself well to a live call-in show on the same topic. Ultimately, the public relations practitioner and supporting team is responsible for cross-promoting all social media efforts so that customers can see, hear, and interact on as many platforms as possible.

Hosting live call-in shows has the ability to promote straightforward, genuine dialogue with consumers, employees, vendors, the media, and just about every external stakeholder. BlogTalkRadio is a great accompaniment to any social strategy.

Wikis

Wikis are an exceptionally useful tool for further involving internal and external audiences with your company. Because wikis are so dynamic in nature, they offer users an unprecedented ability to connect with a company. The most widely known wiki is the online encyclopedia Wikipedia; however, a large number of companies already use wikis in conversing with their online communities.

As an example, Ford of Europe sponsors the wiki Where Are the Joneses?—a fictional interactive comedy that chronicles the adventures of Dawn and Ian Jones. The ingenious aspect of this wiki is that the public participates in shaping the storyline and decides what happens to the couple as they travel on their Ford-sponsored European road trip.[53] Episodes are available on YouTube and are supported by a blog featuring videos from viewers, images, and diary entries written by both the characters and the audience by means of comments. This wiki has been a huge success. The supporting blog logged 141,455 overall visits, with the wiki totaling 15,367 visits during Dawn and Ian's adventures, with an average of fifteen minutes spent on the website per visitor.[54]

Ford is renowned for engagement with its consumer base through the use of original, unique, and innovative methods. The company is adept at establishing close connections between its audience and its brand. The success of Where Are the Joneses? stems from this innovative mind-set and approach. Other companies are also taking fresh and original approaches to their wikis. In addition, wikis can be a platform to gather uncensored customer feedback, provide customer service, extend the brand through user-generated experiences, and work to create and sustain knowledge.[55]

Socializing Business

As organizations move toward a social, integrated way of conducting business, public relations professionals and social media strategists must rethink a customer's journey and relationship with a brand. Blogs, podcasts, and wikis allow customers to engage and interact with brands that they know and trust in ways that move them from passive to active interaction with companies. It is time for a sweeping change, a reorganization of how companies share what they know with their consumers. Adoption of a more social, integrated customer experience using an evolved communication process will drive companies to better position themselves as part of customers' experience with their brands.[56]

As our society becomes more mobile, consumers now gravitate toward and desire on-demand content. Blogs, podcasts, and Internet radio shows are excellent social tools that allow businesses to connect with consumers and promote themselves.

These tools can also go a long way to establishing you as a thought leader within your industry. Hosting an Internet radio show can nicely complement other social tools due to the relative simplicity and low cost. The right choice of topics can nicely harmonize with the strengths of your company, as well as promote thoughts and ideas that you and your target audience are passionate about. That passion, and the time committed to establishing a deeper connection with your customers, will shine through and provide ample content to share as the use of these tools evolves within your business.

#LRNSMPR

Learn More: Sharing Expertise

- "10 Social Media Marketing Podcasts That You Need to Hear": http://bit.ly/1SAOB7R
- "40 of the Best Corporate Blogs to Inspire You": http://bit.ly/1c318LO
- "Blog Lingo": http://bit.ly/12VxSCB
- "Become a Content Curation King": http://www.clickz.com/clickz/column/2104954/content-curation-king
- PodioBooks give listeners the ability to hear free audiobooks distributed via RSS, much like a podcast: http://podiobooks.com
- "Podcatcher Rundown: A Look at the Top 4 Podcast Apps for iOS": http://bit.ly/1beKV2m
- "Throw Out Your Social Media Policies": http://bit.ly/13U8iYl

Notes

1 B. Gates, "Content Is King," *Internet Archive Wayback Machine*, January 3, 1996, http://www.microsoft.com/billgates/columns/1996essay/essay960103.asp.
2 Brandon Gaille, "How Many Blogs Are on the Internet," WPVirtuoso, November 20, 2013, accessed November 2, 2015, http://www.wpvirtuoso.com/how-many-blogs-are-on-the-internet.
3 "Buzz in the Blogosphere: Millions More Bloggers and Blog Readers," Nielsen, last modified March 8, 2010, accessed July 26, 2013, http://bit.ly/16i9ZC1; see the websites of WordPress (www.wordpress.com), Blogger (www.blogger.com), and TypePad (www.typepad.com).
4 L. Safko, *The Social Media Bible: Tactics, Tools and Strategies for Business Success* (New York: Wiley, 2010), chap. 7; E. Terra, "What Is a Podiobook?," *Podiobooker*, September 21, 2012, http://blog.podiobooks.com/frequently-asked-questions.
5 P. Smudde, "Blogging Ethics and Public Relations: A Proactive and Dialogic Approach," *Public Relations Quarterly* (2005): 34.
6 B. Solis, *Engage: The Complete Guide for Brands and Businesses to Build, Cultivate, and Measure Success in the New Web* (New York: Wiley, 2011).
7 J. Bernoff, ed., "Time to Rethink Your Corporate Blogging Ideas," Forrester Research, 2008, accessed August 2, 2013, http://www.forrester.com/marketing/campaign2.1,6538,1946,00.html.
8 Solis, *Engage*.
9 E. Robertson, "The 80/20 Rule for Social Media Success," Marketing of a Different Color, August 2012, http://www.marketingofadifferentcolor.com/2012/08/the-8020-rule-for-social-media-success.
10 P. Smudde, "Blogging Ethics and Public Relations: A Proactive and Dialogic Approach," *Public Relations Quarterly* (2005): 34.
11 W. Waddington, *Share This: The Social Media Handbook for PR Professionals* (West Sussex: Wiley, 2012), chap. 11; K. Hanson, "Should the Boss Be Blogging?," *Strategic Communication Management* 10 (2006): 6–7.
12 Robertson, "The 80/20 Rule for Social Media Success."

13 Solis, *Engage*; Robertson, "The 80/20 Rule for Social Media Success"; N. Harbison and L. Fisher, "40 of the Best Corporate Blogs to Inspire You," *Ragan's PR Daily*, September 13, 2012, http://www.prdaily.com/Main/Articles/40_of_the_best.

14 See the Southwest blog at http://www.blogsouthwest.com.

15 Solis, *Engage*.

16 See the Dell corporate blog at http://dell.to/14dfqUo; Robertson, "The 80/20 Rule for Social Media Success."

17 "Crafting & Sewing," Fiskars, http://www2.fiskars.com/Products/Crafting-and-Sewing.

18 General Electric, "About," GE Reports, last modified 2013, accessed August 5, 2013, http://www.gereports.com/about.

19 "Buzz in the Blogosphere."

20 "Buzz in the Blogosphere."

21 "Buzz in the Blogosphere."

22 H. Cohen, "9 Must-Have Elements for Company Blogs," Content Marketing Institute, November 24, 2010, http://contentmarketinginstitute.com/2010/11/company-blog-elements.

23 Solis, *Engage*.

24 Waddington, *Share This*, chap. 11.

25 Solis, *Engage*; Robertson, "The 80/20 Rule for Social Media Success"; General Electric, "About."

26 Smudde, "Blogging Ethics and Public Relations."

27 See the NYC PR Girls website at http://nycprgirls.com.

28 General Electric, "About."

29 General Electric, "About."

30 R. Luttrell, "Throw Out Your Social Media Policies!," Gina Luttrell PhD, July 26, 2013, http://ginaluttrellphd.com/2013/07/26/throw-out-your-social-media-policies.

31 Luttrell, "Throw Out Your Social Media Policies!"

32 B. Kanter, "Content Curation Primer," *Beth's Blog*, October 4, 2011, http://www.bethkanter.org/content-curation-101.

33 Solis, *Engage*; General Electric, "About."

34 Safko, *The Social Media Bible*.

35 J. Van Orden, "7 Reasons to Create Your Own Podcast," How to Podcast Tutorial, last modified 2013, accessed August 7, 2013, http://www.howtopodcasttutorial.com/seven-reasons-to-create-your-own-podcast.htm.

36 C. King, "6 Podcasting Tips from the Pros," Social Media Examiner, September 8, 2012, http://www.socialmediaexaminer.com/6-podcasting-tips-from-the-pros.

37 Safko, *The Social Media Bible*.

38 Terra, "What Is a Podiobook?"

39 Safko, *The Social Media Bible*.

40 Van Orden, "How to Podcast Tutorial IS."

41 Van Orden, "How to Podcast Tutorial IS."

42 Solis, *Engage*.

43 Safko, *The Social Media Bible*, chap. 10.

44 See the FIR Podcast Network at http://forimmediaterelease.biz/index.php.

45 Rosanne Mottola, "PRSA 2013 Health Academy Conference Preview with Founders of Healthy TXT," PRSA, April 18, 2013, http://podcast.prsa.org/podcast.

46 "All Things Press Release," iTunes, https://itunes.apple.com/us/podcast/all-things-press-release/id323723658?mt=2.

47 Michael Stelzner, "Blog Comments Revisited: Why Major Bloggers Are Turning Comments Back On," Social Media Examiner, April 1, 2016, http://www.socialmediaexaminer.com/category/podcast-episodes.

48 "Social Pros Podcast," Convince and Convert, http://www.convinceandconvert.com/social-pros-podcast.

49 "A Brief History Of Podcasting," New Media Europe, http://newmediaeurope.com/2015/a-brief-history-of-podcasting.

50 Staff Writer, "Howard Kurtz—with BlogTalkRadio, the Commentary Universe Expands," *Washington Post*, accessed June 23, 2014, http://www.washingtonpost.com/wp-dyn/content/article/2008/03/23/AR2008032301719.html.

51 See the Blogger website at http://www.blogger.com.

52 See the Imagination website at http://www.imagination.com.

53 "Where are the Joneses? Ford," Imagination, http://www.imagination.com/en/our-work/where-are-joneses-ford.

54 Where are the Joneses? Ford."

[55] K. Colley, *Using Wikis in Marketing and Media Relations* (lecture, Texas Wesleyan University, 2009), http://www.slideshare.net/klcolley/Using-Wikis-in-Marketing-and-Media-Relations.

[56] M. Fidelman and D. Hinchliffe, "Rethinking the Customer Journey in a Social World," *Forbes*, November 26, 2012, accessed August 8, 2013, http://www.forbes.com/sites/markfidelman/2012/11/26/rethinking-the-customer-journey-in-a-social-world.

Social Networks 6

In today's digital age, the frequency of individuals using social networking sites to connect with brands they love increases daily. Influencers initiate conversations with other influencers about what's trending, what's hot, what's new, who's who, and where to go for the best sushi. These conversations allow some brands to excel at connecting and resonating with their social users, while other brands flounder in the social web of confusion. This chapter focuses on the top six social networking sites and companies who understand their audiences.

Setting the Stage

It seems as though we are being introduced to a new social networking site or tool in the social web on a daily basis. Some have staying power, some linger a bit, and some simply fizzle out as quickly as a new one gains traction. Currently, there are hundreds of social networking sites on the social web. This chapter focuses on what we refer to as the "Big 6": Facebook, Google+, Twitter, LinkedIn, Pinterest, and Snapchat.

With so many avenues to approach and design a brand strategy, it is always beneficial to the success of the strategy to plan ahead. Social media strategies should be synergistic with the overall corporate communications, public relations, and marketing plans. Successful social strategies include elements from every department within the company. A few elements to keep in mind as you begin to design your social media strategy include the following:

- *Goal Plan:* When companies decide to embark upon a social strategy, including setting up a Facebook fan page, creating a Pinterest board, or initiating a Twitter account, they must first define what they want to achieve. Set clear goals and be sure to consider how this activity fits within the overall communications strategy. You also need to take the time to determine whether your customers utilize the particular social networking site(s) that you plan to utilize.
- *Content Plan:* Formulate a plan for maintenance of your content. Social sites must be continually maintained or consumers will become uninterested and leave. Your social strategy should outline the frequency that devised content will be uploaded—hourly, daily, weekly, or monthly. Consistency is key; however, posting relevant content is equally important.
- *Conversation Plan:* Companies must determine the types of conversations that they are seeking to have with their consumers. It is also helpful to consider any anticipated responses that will materialize. Is a retweet good enough, or is the expectation to converse back and forth between customers and your brand? Is liking a post on Facebook okay, or does the company want consumers to share the information with their audiences too?
- *Operation Plan:* Who is going to manage the social site? Planning is always fun, but once the planning is over, someone must curate content and maintain the

site. Protocols, reputation management guidelines, and rules for conduct are all essential.

- *Evaluation Plan:* As with all public relations planning, the "evaluate" stage is critical. One method of measurement is to record the number of conversation starters. For example, you can track the number of status updates, videos, or links that a company shares to generate conversations. Companies can also track the number of fans, increases in fans, likes, and posts generated by fans. Measuring outcomes that correlate with corporate goals and communication goals is also a good way to evaluate the success of a social strategy.

As noted, social strategies should support the overarching goals of the communications plan and those of the company. Any metrics collected should be weighed against those goals to understand the level of success that each initiative has achieved.

Facebook

With more than 1.19 billion people using Facebook and more than 874 million active daily users spending 700 billion minutes on the website each month, Facebook is considered one of the most influential social networking sites in the world.[1] Facebook provides users with the ability to share information and communicate with family and friends, while also promoting openness and connectivity. More than 70 billion pieces of content, including web links, news stories, blog posts, status updates, photos, and other sources, are shared through this platform.[2] Facebook provides a place to not only share information but also to interact with it. News organizations, for example, allow people to post their stories directly to their Facebook walls to share with friends. Brands use Facebook to build communities and engage with consumers in a more personal and meaningful manner. Facebook is also accessible through mobile phones, iPads, and other tablet devices. It makes sense to include Facebook in a company's social strategy considering that the average Facebook user is connected to eighty pages, groups, and events.[3]

Back to Basics

Understanding the fundamentals will go a long way in establishing a strong presence on Facebook. Certain terminology is used frequently, and therefore it is important for public relations professionals and social media strategists to have a firm grasp of the language used and its meaning. A list of the most frequent terms used when referring to Facebook is provided below:[4]

Brand Page/Profile: the official presence of a business, artist, political official, brand, cause, or product where the owner shares information and interacts with fans on Facebook. Pages create a culture that allows businesses to interact and engage with their fans one-on-one.

EdgeRank: an algorithm used to determine the content that appears in a person's newsfeed.

Fan: a Facebook user who "likes" a corporation's business page.

Friend: (v) to add a person as a connection to your personal profile; (n) a personal connection on Facebook.

Friend List: an ordered sorting of friends.

Group: an organized group of users with a common connection or similar interests—for example, "coworkers" or "family." Groups can be public or private.

Insights: the metrics used to analyze demographic data about the user's audience. Insights also highlight how people see, discover, and respond to posts.

SOCIAL MEDIA CHEAT SHEET
(for brands)

		PROS	CONS
	FACEBOOK The largest social network. 128+ billion users, 475 billion pieces of content shared daily. Virtual necessity for brands investing in social. DEMO: 65% 35+ yrs old; 60% female.	- Fans are 79% more likely to purchase than on other networks. - Contains advanced ad targeting capabilities for massive audiences. - Powerful and valuable analytic insights	- Low organic reach (pay to play). - Saturated by brands, so it's difficult to stand out.
	TWITTER 271 million active users post text, links, images, and 6 second videos (Vines) in 140 characters or less. DEMO: 18-20 yrs old; increasingly female.	- Strong customer service tool. - Strong analytics.	- Expensive, limited ad platform. - Short lifespan of posts.
	INSTAGRAM Primarily mobile app with 200+ million users who share pictures and short videos. DEMO: 37% 18-29 yrs old; 68% female.	- Untapped audience by many brands. - Facebook owned, so great potential.	- No links, analytics, or scheduling capabilities. - Advertising capabilities in their infancy.
	PINTEREST Online collaging resource for sharing inspiration and bookmarking links. 70 million users. DEMO: 79% female.	- Strong, receptive audience with buying power. - Generates over 400% more revenue per click than Twitter and 27% more than Facebook.	- Not effective for brands with limited web presence or e-commerce. - Skews highly female.
	GOOGLE PLUS Niche social network of 300 million users (though not very active). DEMO: 31% are 25-34 yrs old; 62% male.	- Great SEO benefits because it's owned by Google. - Ties to Google AdWords and YouTube.	- Uncertain future. - Largely inactive user-base.
	LINKEDIN Network of 300 million users. Exists for company information, updates, and recruiting Demo: White collar, urban or suburban users, balanced between genders.	- Best used to establish your brand as industry leader/authority. - Valuable recruiting tool.	- Unlikely to drive sales, unless B2B.
	SNAPCHAT Mobile app for sharing pictures between friends. 100 million users and rapidly growing. DEMO: 71% under 25 yrs old; 70% female.	- Find your customers where they live.	- Resource intensive. - Creativity required.

Source: Infographic courtesy of Likeable Media (www.likeable.com).

Like(s): (v) to become a fan and "like" a business's page or to "like" a comment posted by a friend or business; (n) the number of users who "like" your page.

Network: a collection of Facebook users, who may be related to a school, location, place of employment, or category such as "engineer," "nurse," or "educator."

Newsfeed: the center column of a user's home page. The newsfeed is continually updated with status updates, photos, videos, links, likes, and app activity from friends and pages that users follow. This section can be broken down by "top news" or "recent news."

Personal Profile: pages for individuals, not businesses, who have an account from which they are able to share information and interact with brands.

Timeline: a collection of the photos, stories, and experiences that users or brands post.

Constructing Your Brand Page on Facebook

Setting up a brand page on Facebook is fairly straightforward and easy. Facebook has very simple and uncomplicated instructions for novices (http://on.fb.me/1c9gVFr). Brand pages offer "insights" that include statistical data that can be useful in measuring growth. As a company's social strategy develops and matures over time, analytics will become increasingly important. Which promotions work and which may need tweaks and promotional "reach" can be evaluated through insights.

A brand page also affords a company an additional opportunity to highlight important information that the customers might find important. The company address, telephone number, website, and email address, as well as other social networking sites that the company is on, are all excellent pieces of information that a company should include. The company logo should be the profile photo for the brand page. Purina Dog Chow, General Electric, Maybelline New York, Adidas, Mattel, and even television shows such as *Scandal* and *Transparent* are examples of brands that incorporate their logos as their profile photos. This helps reinforce the company brand. A company may also elect to set up customized Facebook landing pages that require users to "like" the company page before they are able to access certain features. Pier One Imports and Victoria's Secret require users to "like" their pages before they can receive a coupon during certain promotions.

Attractive, Interactive, and Fresh

Brand pages should be attractive to your audience and provide enough information to generate interest in your products, services, and company. One of the benefits of a brand page is that it allows for mutual interaction. Set up a photo gallery, update the company status regularly, post videos, share links, and invite consumers to events. Facebook events can be used to promote anything from product demos to Internet shows, community events, and open houses. Invite users to the event so that they can then share it with their friends. This is an excellent technique to generate buzz about upcoming special occasions. Keep content fresh. Write fun, creative posts daily and employ the eighty/twenty rule, also known as the Pareto principle. Businesses should post content that is relevant to their audience at least 80 percent of the time and content explicitly about the company or products no more than 20 percent of the time.[5] Companies understandably want to make fans aware of their products and services, but it is important to make use of customer stories, photos, videos, and other interesting and informative responses when establishing the community.

Customized URL Address

Custom URLs make it easy to direct people to your brand page. Facebook allows brands to choose a specific URL address. For example, *The Ellen DeGeneres Show* uses https://www.facebook.com/ellentv, where "ellentv" is the customized portion of the show's Facebook URL. Companies should use the same username, or a very similar username, on all social networks to reinforce consistency within the brand. Keep it short so that consumers are able to remember it.

Badges, Widgets, and Apps

Once a user likes a company brand page, a company then has access to that fan on a consistent basis. Badges, widgets, and apps are excellent techniques to connect on a more in-depth level. There are four types of badges for sharing different information. "Profile" badges are used to share profile information, a "like" badge showcases pages that users have liked, a "photo" badge shares Facebook photos, and a "page" badge advertises a company page on Facebook.

Brands will often want to expand the audiences that their Facebook pages reach. Adding third-party widgets from Facebook's App Center allows companies to run contests on their pages, collect data with forms, import external feeds, and customize content through HTML coding.[6] Facebook apps allow for a deeper incorporation into the core Facebook experience and even tap into Facebook algorithms to help reveal the best content for users.[7] Apps fully integrate with Facebook.com, the newsfeed, and the notifications—all of which drive traffic and engage users.

Live Streaming

Facebook recently launched a live-streaming function. Users are now able to use a redesigned status menu to select "live video." The number of live viewers, the names of friends who are watching, and real-time comments are displayed while using this function. Unlike with the live-streaming pioneers such as Periscope and Meerkat, Facebook's videos are saved to a user's timeline and stay there unless the user chooses to delete them.

Top Fan Brand Pages

Generating buzz using creative incentives such as "liking" a page or reaching a certain number of "shares" allows fans to become brand advocates. Fans naturally want to engage with brands that resonate with them. By sharing a post or liking a company status update, a fan is promoting your business.

The first priority of a public relations or social media practitioner is to listen to customers and communicate by engaging in conversations with them. Unlike traditional advertising or marketing, a Facebook strategy requires a deeper and more meaningful level of interaction. Here are some brands that are building formidable relationships on Facebook:

1. *TOMS Shoes:* The brand has tapped into its core belief system of the one-to-one principle. It follows the eighty/twenty rule by balancing fan responses and interactions with promotion of its products.
2. *Domino's Pizza:* The brand has created a "Fancentric" experience. Rarely does the company overtly promote its products; rather, it engages its fans with humorous posts that promote interactivity. Here are two posts that generated hundreds of responses and thousands of likes: "1,2,3,4 I declare a last slice war. #GameOn," and "When has the power of pizza helped you the most? #poweredbypizza."

3. *Burberry:* This brand excels at hitting its target market with content that its users want. Elegant, simple, and stylish images present everything fans love about the brand. The company also connects with fans by showcasing past campaigns from previous years.

4. *Starbucks:* This Facebook brand page includes photos and updates from local stores. The company connects with fans by illuminating the intimacy of friends enjoying the coffee experience together.

5. *Ford:* The brand excels at having meaningful conversations with fans. The company promotes content that highlights the history of the Model T to Ford enthusiasts

Theory into Practice

The Outdoor Advertising Association of America

Social Media for the Largest Outdoor Art Show Ever Conceived

Overview

The Outdoor Advertising Association of America (OAAA) partnered with the Art Institute of Chicago, the Dallas Museum of Art, the Los Angeles County Museum of Art, the National Gallery of Art, and the Whitney Museum of American Art to bring Art Everywhere to the United States. Art Everywhere US exhibited great American art on thousands of out-of-home advertising displays across America. The objective of the campaign was to demonstrate the capabilities of outdoor advertising in a way that created a positive association with the medium among advertisers, elected officials, regulators, and the general public.

Strategy

Art Everywhere US was officially unveiled in August 2014 at a press event in Times Square, New York. The public was able to vote online for their top art choices. Votes were tallied, and the top 50 pieces of art were featured throughout the campaign.

Art Everywhere US also utilized Facebook, Twitter, Instagram, Pinterest, and YouTube channels prior to and during the event to attract media attention and promote the campaign.

Tactics

Using the hashtag #ArtEverywhereUS, social media users tweeted about their favorite pieces of art and shared photos via Instagram, Facebook, Twitter, and other photo sharing platforms. The campaign's website featured an interactive map, where public photos appeared near Art Everywhere US installations.

Daily social media outreach encouraged engagement and conversation, with staff sharing news articles and photos of live installations across the country. A social media contest was also launched, asking the general public to photograph themselves (snap a selfie) with gallery installations across the country and Tweet or Instagram them using the hashtag #ArtEverywhereUS.

Results

- From April 6, 2014–November 12, 2014, Art Everywhere US gained 5,837 Facebook likes; 1,978 Twitter followers;
- The campaign generated more than 50 million social media impressions and more than 1,000 media clips were in print or posted online, including 1,529 Instagram followers; 303 Pinterest followers; and over 26,000 YouTube video views.
- In addition, Art Everywhere US created buzz in Congress. U.S. Representatives and Senators posted on social media about art connections to their states. Representatives Billy Long (R-MO) and Steve Cohen (D-TN) published statements in the *Congressional Record* on June 25 and July 28, respectively, highlighting local artists represented in the national art show.
- To date, Art Everywhere US social media channels continue to grow and support conversation and have been valuable tools in promoting awareness of OAAA and its member organizations.

Source: Peter Rush, "Social Media Impact Study for Associations 2015," Kellen Company, 2015, accessed November 15, 2015, http://kellencompany.com/wp-content/uploads/Kellen-Social-Media-Impact-Report-for-Associations-2015-digital.pdf.

of today. Fans can download wallpaper or earn badges to declare their allegiance to their favorite Ford car—the Mondeo, the Mustang, and even the Escort.

Facebook may currently dominate the social connectivity market in terms of popularity and familiarity, but Google+ is making headway in establishing its own sizeable global audience as well. In the years since Google+ was introduced, it has surpassed both YouTube and Twitter in becoming the second-largest social platform that hosts active users.[8]

Google

Recently Google announced that it was splitting Google+ into separate services. This decision has been met with mixed reviews from consumers so far. It cannot be denied that Google's network is far-reaching and incredibly valuable. Google's strength has always been its search function, with features that are linked to Google Search continuing to be vital when connecting with consumers. In this move to separate services, Bradley Horowitz was charged with heading Google's Photos and Streams products—two of the most widely used services offered by Google+. As practitioners, it is important to properly understand how these changes impact the ability to reach users. Even with the changes, many of the functions that consumers know and love are still in use.

The Venn Connections

Among its many distinguishable features, Google+ boasts the ability to separate friends from "friends." Facebook does not truly allow users to separate their personal lives from their professional lives or the brands that they connect with online. One may argue that the Facebook "lists" feature accomplishes this, but it simply is not so. Mothers, brothers, sisters, and cousins are "friends" and comingle with coworkers, bosses, neighbors, the book club, and the brands that users follow and enjoy. Ultimately, the major differences between Facebook and Google+ boil down to these two principles:

1. Facebook centers on connecting a user with existing "friends" and the user's relationships with them, lumping all users into a single group.
2. Google+ Circles helps users build new connections, find interesting people, and discover personalized content, while at the same time keeping connections separate yet equal.

A key differentiator for Google+ Circles is in the way that it approaches revolutionizing online connections. Google+ Circles empowers users to create their own customizable circles of connections and group them depending on the specific relationship that they have with a particular person, group, or entity. For example, a user can create a circle of family members, a circle of friends, a circle of coworkers, other public relations professionals, and journalists, or even a circle of cupcake enthusiasts. This feature becomes increasingly valuable when promoting a brand. Not all brands have the same type of consumer. A company can now create various circles based on its consumers' buying habits, needs, and affinity with the brand. Brands can post content to one circle or to all of the circles that they manage. Google has even introduced the "+1" button. This feature is based on the premise that consumers turn to friends and family when making decisions.

The Power of +1 and Search

The +1 button combines the value of personal recommendations with the influence that Google offers. Recommendations with +1 appear on websites, display ads, search ads, Google Search results, and now Google+ pages. This facilitates easy integration across all of Google's platforms and services, including Google Search, Gmail, and YouTube.

Since Google was built on the power of search, it should not come as a surprise that Google+ also has a built-in search feature and ranking ability. Google can more easily monitor a real profile from one that may belong to a spammer. For public relations professionals and social media strategists, the ability to pull data and analytics from these rankings provides a brand with the power to create strong and formidable Google+ campaigns.

Let's All Hang Out!

Another inventive feature in Google+, Google Hangouts, allows brands to essentially "hang out" with users in real time. This is a function that has not easily been available on any platform. Facebook currently offers video chat functionality through a partnership with Skype, but this is only available for one-on-one calls. In comparison, Google Hangouts allows up to fifteen people to converse at once and opens the viewing for as many people as the host allows. Connecting with consumers is simple since downloads are not necessary to use the Hangouts feature. It can be launched directly from a user's Gmail account or from a Google+ page. Hangouts can be aired in real time or saved to a company YouTube channel for viewing at a later date. A Los Angeles–based digital publishing platform for cooking enthusiasts, BakeSpace, is an example of a Google+ success story. The company has more than 360,000 people in its circles on Google+ and has hosted approximately forty Hangouts with topics ranging from tutorials on cupcake decorating to conversations with the founders of Chameleon Cold-Brew Coffee.[9]

Google+ Pages with Power

As with any social media platform or tool, some brands have integrated Google+ with a greater degree of success. Connecting to customers using Google+'s features tends to humanize the brand, make it more accessible to consumers, and have long-lasting effects. Here are two stellar examples:[10]

1. *H&M:* Heralded as the poster child for Google+, the clothing store responds to and shares posts from followers to build an ongoing dialogue. This keeps H&M's customer base engaged. The company continually posts content that focuses on inspirational fashion motifs, including videos and images. It invites followers to share their personal experiences and truly values their feedback and opinions. On average, H&M achieves seventy-two +1s per post, eleven reshares, and twenty-two comments. The most popular posts to date involve the brand's top collections by Victoria Beckham, Versace, and Marni. Google reported that H&M's AdWords campaigns increased by 22 percent due in part to its Google+ social extensions.

2. *Cadbury:* The company has made social media central to its overall promotions strategy. On Google+, daily updates are posted that keep fans engaged by asking questions and sending teasers about new products. Cadbury uses Google Hangouts regularly for celebrating events, such as reaching the milestone of five hundred thousand followers and hanging out with Cadbury's Olympic brand ambassador Rebecca Adlington.

Google+ empowers both the company and the consumer to share their interests through their stories, recommendations, opinions, and relationships, all of which contribute to making the social sphere better. With the addition of Google+ Collections, users can now categorize their updates by topic, which helps followers quickly find updates for the topics they're interested in.

Another social tool, Twitter, is often incorporated into a social strategy because it is a great way to start a conversation with your target market and build and manage connections with customers, prospects, bloggers, and a myriad of other influencers.

Twitter

Launched in 2006, Twitter is a powerhouse in the social sphere. People clamor to connect with one another, update their statuses, learn about new products, share ideas, and create connections on Twitter. Since 42 percent of Twitter users follow various brands or companies using this social tool, it is certainly time for brands to take action.[11] With more than 500 million active users sending more than 500 million tweets per day, Twitter has become a crucial social media tool.[12] Businesses, both big and small, use Twitter for a variety of reasons, including lead generation, customer service, and even competitive intelligence. The rationale for introducing Twitter in the social strategy will vary based on individual company goals and outcomes.

Twitter is known as a "microblogging" service, meaning users can post short updates constrained to 140 or fewer characters. Originally intending tweets to be compatible with mobile phones and texting, the creators of Twitter limited how much an individual could write. Today, the 140-character limit is a signature feature, allowing for concise information to be shared.

ABCs and 123s of Twitter

Paralleling other social networks, Twitter also uses a set of common terms, symbols, and language—often dictating how users behave. The following are key terms that all Twitter users should know:[13]

Twitter Handle: an individual's or entity's username. This is the name used to represent an individual or a company on Twitter. For example, Edelman, the world's largest public relations firm, tweets from the Twitter handle @ EdelmanPR.

@ symbol: probably the most common symbol used on Twitter. This signifies that you are commenting or conversing with another Twitter user directly. For example, "@McLean_Don @RGA gotta say @HVSVN was pretty clever! Not surprised if we see more moves like this" indicates that the Twitter user is speaking directly with the people who tweet under the Twitter handles @ McLean_Don, @RGA, and @HVSVN. Messages that are tweeted to other users will show up in their Twitter feed and in their "@" connections.

RT: retweet. When a user RTs a fellow user's tweet, it is essentially like forwarding that tweet to all of the people in that user's own Twitter stream. In business, RTs spread the information that a company wants to share with others, including links to articles, blogs, newspapers, websites, journals, contests, and coupons. When retweeting, a user should always credit the original user. For example, that would look like "RT via @eharrisondotorg Check out the Peer-to-Peer Learning Handbook by @hrheingold & self-organizers with the #Peeragogy.org project http://peeragogy.org." If you simply click the retweet button, this will happen instantly. Users can also "favor" tweets, which is similar to "liking" a Facebook status update.

Hashtag: one of the most valuable assets that a Twitter user possesses. Twitter uses hashtags to aggregate a conversation surrounding an event, topic, or theme. For example, this book uses #LRNSMPR to share links about social media and public relations. Hashtags are created by combining the "#" symbol with a word, phrase, or acronym. When a tweet contains a hashtag, it then becomes searchable.

Like: represented by a small heart icon in a tweet. These are most commonly used when users like a tweet. Liking a tweet can let the original poster know that his or her content resonated with you, or you can save the tweet for later.

DM: direct message. A private message from one Twitter user to another. A DM can only be sent if both Twitter users follow one another.

Status Update: a tweet.

Twitter Stream: a list of a user's real-time Twitter updates.

Twitter Chat: an event held entirely online and intended as a forum for people to exchange ideas and discuss a specific topic. Twitter users connect with other like-minded Twitter users. Twitter chats are casual events that do not require registration and are generally organized by an individual or small group, an organization, or company. The intention of any Twitter chat is to be educational and informative. Twitter chats are not forums to promote products or sell wares. A popular Twitter chat among public relations professionals and public relations students is #PRStudChat. This event is designed to bring together public relations students, professionals, and educators for energetic conversations surrounding the public relations industry and to provide opportunities for learning, networking, and mentoring. Monthly charts are organized by cofounders Deirdre Breakenridge (@dbreakenridge) and Valerie Simon (@valeriesimon).

Twitter List: a curated group of Twitter users that is organized by the commonalities among its participants. Lists help individuals and companies organize their followers into categories or groups. This allows a user to easily view tweets from a specific group without having to scan your entire feed.

URL Shorteners: used to shorten and share links due to the 140-character tweet limit. The most frequently used shorteners include Bitly (www.bitly.com), Google URL Shortener (http://goo.gl), and TinyURL (www.tinyurl.com).

The Business of Twitter

There are numerous lists available that identify the ways in which businesses are using Twitter to connect and, yes, even monetize their strategies. Just when we thought the "Top Twenty-One Twitter Tips" from *Forbes* could not be outdone, the experts at MonetizePros came up with "101 Twitter Monetization Tips."[14] Whether a company pulls ideas from the top five tips or the top one hundred, public relations practitioners should encourage their companies to share their expertise by tweeting useful resources, insightful ideas, and helpful tips that will ultimately benefit their followers. Establishing company representatives as leaders within an industry is common in public relations. Tweeting company resources, including white papers, blogs, and ebooks, is an excellent way to illustrate that a company representative is a thought leader. It is important to understand that following social media strategies and connecting with others on the social web is not just about your company. Take the time and commit the effort to make sure to link other resources within communications to your consumer base beyond those only written by the company.

In the business realm, it is important to remember that using Twitter is more than merely tweeting content. A company Twitter page is like any other piece of collateral. It must be branded. The first thing a company should do when initiating a Twitter handle is to upload an image as the profile picture that represents the company and what the company has to say. Many companies opt to use a branded logo. Some small businesses or sole proprietors opt to use a photo of the person who maintains the Twitter account. Regardless of the image chosen, it should represent the professional image of the company. The profile background and header image should blend together well, since they also represent the brand. You want to make it easy for users to find what they are seeking when they search for you or your company on Twitter. It is important to detail your real name and location or the name of your company and where it is headquartered. Finally, write the best, most succinct bio that you possibly can. What captures your company attitude? Companies should have fun and be creative when writing the 160-character biography. Some companies include other Twitter handles managed by the company and even Twitter chats that the company hosts. The Coca-Cola Company, for example, has distinct accounts for specific products and independent channels. Twitter users who follow @CocaColaCo can learn about what's happening within the company itself. Those who follow @CocaColaZero can get the latest updates on their favorite soda, while users who follow @WorldofCocaCola can experience the story of the company, interact with the Coca-Cola polar bear, and learn more about the more than one hundred flavors the company offers across the globe.

Managing a company brand on Twitter is fairly straightforward and is accomplished by monitoring what is happening with your brand and what is going on within your industry. Staying abreast of the conversations on Twitter help brands connect more intimately with their customers, while at the same time eliminating surprises, including disgruntled customers and faulty products. When a company appoints an individual to manage its Twitter account, that person should be knowledgeable, a good listener, and trustworthy.[15] Twitter is not an advertisement, marketing campaign, or fad. Any company that enacts a Twitter strategy would benefit from appointing individuals whom it trusts completely with its brand reputation, since Twitter users expect to interact with a real person. Twitter accounts that are abandoned are not seen as credible in the eyes of the larger online community. Cheerios (@cheerios), for example, lacks sustainability. The company Twitter account goes days, even months, without sending a tweet.

Bonding with Followers

The value of any interaction on social media is the conversation and relationship that is cultivated with real people and real customers. Using Twitter, there are plenty of ways to interact with your customers and engage in meaningful conversations.

- Special offers and coupons are often used. Companies can easily tweet exclusive offers to their followers. A benefit of using Twitter to support this strategy is when the offer is compelling enough; the follower will not only redeem the offer but also share it with his or her followers. A good habit to get into is to link back to a company landing page where customers can download the coupon, ebook, or free code to the latest webinar the company has hosted. When companies steer customers back to a specified webpage, they create an opportunity to expose customers to the company website, where they may be inclined to look at or purchase other products.
- Customer service is often an avenue of connection on Twitter. When customers have questions for the company, they rely on Twitter. When customers

have complaints, they rely on Twitter. Simply Measured conducted a study that showed that 99 percent of brands are on Twitter, and 30 percent of them have a dedicated customer service Twitter handle for customer interactions.[16] One of the leading brands supporting excellent customer service via Twitter is the team at Nike. They monitor the @NikeSupport Twitter handle, where their sole purpose is to respond to customers who need help. They boast a 73 percent response rate, which is three times higher than the closest brand.

• Team recruitment isn't saved for LinkedIn alone. Recruiting and hiring managers turn to Twitter to post open positions, leverage their network of followers, and view potential employee profiles.

• Philanthropic endeavors permeate the social sphere on Twitter. Twitter has been used to raise hundreds of thousands of dollars for charities and benevolent causes. In addition, Twitter has been a critical component to spread awareness about social issues. For example, the world came together to globally support the complex struggles of the Egyptian and Libyan populations using Twitter.

The key here is to take a look around the next time you wonder what you should tweet. Is there anything of note happening in the office that your customers may want to see? Maybe you could share a sneak peek at the latest photo shoot or the guest speaker who is spending a day at the office. Simply pull out that smartphone, snap a photo, and tweet it. Perhaps your company has an upcoming conference or webinar it is hosting—tweet the link to that event. Tweet the company's latest blog post. You could also post a link to another industry leader's content that your customers may find relevant. Finally, and this is especially important in building brand awareness, just chat with your network. After all, Twitter is "a real-time information network that connects you to the latest information about what you find interesting."[17]

As consumers continue to flock to the social sphere in droves, so are businesses and brands, because it has been demonstrated time and again that these sites drive traffic, increase authentic engagement, and build brand

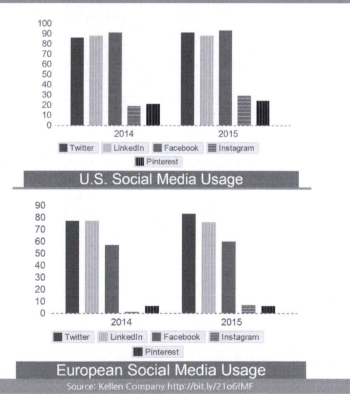

Impact of Social Media on Corporations in the U.S. and Europe

The utilization of nearly all major social media channels increased in the past year throughout the U.S. and Europe. Platforms involving images and videos experienced the largest growth in both regions, with Instagram seeing the greatest adoption rates.

U.S. Social Media Usage

■ Twitter ▥ LinkedIn ■ Facebook ▤ Instagram ▥ Pinterest

European Social Media Usage

■ Twitter ▥ LinkedIn ■ Facebook ▤ Instagram ▥ Pinterest

Source: Kellen Company http://bit.ly/21o6fMF

From 2014 to 2015, U.S. and European companies expanded their presence on almost all major social media platforms.

loyalty. The recent changes that LinkedIn implemented created more opportunities for businesses to launch a brand page, and the results are paying off.

LinkedIn

An astonishing 400 million members in over two hundred countries and territories are on the professional social networking site LinkedIn.[18] This social network boasts 97 million unique monthly U.S. visitors and 3 billion users globally.[19] If you look a bit closer at these statistics, professionals are signing up on LinkedIn at a rate of approximately two new members per second.[20] There are over 39 million students and recent college graduates on LinkedIn, making them the fastest-growing demographic.[21] This makes LinkedIn the world's largest professional social network. Creating a company profile with a company page on this network just makes sense.

Professionals come to LinkedIn for a variety of reasons. Some are looking for a new job, while others join groups to network with. LinkedIn's membership includes individuals spanning numerous sectors, including employees, potential customers, purchasing managers, clients, and users who are simply interested in observing what is going on in industries. LinkedIn members typically follow companies to keep abreast of new developments, compare products and services, track potential business opportunities, and keep a lookout for job openings. When members want to know more about a company, they seek out company pages and access specific profiles.

Central to the Brand

Businesses should consider their company pages as anchors within LinkedIn. A company's page is the first place a member lands to see company status updates, the latest blog post written by thought leaders within the business, Twitter updates, and special offers and to network with other professionals. Company pages bring life to a brand, reveal the human side of a business, and reach millions of professionals through word-of-mouth recommendations. Businesses can manage and measure all facets of the company brand on LinkedIn, including product brands and employment brands. There are four tabs on every company page on LinkedIn: overview, careers, products, and insights.

Overview Tab

The overview tab is akin to a front receptionist in a typical brick-and-mortar business. A receptionist will often greet visitors and make them feel welcome. A company page should accomplish the same goal. This is the first impression that a newcomer will have of your business. A high-level overview of the company should be included on the overview tab along with a cover image that represents the company and brand. Be mindful of how the company description is written and the images used to represent the company. Any text and photography should be consistent with the company's brand position across multiple channels. Unilever (http://www.linkedin.com/company/unilever) has created a strong image that represents not only some of the brands that it sells but also its people, philanthropy efforts, and followers. The overview tab gives members the opportunity to connect with a company on various levels:

- Follow the company to stay abreast of significant developments, updates, employment opportunities, and landmark events.
- Access the latest news through the company Twitter feeds and blog posts.
- Connect with employees of the company.

Get Inspired: Five Steps to a Successful Company Page on LinkedIn

1. *Be Creative:* Be creative with how you present your company. Upload an image that welcomes visitors to the company page and reinforces the presence of the brand. Create and share videos that resonate with your target audience. Members are more likely to share information that they think their sphere of influence will appreciate.
2. *Start Conversations:* Post regular updates that spark conversations with members.
3. *Share with Others:* Share all of your status updates, and encourage members within your company to add the company page to their personal profiles. It should become common practice for employees to "like" and "share" the content published on the company page. Sharing drives traffic to the company page and increases the number of people who see your content updates.
4. *Show Off a Little:* Add your product or services so that LinkedIn members can see what you have to offer. Include recommendations to further highlight the reasons why your products and services are special.
5. *Extend Your Reach:* Feature relevant groups to reach a broader audience.

- Access essential data on the company.
- View the "employee statistics" area to gain a better understanding of the company makeup. There is no better ambassador for a company than its own employees. Connecting with employees humanizes a company.

The feed on LinkedIn is a company's way of communicating important messages to its audience. Some businesses are more effective than others at using images to tell their stories, providing rich content, writing compelling status updates, and engaging in meaningful dialogue with their target audiences. Walt Disney (http://lnkd.in/WaltDisney), Xactly (http://lnkd.in/xactly), IT Media Group (http://lnkd.in/ITMediaGroup), and Adobe (http://lnkd.in/adobe) are among the few that understand the best practices for creating an effective company page.

Careers Tab
Premium careers pages, a paid subscription section within LinkedIn, allow businesses to promote general job opportunities as well as post specific jobs that target candidates using an automated job-matching system. This tab also allows a company to highlight awards, showcase the company's best employees, and even determine various career paths available within the company. Customized modules like this help complete the corporate story by providing a company with an opportunity to share its mission, vision, and goals.

Products Tab
The company products tab is particularly important because it accomplishes three goals: it (1) enables a business to showcase its best products and services to a highly targeted audience, (2) creates a place to feature product recommendations, and (3) facilitates meaningful conversations with current and prospective customers.

It would be prudent for a business to take advantage of the features provided in this tab. One such feature allows a company to capture the significant features of its products by incorporating powerful images and video clips that promote interactivity. Some businesses also include the contact details of the people behind the products in case members would like to connect directly with a designer or simply learn more,

LinkedIn Lingo

LinkedIn is a social networking site dedicated to professionals and businesses alike. The following glossary of commonly used terms is provided to help ground users in the LinkedIn lingo.

1st Degree Connections: These are users that you choose to connect with personally. In general, these are the individuals whom you have established a personal relationship with prior to connecting on LinkedIn. These can be school-related connections, previous colleagues, or personal friends.

2nd Degree Connections: These are contacts of a 1st degree connection.

3rd Degree Connections: These are contacts of a 2nd degree connection.

Activity Feed: This feature of LinkedIn displays the current activity of any of your connections—generally other users or groups that you are a part of. This would also include activities related to joining or starting groups, comments that you have made, changes to your profile, and application downloads.

Activity Broadcasts: This includes content that appears on the Activity Feed and is visible for other users to see and comment on. This section can be edited.

Anonymous Viewers: These are LinkedIn members who have chosen to keep part or all of their profiles private.

Applications: Applications allow members to integrate other social media networks with their LinkedIn account, including Twitter, Facebook, and WordPress.

Basic Account: This is a free LinkedIn account.

Connection: A connection is another LinkedIn member who has accepted your invitation to connect, network, and view each other's profiles and networks.

Groups: Groups allow professionals to develop their careers by sharing expertise, experience, and knowledge.

Invitation: This is a request from an existing member or individual not on LinkedIn to join or make a professional connection.

InMail: These are private messages that allow a member to directly contact any LinkedIn user, while protecting the recipient's privacy. This is a fee-based service.

Network: This is a group of users who can contact you via connections up to three degrees away.

Open Link Network: Premium members can join this network, which allows any LinkedIn member to send them an InMail free of charge, regardless of relationship.

Premium Accounts: This is an upgraded LinkedIn account where members can pay a monthly or annual subscription fee. Paid account benefits include InMail, better profile search results, expanded profiles, and larger storage space.

Recommendations: Similar to letters of recommendation, recommendations are references that are written to recommend a colleague, business partner, or someone whom you have done business with.

Job Seekers Account: LinkedIn members can choose between three levels of fee-based job-seeking accounts: basic, standard, and plus. The aim of this service is for the member to gain increased exposure to potential employers.

LION: This acronym, meaning "LinkedIn open networker," is sometimes visible on a member's profile. It simply means that the particular member agrees to connect with anyone, regardless of industry or connection.

buy a product, or contract with a company for work. Companies that understand how to connect with their members on LinkedIn create personalized content that is geared toward that specific target market. Using this technique, companies retain the ability to show different content to different members based on their preferences and needs. Currently, LinkedIn offers users up to thirty specific audience segments (based on date), including segmentation by industry, geography, company size, and more. Companies need to capitalize on the fact that recommendations from family, friends, and peers are greatly influential in our decision-making process.[22] By featuring recommendations from trusted third-party entities, organizations, and LinkedIn members, companies can potentially benefit from these influences related to specific products or brands.

Insights Tab

Analytics are invaluable to all social media strategies. Analytics are how most public relations professionals and social media strategists track the successes and failures of their campaigns. Each LinkedIn company page is outfitted with an insights tab that is only visible to administrators. Company administrators can analyze the number of visits to their company pages and the demographics of followers, and they track new followers, see which areas have the most hits, and monitor overall page growth. Using these analytics, administrators can easily populate graphs, providing insights regarding traffic, user-pattern page clicks, likes, comments, shares, and percentages related to a number of valuable metrics.

Proof Is in the Pudding

Successful companies lead by example. LinkedIn is a great illustration of how a social networking platform can best utilize each offered feature to support business initiatives. On average, LinkedIn posts fresh, engaging content approximately 150 times each month to its members. Fresh videos, images, status updates, and blog posts keep members coming back for more and incidentally also promote increased sharing among members. From a social site whose original goal was to provide networking opportunities and recruit talent, LinkedIn has become a powerhouse in search, content, and influence.

Another social media platform, Pinterest, has seen its adoption continually increase since its inception and now takes its place as a "go-to" social media tool alongside other veteran social networking sites like LinkedIn and Facebook.

Pinterest

Pinterest has quickly become one of the biggest social traffic referral sites, recording more traffic than YouTube, Google+, and LinkedIn combined.[23] The astonishing growth of Pinterest has led to widespread media coverage and an abundance of articles, blog posts, forum discussions, how-to podcasts, and videos about how this new social network is taking the social web by storm. Keenly adept at what other social networks have done so well, Pinterest connects people and triggers them to share and communicate, while at the same time facilitating *discovery* rather than having users search for what they want.

The fastest social site to garner 10 million visitors per month in the short history of social media, Pinterest's rise to the top has communications professionals, tech junkies, and social media thought leaders amazed at the power it commands. Strictly speaking, Pinterest is a social network that allows users to visually share, curate, and uncover new interests by "pinning" videos or images to their own pinboards. Through pictorial representations, brands can connect with pinners who share interests and preferences that the brand represents. Pinterest is a social network meant to "collect and organize the things that inspire" its users.[24] With thirty-two categories of pinboards, brands have the ability to connect on many levels. There are five types of pinners:

The Influencing Pinner: Influencers' activity affects the decisions of those who follow them. If an influencer pins or repins an image from your brand, others are likely to follow suit. Influencing pinners recommend products, websites, contests, and social connections that they believe other Pinterest users will also enjoy. These individuals have the ability to sway the decision-making power of their followers.

The Purchasing Pinner: These pinners express themselves through pictures and images relevant to items that they have purchased or plan to purchase.

The Almost Purchasing Pinner: Pinners who use Pinterest as a social bookmarking site or simply as a wish list fall into this category. These users pin images as a reminder of what they want to do, buy, plan, share, or come back to at a later date.

The "In It for the Long Haul" Pinner: Pinners in this category use Pinterest to explore and conduct research on products or projects that they know will eventually be purchased or implemented. Pinners who are "in it for the long haul" know what they want. For example, perhaps they are planning a wedding. These individuals know that they need invitations, but they do not quite know what type of invitation they like. They will create a board and save images that approximate what they are looking for. These users will keep collecting pins until they find the perfect pin.

The Instantaneous Pinner: Instantaneous pinners are precise in what they search for on Pinterest—for example, "hand-painted, classic, do-it-yourself wedding invitations" rather than "wedding invitations."

Pinteresting Campaigns

Branded profiles allow businesses to develop promotions that encourage users to follow the profiles of individual brands and pin items from their websites. Whole Foods Market, an early adopter of Pinterest, has amassed close to 272,500 followers on this platform.[25] With fifty-seven boards ranging in topic from organically grown foods—"How Does Your Garden Grow?"—to gift-giving ideas—"Great Gifts (. . . You May Not Think Of)"—the company presents itself to a variety of audiences. However, Whole Foods Market does not overly promote its products within these boards. Its pins relate to the core values of the company: being all natural, sustainable, and organic.

When defining a social strategy for Pinterest, brands should focus on creating genuine interactions that result in a community of dedicated and loyal followers. Think of pins in terms of "likes" and every comment and follow as a symbol between two people building a long-term friendship.[26] The social strategy for Whole Foods Market is to pull content from blogs and other online sites that align with its mission.

Other brands, including Bare Minerals and Lands' End Canvas, ran Pin It to Win It campaigns using Pinterest.[27] Fans of Bare Minerals were asked to follow the brand's pinboard, set up a themed board of their own following the company's set of directions, and then simply tag pins with #BareMinerals and #READYtowin. Lands' End asked followers to pin images from LandsEndCanvas.com for a chance to win one of the pinned items.

One of the most successful Pinterest campaigns to date was created by the brilliant minds at Honda. The You Deserve a Pintermission campaign promoted the CR-V's young, hip, live-life image by reaching out to five influential pinners and challenging them to a #Pintermission.[28] They were asked to take a twenty-four-hour break from Pinterest so they could bring something from their personal pinboards to life. To help the influential pinners complete the activity, Honda gave each $500.

Pinterest Patois

Although other social networking sites require mastery of a long list of essential definitions, Pinterest only has a few phrases that matter.

Follow: Following means that a user wishes to pay attention to whatever another user is posting. Two levels of following exist:

- *Following the Overall User:* Any time a particular user posts anything on Pinterest, it will show up on your newsfeed.
- *Following an Individual Board:* Any time something new is pinned to that specific board, it will show up on your newsfeed.

Pin: This is an image added to Pinterest using the "Pin It" button. Pins are generally uploaded from your computer or from a URL. A pin can be an image or a video. Pins typically link back to the site that they originate from.

Pinboard (aka Board): A board is a themed collection of pins. Pinners can create as many boards as they wish and as many categories as they can think of. Boards can be edited at any time.

Pinning: This is the act of adding an image to a board.

Pinner: This is a user who shares content on Pinterest.

Repin: This is the act of reposting another Pinterest user's image to one of your own boards (similar to retweeting).

Once the pinners were selected, Honda uploaded personalized posters to individual boards within the company's profile. Honda also had the pinners create their own #Pintermission boards and add Honda as a collaborator. The results from this initiative were astounding, primarily because these five "chosen" pinners were so influential within the target community. The #Pintermission boards attracted more than 4.6 million visitors, resulting in more than five thousand repins and nearly two thousand likes. The campaign was so popular that it migrated to Twitter, resulting in hundreds of tweets and generating more than 16 million media impressions.

Watch John Watts, Honda's head of digital marketing, discuss why the campaign was so successful: http://bit.ly/15jXPeD.

These types of campaigns illustrate that contests can be powerful draws using Pinterest if they are executed correctly. They create a more engaged fan base, broaden a brand's online reach, and foster longer-term relationships.

Traditionally, younger users are typically a rich resource for what's hot and what's not. In fact, much of the success that the company UsTrendy has realized is because founder and CEO Sam Sisakhti implements the social platforms his interns use. So when his interns started praising Snapchat, he took notice.[29]

Snapchat

As noted throughout, not every organization needs to have a presence on every social media platform. Even fewer need to be on Snapchat. However, if your business is targeting younger consumers falling in the thirteen-to-twenty-four age demographic, you might want to pay attention. Initially, Snapchat began infamously as a one-to-one mobile messaging app known for sexting—because its messages disappeared in seconds—but today it's a one-to-many platform used daily by more than 100 million active users and 200 million monthly users.[30] This social platform is ahead of its competitors after just four years.

It sometimes takes years for a brand to fully understand how to organize and create content for some of the more established social platforms, including Twitter and Facebook. When a social platform like Snapchat comes along, public relations professionals are faced with the challenge of engaging consumers through an app in which the content disappears in seconds.[31]

Brands seem to be most interested in using Snapchat to engage with the most elusive age demographic: tween to young adult. Any platform that promises a direct path to a younger audience is surely one that brands want to be on.[32] The challenge becomes figuring out an application that makes strategic sense.

Here are a few examples of top brands investing time and creative efforts into developing a strategy around Snapchat:

McDonalds: The brand is a force to be reckoned with on Snapchat. The company understands its audience and what its audience wants. McDonalds has snapped out behind-the-scenes photos of LeBron James and commercial footage with athletes like Richard Sherman and Johnny Manziel, as well as creative food snaps and contests. McDonalds uses Snapchat as a way of providing fans unique looks at their favorite athletes and is a simple way to add value to its social presence. "We're really excited to explore the 'chat' and 'here' features more," noted Lainey Garcia, McDonald's U.S. Snapchat lead. "The instant face-to-face video chat has a number of possibilities for us, too. The more one-to-one conversations we're able to have with our fans the better."[33] When McDonald's announced its Pay with Lovin' promotion, it combined the power of Twitter and Snapchat to take the promotion to the next level. Using Snapchat, the company spread its campaign messaging with a post during the Super Bowl. The snap showed three friends on the couch watching football and reflecting on the Pay with Lovin' promotion. The creative seemed to match what most of McDonald's audience might be doing at that moment—sitting on the couch.[34] McDonald's may have

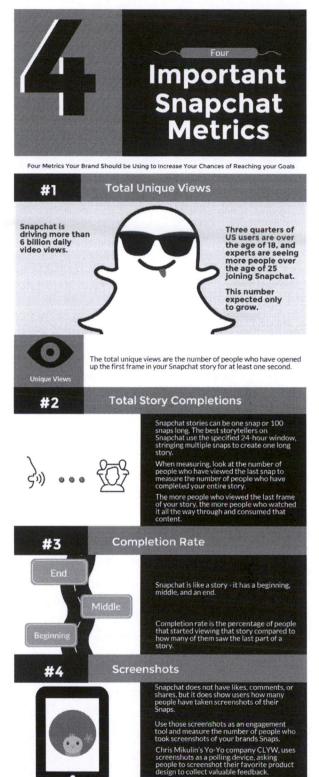

Four

Important Snapchat Metrics

Four Metrics Your Brand Should be Using to Increase Your Chances of Reaching your Goals

#1   Total Unique Views

Snapchat is driving more than 6 billion daily video views.

Three quarters of US users are over the age of 18, and experts are seeing more people over the age of 25 joining Snapchat.

This number expected only to grow.

Unique Views

The total unique views are the number of people who have opened up the first frame in your Snapchat story for at least one second.

#2   Total Story Completions

Snapchat stories can be one snap or 100 snaps long. The best storytellers on Snapchat use the specified 24-hour window, stringing multiple snaps to create one long story.

When measuring, look at the number of people who have viewed the last snap to measure the number of people who have completed your entire story.

The more people who viewed the last frame of your story, the more people who watched it all the way through and consumed that content.

#3   Completion Rate

End

Middle

Beginning

Snapchat is like a story - it has a beginning, middle, and an end.

Completion rate is the percentage of people that started viewing that story compared to how many of them saw the last part of a story.

#4   Screenshots

Snapchat does not have likes, comments, or shares, but it does show users how many people have taken screenshots of their Snaps.

Use those screenshots as an engagement tool and measure the number of people who took screenshots of your brands Snaps.

Chris Mikulin's Yo-Yo company CLYW, uses screenshots as a polling device, asking people to screenshot their favorite product design to collect valuable feedback.

Brands can encourage people to screenshot three choices, in a "choose-your-own adventure" type of story.

Embrace Snapchat

Source: Nick Cicero http://www.convinceandconvert.com/social-media-measurement/snapchat-measuring/

been the only advertiser to synchronize its Super Bowl TV and Twitter ads with its Snapchat content during the game.

Free People: This company uses Snapchat to engage its audience on multiple levels. It provides fans with a first look at new collections and behind-the-scenes looks inside the office; it also takes the opportunity to engage fans by asking questions regarding their weekend plans. It has even implemented Question Wednesdays, whereby users can ask questions to Free People employees. Staffers have been asked an array of questions ranging from "What was the first concert you've ever been to?" to "If you're an alien what would you look like?"[35]

Exclusive, unique content always resonates with fans. Kathryn O'Connor, marketing director for Free People, says, "We keep followers guessing, so that when they go to open a Snap, we have 100% of their attention. It's a channel where followers get real insight into the brand and what we're doing. There is a true delight factor in that."[36]

The Maze Runner: #SurviveTheNight:[37] The objective of this initiative was to bring the movie *The Maze Runner* to life in a way that actively engaged the

The Chitchat of Snapchat

Snap, when used as a verb, refers to taking a picture or video with Snapchat and sending it to another individual. **Snap**, when used as a noun, refers to the actual picture or video that is received from another user. Snaps cannot be viewed for longer than ten seconds.

Stories are collections of snaps that are specifically added to the story and are available for twenty-four hours.

Filters are applied to a snap after it is taken to change the snap's appearance. Filters have also been added to allow users to show their location, their speed, or the time or temperature when the snap was taken. Video filters have also been added that recognize an individual's face and create fun videos.

Geofilters are special overlays for snaps that can only be accessed in certain locations.

Replay is a feature that allows a user to view a snap again. The replay feature can only be used once a day.

Front-facing flash allows a user to snap in the dark using a front-facing camera by lighting up the screen while taking a snap.

Best Friends is a list that Snapchat creates of the friends with whom you exchange the most snaps.

The number of best friends shown can be adjusted using the settings.

Snapstreak is used to highlight when you have snapped a person back and forth for two or more days. If one person does not send a snap within twenty-four hours, the streak will break. The snapstreak is represented by a flame emoji next to the friend's name.

The **Trophy Case** gives users virtual trophies that can be unlocked when they achieve a goal on Snapchat. Examples of goals that unlock trophies are sending a video snap, using a filter on a snap, and reaching a ten thousand Snapchat score.

Snapchat score is the total number of snaps that a user has sent to friends. Friends can see the score and compare their own.

Discover is a feature that allows users to see stories from news outlets or locations around the world. ESPN, Comedy Central, the Food Network, CNN, and other outlets supply interactive snaps with users and can keep users up to date with things that apply to the outlet.

Sources: "Snapchat FAQ," Snapchat, accessed November 11, 2015, https://support.snapchat.com/a/geofilter-faq; Derek Kerr, "The Language of Snapchat" (class presentation, "Fundamentals of Social Media," October 1, 2015).

movie's fan base using Snapchat in a new and interesting way. The result was an overnight Snapchat challenge that mirrored events in the movie. For one night only, from sundown to sunrise, @mazemovies hosted a Snapchat battle with Kenny Holland and Amymarie Gaertner, two established social media influencers. Throughout the night, the two competed in various challenges on Snapchat. The activity was supported entirely by fans who were responsible for voting and helping their favorite influencer complete each challenge using the hashtag #SurviveTheNight.[38] To incentivize viewers and drive awareness of the movie release, fans were rewarded with links to exclusive content after select challenges. The winner of #SurviveTheNight was determined by the influencer who activated a larger majority of *The Maze Runner*'s fan base. In just twelve hours, this Snapchat campaign garnered 5.5 million Snapchat impressions, 95,000 Snapchat screenshots, over 41,000 Snapchat followers gained, and 33,000 views of exclusive content.[39]

Social Networks: The Platform/Social Networking Sites: The Channel

Loyalty is the foundation for successful relationships in life. Relationships between a business and customers are no different. Customers who are loyal to a specific brand, product, or service tend to stay loyal throughout their lives. They even become brand champions and look for ways to share their love of a brand with others. The dynamics between a customer and a business have created an ever-evolving relationship that promotes and fosters loyalty.

People connect with brands on social networks using various social networking sites because they want to learn something about a brand, share valuable content with others, define who they are, grow and cultivate their online relationships, and support causes that resonate with them. Social media campaigns help businesses accomplish these goals while also building brand and company loyalties. Selecting the correct social platform to promote a business and incorporating the necessary elements that make sense is also core to building a successful social strategy or campaign. Analyzing these strategies and campaigns a bit more closely, one can see that businesses successful in building a community of brand advocates have incorporated many of the valuable principles highlighted in the Circular Model of SoMe for Social Communication (*S*hare, *o*ptimize, *M*anage, *e*ngage) when interacting with their consumer bases. Genuine, authentic interactions with consumers can be a company's best asset for enhancing relationships and expanding a brand. Social networking sites are easy, available channels for customers to reach out to a brand and, in turn, for a company to respond.

#LRNSMPR

Learn More: Effective Uses of Social Networking Sites

- Peach: The Latest Social Networking Site: http://bit.ly/1SiuEBw
- "Snapchat Marketing, a Beginners Guide": http://bit.ly/1MnU4qh
- "Slack: A Communication Tool Every Team Should Use": http://bit.ly/1P1bbVu
- "25 Brand-Building Ways to Use Periscope": http://bit.ly/1OramQe
- "Why Every Employee at Your Company Should Use LinkedIn": http://onforb.es/1SFqh1t

Notes

[1] Associated Press, "Number of Active Users at Facebook Over the Years," Yahoo! News, last modified May 1, 2013, accessed August 22, 2013, http://news.yahoo.com/number-active-users-facebook-over-230449748.html; "Social Networking Statistics," Statistic Brain, last modified November 12, 2012, accessed August 23, 2013, http://www.statisticbrain.com/social-networking-statistics.

[2] "Social Networking Statistics."

[3] "Facebook Statistics," Statistic Brain, last modified June 23, 2013, accessed August 23, 2013, http://www.statisticbrain.com/facebook-statistics.

[4] R. Wilson, *Share This: The Social Media Handbook for PR Professionals* (West Sussex: Wiley, 2012), chap. 7; A. Sibley, "An Introduction to Facebook for Business," HubSpot, last modified 2013, accessed August 23, 2013, http://hubspot.uberflip.com/i/152427.

[5] R. Luttrell, "Are You Abiding by the 80/20 Rule?," Gina Luttrell PhD, August 9, 2013.

[6] R. Menezes, "How to Add Widgets to Facebook," eHow.com, 2013, http://www.ehow.com/how_5086646_add-widgets-facebook.html.

[7] "Games on Facebook Overview," Facebook, last modified 2013, accessed August 26, 2013, https://developers.facebook.com/docs/guides/canvas.

[8] Wing Kosner, "Watch Out Facebook, with Google+ at #2 and YouTube at #3, Google, Inc. Could Catch Up," *Forbes*, http://www.forbes.com/sites/anthonykosner/2013/01/26/watch-out-facebook-with-google-at-2-and-youtube-at-3-google-inc-could-catch-up.

[9] Todd Wasserman, "Should Your Business Use Google Hangouts?," *Mashable*, May 19, 2013, http://mashable.com/2013/05/09/google-hangouts-business.

[10] D. Moth, "10 Brands with Great Google Pages," Econsultancy, October 9, 2012, http://econsultancy.com/us/blog/10845-10-brands-with-great-google-pages.

[11] M. Monahan, "Marketing Your Business with Twitter," *Summing It Up Blog*, February 7, 2013, http://www.sigmawebmarketing.com/blog/bid/171523/Marketing-Your-Business-With-Twitter.

[12] C. Smith, "By the Numbers: 24 Amazing Twitter Stats," *DMR Digital Marketing Ramblings*, August 18, 2013.

[13] R. Luttrell, "Twitter Basics," Gina Luttrell PhD, July 30, 2012, http://ginaluttrellphd.com/2012/07/30/twitter-basics.

[14] D. Adler, "Twenty-One Top Twitter Tips," *Forbes*, July 31, 2009; M. Johnston, "101 Ways to Make Money with Twitter," MP: Monetize Pros, July 13, 2013, http://monetizepros.com/blog/2013/101-ways-to-make-money-with-twitter.

[15] J. Duffy, "How to Use Twitter for Business," *PC*, April 16, 2013, http://www.pcmag.com/article2/0,2817,2383408,00.asp.

[16] A. Stadd, "How Are Top Brands Doing with Twitter Customer Service?," *All Twitter*, May 10, 2013, http://www.mediabistro.com/alltwitter/twitter-customer-service_b42180.

[17] "About Twitter," Twitter, https://twitter.com/about.

[18] See the LinkedIn website at http://www.linkedin.com.

[19] See QuantCast search results for LinkedIn at https://www.quantcast.com/search?q=linkedin.

[20] S. Rayson, "9 Ways to Improve Your LinkedIn Marketing," *Social Media Today*, July 22, 2013, http://socialmediatoday.com/steve-rayson/1611011/improve-linkedin-marketing-9-ways.

[21] "About Us," LinkedIn Newsroom, accessed November 2, 2015, https://press.linkedin.com/about-linkedin.

[22] B. Solis, *Engage: The Complete Guide for Brands and Businesses to Build, Cultivate, and Measure Success in the New Web* (New York: Wiley, 2011).

[23] Eric Gilbert et al., "I Need to Try This? A Statistical Overview of Pinterest," in *Proceedings of the SIGCHI Conference on Human Factors in Computing Systems*, 2427–36 (New York: ACM, 2013).

[24] See the Pinterest website http://about.pinterest.com.

[25] S. Guneulis, "5 Brands Using Pinterest Brilliantly," *SproutInsights*, February 13, 2012, http://sproutsocial.com/insights/2012/02/best-pinterest-brands.

[26] L. Indvik, "How Brands Are Using Promotions to Market on Pinterest," *Mashable*, March 7, 2012, http://mashable.com/2012/03/07/pinterest-brand-marketing.

[27] S. Mallon, "5 Brands Using Pinterest Right and How to Learn from Them," *Online Marketing Insights*, May 15, 2013, http://www.onlinemarketinginstitute.org/blog/2013/05/pinterest-marketing-examples.

[28] K. Piombino, "Honda's Shoestring Pinterest Campaign Attracts Millions," *Ragan's PR Daily*, February 21, 2013, http://www.prdaily.com/Main/Articles/Hondas_shoestring_Pinterest_campaign_attracts_mill_13883.aspx.

[29] Brian Solomon, "How to Use Snapchat: A Small Business Guide," *Forbes*, August 25, 2015, accessed November 2, 2015, http://www.forbes.com/sites/smallbusinessworkshop/2015/08/25/how-to-use-snapchat-a-small-business-guide/#7564dd4167bd.

[30] Solomon, "How To Use Snapchat."

[31] Jeff Beer, "How 12 Brands Used Snapchat," Co.Create, August 12, 2014, accessed November 11, 2015, http://www.fastcocreate.com/3033793/how-12-brands-used-snapchat.

[32] Beer, "How 12 Brands Used Snapchat."

[33] Beer, "How 12 Brands Used Snapchat."

[34] Nick Cicero, "Here's What Innovative Brands Did on Snapchat for the Super Bowl," Marketing Land, February 3, 2015, accessed November 11, 2015, http://marketingland.com/heres-brands-snapchat-super-bowl-116933.

[35] Beer, "How 12 Brands Used Snapchat."

[36] Beer, "How 12 Brands Used Snapchat."

[37] Amanda Huggins, "The Maze Runner: #SurviveTheNight—Shorty Awards for Brands, Agencies, and Organizations," Shorty Awards, accessed November 11, 2015, http://industry.shortyawards.com/nominee/7th_annual/o20/the-maze-runner-survivethenight.

[38] Huggins, "The Maze Runner."

[39] Huggins, "The Maze Runner."

Photo Sharing 7

The overwhelming acceptance and widespread use of popular photo-sharing sites have inspired all types of brands to explore this new platform as a way to further connect with customers. Visual content is allowing companies to show, not tell, about their brands, businesses, and stories.

Before Instagram and Flickr

The use of images on Instagram, Flickr, and other mainstream social networking sites, including Facebook, Pinterest, Tumblr, and Twitter, is on the rise. It is quite common for public relations professionals to use images in promoting campaigns. Brochures, newsletters, annual reports, websites, and press kits include a bevy of images that complete a story, show off products, or highlight specific services. The evolution and mass acceptance of the digital camera has played an important role in how we share images online. The advent of the point, shoot, and upload philosophy allows anyone to take high-quality images with ease, upload them to a computer, and then use them for professional or personal use.[1] Prior to the age of digital photos, the process of incorporating photos within collateral material or on a website was tedious and time consuming. As digital photos started becoming more mainstream, but before the advent of social networks like Instagram, Flickr, Pic Stitch, and Tumblr, consumers flocked to photo-sharing websites such as KodakGallery.com and Snapfish.com. These types of web-based photo-sharing and photo-printing services allowed users to create private accounts, upload images from their digital cameras, buy prints, and share their albums with others. Essentially, these websites paved the way for what we now use today.

Show, Not Tell

At any given moment there are thousands of people on the web searching for photos. The vast majority of these photos are more than likely located on photo-sharing websites that are associated with a specific company, brand, celebrity, hot-spot destination, must-attend event, or anything else that a person can imagine. Think about the numbers: Flickr alone has 17.49 million monthly visitors, while Instagram boasts a whopping 300 million users who have shared more than 20 billion photos since the platform launched in 2010.[2] Companies utilize channels like Flickr and Instagram to successfully connect with online influencers, investors, stakeholders, consumers, and prospects. Mirroring other forms of social media, photo-sharing sites allow users to share their love and affinity for a company's brand with others inside their sphere of influence. Photo-sharing websites are another example of a powerful tool that allows direct interaction with your consumer base.

The more a company shares with its consumers, the more likely those consumers are to share with others. Two-way communication is at the epicenter of social media. Sharing photos with those on the social web, while also encouraging them to share, comment, and interact with a company, supports the very spirit of social

5 REASONS TO USE PHOTOS IN SOCIAL MEDIA CAMPAIGNS

People Are Visual Beings
Photos allow a company to tell a story that they otherwise could not have accomplished through other, more traditional mediums. Integrating photos as a means to inform your audience can create engagement and interaction.

Share Photo Streams
Since it is so easy to share photos across multiple social media platforms, encourage the company's online community to distribute photos across multiple sites.

Tag It
Tags assigned to photos are used in SEO. Tags allow users to more easily find your brand, products, and services. This not only supports growth of your base audience but also affords a more genuine level of interaction with them.

Creative Commons
Employ a Creative Commons (CC) License on the photos that a company uploads. The social web is about sharing, being both transparent and authentic. CC License gives individual creators, large companies, and institutions a simple, standardized way to grant copyright permissions to their creative work.

Chat, Chat, Chat
Image platforms, such as Instagram, allow for users to post comments on photos that are uploaded. Take the time to interact with your consumers by replying to their comments and also share what they have to say.

media. Instagram and Flickr allow companies to create communities, share images, build trust, and develop genuineness with consumers—just like every other social media platform that has been discussed.

Instagram

The allure of Instagram is the ability to create, manipulate, and share photos with family, friends, coworkers, and anyone else interested in taking a peek at those sepia-tinted, vintage-style, toaster-hued digital images. With Instagram's mass appeal, unprecedented usage, and popularity, the company has positioned itself as a social network in its own right and not merely a photo-sharing app. The success and mass appeal of Instagram has not escaped the attention of many popular brands that have incorporated the platform into their social strategies. MTV, Nike, Starbucks, Forever 21, Burberry, and Victoria's Secret are among the most popular

Theory into Practice

Ford Fiesta

Challenge

The Ford Fiesta is known for its award-winning sleek, sexy design and sophisticated exterior. However, the Fiesta is not as well known for its intuitive tech-savvy features, which include keyless entry, MyKey technology, EcoBoost, and auto start-up features, to name a few. Ford set out to change all of that. Nicholas Oliver and Tom Gibby of Blue Hive, a London-based marketing firm that worked with Ford to execute the campaign, were charged with creating the captivating campaign.

Strategy

In October 2012, Ford leveraged the power of Instagram and launched "Fiestagram," a six-week contest in which users throughout Europe could submit photos for an opportunity to win prizes. The best photos were selected to be featured in actual photo galleries and digital billboards all across Europe. Weekly innovative hashtags associated with one of the Fiesta's high-tech features, such as #entry, #music, and #hidden, were revealed. Fans could then submit photos on Instagram, tagged

(continued)

with "#Fiestagram" and that week's particular hashtag. Photos needed to hold true to four criteria: (1) relevance to the theme, (2) artistic interpretation of the theme, (3) relevance to the Ford Fiesta technology, and (4) originality of the photos. Judged by Scott Monty, Ford's head of social media, James Day, an internationally renowned photographer, and Philippe Gonzalez, the founder of the Instagramers fan network, winners of the contest were selected and awarded prizes, including iPads and digital cameras. The grand prize was a Ford Fiesta.

Instagram: The Right Social Tool

For this campaign, the key demographic identified as participants on Instagram and within the campaign tended to represent a specific demographic—trend-setting fashion, style, and tech mavens, all of whom are committed, high-volume users of Instagram. The campaign focused on showing the story through images rather than telling it. Images, via Instagram, became the channel to launch and execute a multinational, multilingual campaign.

Results

Considered wildly successful, more than sixteen thousand photos were submitted as a result of the Fiestagram contest, and Ford gained in excess of 120,000 new Facebook fans across Europe. More importantly, Ford successfully attracted the attention of its target demographic: fashion, style, and technology trendsetters. Daily Fiestagram updates and entries were showcased on the "popular" page of Instagram, prominently featuring Ford's name and the Fiesta's technology.

Ford saw unprecedented success using Instagram. Too often, brands stick to what is common, what they know, or what they see other brands doing. Rather than launch its campaign through more established platforms such as Facebook or Twitter, Ford developed and executed a successful social media campaign using Instagram. The overall success of Blue Hive's Ford Fiesta campaign can be attributed to a variety of elements, but five ingenuous tactics really stand out above the rest:

Ease: Users simply had to take a picture, add a preset hashtag, and upload to Instagram for their chance to win a car. Making it easy to participate and easy to share makes participating worthwhile.

Influencers: Relying on the knowledge of previous successful campaigns, Ford again called upon its community of influencers to help promote the contest. Instagram has a vibrant network of super users—called Instagramers. Recruiting Philippe Gonzalez, the Instagramers fan network founder, and tasking him with spreading the word to promote the contest to his massive audience was genius.

Community: The contest unsurprisingly nurtured a community of supportive users. Fans encouraged their friends to add the #Fiestagram hashtag to applicable photos to help spread the word. Ford realized a fairly substantial trickle-down effect from this community participation. Participants could not wait to share the fun with others.

Transparency: Ford has a policy of transparency in all modes of social media. It should come as no surprise that the company utilized its Facebook page to share relevant information with that community as well, including contest rules, processes, and weekly challenges.

Momentum: Weekly giveaways of smaller, highly desirable items like iPads kept users engaged as Ford continued to build toward awarding the Ford Fiesta grand prize. Using this tactic, Ford was able to create continued buzz around the campaign, keep fans interested, and keep them coming back and sharing more often.

Sources: D. Klamm, "How Ford Used Instagram to Promote the Fiesta's High-Tech Features," *Mashable*, February 2, 2012, http://mashable.com/2012/02/02/ford-fiesta-instagram/; S. Balwani, "Presenting: 10 of the Smartest Big Brands in Social Media," *Mashable*, February 6, 2009, http://mashable.com/2009/02/06/social-media-smartest-brands.

brands on Instagram, with followers numbering 1 million or more. Companies engage with customers by sharing snapshots of their products, cultures, and people in an intimate yet informal manner. There are three major features that draw users to Instagram: (1) personalization, (2) lifestyle, and (3) exclusivity.

What Is Instagram?

Owned by Facebook, Instagram is a free photo-sharing application that allows users to take photos, apply a filter to a photo, and also share the photo on Instagram or other social networking sites, including Facebook, Twitter, Foursquare, Tumblr, Flickr, and Posterous.

Personalization

Nike, for example, offers its Instagram followers the opportunity to become custom designers and allows them to create their own shoes using Instagram photos. The NIKEiD campaign utilizes the power of the social community by providing users with a chance to design, share, and purchase customized versions of Nike gear.

Lifestyle

Starbucks is a company that resonates well with Instagram users because followers of the company primarily control the content on this social platform. The Starbucks Instagram account predominantly features images posted by enthusiastic, imaginative fans who love and enjoy everything about Starbucks coffee. The company aims to promote the brand as part of a lifestyle choice and one that should be enjoyed with friends. It should come as no surprise that Starbucks is famous for cross-promoting its social strategies. For example, the company used Instagram to promote a Google Hangout with Maroon 5. This was a great illustration of how the mobile app can be used as part of a multichannel social media campaign.

Exclusivity

Instagram users have also become accustomed to seeing exclusive photos, including behind-the-scenes looks at their favorite companies. Burberry is a company that frequently does this. Whether it is the latest commercial, photo shoot, or iconic images from London, Burberry fans always feel connected to the brand. As a company, Burberry recognizes the impact of this premier access and often rewards followers with exclusive content. This technique builds a community of loyal brand ambassadors.

With these success stories in mind, the first question that a public relations practitioner should ask might be, How might a company best look to harness the power of Instagram? A company's Instagram account can serve multiple purposes, but, above all, it should make users feel included and part of the company culture. Some tactics to consider when planning an Instagram campaign include the following:[3]

- *New Products:* Snap a quick picture of a new product, share a screenshot, or, better yet, share an image of someone using the product on Instagram. Instagram photos should be simple and can promote the desired effect through the use of the many photo filters that are available.
- *Company Culture and Employees:* Use Instagram to humanize the company brand. Highlight the inner workings of the company culture; give followers insight into the day-to-day behind-the-scenes activity. Followers want to see who is running the company, who is tweeting them, and who is blogging—so show them. It is not necessary to post a traditional headshot. This would be too formal for Instagram. Save those for LinkedIn and the company website. Make the photo fun by using a more relaxed image. A peek behind the scenes is not a photo of someone simply sitting at his or her desk. As an example, Centresource,

an interactive agency, uses Instagram to show the details of its company culture. The "Who We Are" page is a running feed of its Instagram account.

* *Trending Topics and Events:* In addition to posting images of company events, illustrate that the company is involved in and informed about events that matter to your followers. Post Instagram photos of news, fun facts, and trending topics that followers are most likely aware of and then engage with them on that topic.

* *Photo Contests:* Instagram users love the app because they can create fun images. Use this passion to a company's advantage. Develop and launch a photo contest in which followers can submit images and earn recognition from a brand they adore. White House Black Market's Sweater Boutique Instagram Contest asked followers to incorporate their pets into photos of themselves dressed in their favorite White House Black Market (@whbm) outfits and to upload the photos to Instagram using the hashtag #feelbeautiful (while also mentioning @whbm). Upon posting the photo to Instagram, participants received one entry into the contest. Three grand-prize winners took home $100 store gift cards. This contest helped build followers, create brand loyalty, and showcase the new clothing line as modeled by real customers, and it also provided a platform for the company to engage with its community of users.

In taking its capabilities one step further, Instagram had social media strategists and public relations professionals buzzing as it extended its photo-sharing features to include video capabilities. This development is another avenue for companies to use in promoting products and services, building corporate culture, and interacting

International Relations

Instagram in Europe

Internationally speaking, over 70 percent of Instagram users are based outside the United States. In the United Kingdom alone, over 14 million Instagram account holders are accessing the social image-sharing platform on a monthly basis. The following list highlights some of the more successful European brands that are rocking the power of Instagram:

John Lewis

John Lewis, a London-based fashion brand, wanted to appeal to a younger female demographic. In partnering with influential fashion bloggers, the company launched an Instagram campaign that showcased the bloggers wearing John Lewis clothes in a series of simple fashion shoots. As a result, the brand increased its reach by a full fourteen points among the twenty-five-to-thirty-four female demographic, along with a 10 percent increase in ad recall.

Turkish Airlines

Turkish Airlines, a successful and popular global airline, recognized that it was suffering from poor brand awareness, specifically in the United Kingdom. Armed with the knowledge that food is one of the best ways to experience a variety of cultures, Turkish Airlines took to Instagram in early February 2015 with a four-week #EpicFood campaign. By subtly displaying its logo in the background and focusing the images on the food, this campaign led to a 28 percent increase in message recall and 13 percent increase in overall brand awareness.

Ben & Jerry's

When Ben & Jerry's turned to Instagram to spread awareness of its new *Anchorman*-inspired Scotchy Scotch Scotch ice-cream flavor, the company reached 9.8 million users. Of the users who saw the Instagram images, 17 percent became aware of the new flavor and associated it with Ben & Jerry's.

Source: Christopher Ratcliff, "How Brands Are Using Instagram Ads," Econsultancy, July 13, 2015, accessed November 15, 2015, https://econsultancy.com/blog/66689-how-brands-are-using-instagram-ads.

with their customer bases. The video feature in Instagram allows for fifteen seconds of video recording with a built-in editing capability, the ability to decide which image to use for the cover image, instant integration with the existing Instagram app, Facebook in-line viewing, and, of course, those filters we have all come to love.[4]

Brands are already using Instagram video in some pretty ingenious ways. Charity Water, for example, brings its mission to life by capturing the story of a woman who benefited from the nonprofit organization, using a short, impactful video of her life.[5] This example has Charity Water using the video feature, along with the introduction of captions, thereby maximizing both the technological features and the searchability of the video. Ben and Jerry's gave fans a peek into its kitchens by showing them how it makes its dangerously delicious ice cream, while famous chef Jamie Oliver whipped up a simple how-to video teaching fans how to make salad dressing in his traditional, crazy style.[6]

The power of Instagram is that it allows companies to use this video feature in countless creative ways. Shooting a product demo, answering some frequently asked questions, featuring events and special offers, creating a video portfolio of the company's products, and encouraging fan submissions are some examples of ways that a company can take advantage of video storytelling.[7] Both customers and fans want to see a humanized brand, one that captivates them and keeps them connected to the brand.

Measuring Matters

Being able to illustrate results and understand metrics properly is important in all social media platforms because the analytics can drive social media strategies. Statigram, a tool specifically developed for Instagram users, allows brands to measure their efforts through viable metrics. With Statigram a company can manage both comments and the community simultaneously and also analyze the company activity within Instagram.

Flickr

While not necessarily at the center of every social media campaign, Flickr should not be discounted as a way to connect with consumers. Flickr's subscribers are made up of amateur as well as professional photographers who want to share their photos with others, who engage Flickr's active community of users, and who are also interested in obtaining feedback from other users. The culture and draw of Flickr is much different from that of other social communities because Flickr has rules that explicitly forbid companies from uploading photos that are posted with the sole purpose of advertising or marketing products.[8] Two of the most effective ways to use Flickr include commenting on photos that are uploaded by other users and participating in Flickr groups. Each time a user leaves a comment on the site, the username (alongside the comment made) links back to his or her personal profile, which in turn contains links to that user's photo sets, videos, and additional biographical information. Flickr Groups provide an area for members to upload photos and videos and also a platform for users to engage in discussions with other members on a specific topic. Creating a group, adding photos, and participating in the discussions are great ways to gain exposure and establish a community with a company's followers.

Authorized Resources on Flickr

Brands that use Flickr tend to implement strategies that help build a community base and act as a resource center for their consumers. Graco and Nikon are two companies that have successfully utilized Flickr to connect with their consumers. Nikon provides a "Digital Learning Center," allowing fans access to step-by-step tutorials, photography tips, discussion forums, and advice from Nikon photo experts.[9] With more than seventy-two thousand registered members, Nikon gives its Flickr users access to a variety of hardware-related experts, as well as exposure to authentic Nikon supplies. Nikon's use of Flickr illustrates the concept that there is now an opportunity for companies to act as branded resources and to provide an additional outlet for consumers who want to hear from qualified experts.

Graco is another company that has built a community around its products using Flickr reviews. By posting photographs from members using Graco products and photos that provide behind-the-scenes access to the people behind the brand, Graco is humanizing the brand.[10] The company has even combined offline tactics in its strategy by hosting a number of community gatherings. The images from these events are also posted to the company Flickr page and contribute to bringing a more intimate and personalized feel to the brand.

Photos, and the resulting discussions they stimulate, can be an incredible way to share ideas and stories, give advice, and receive feedback from your customer base. Brands that have successfully incorporated photo-sharing platforms into their social strategies have yet to blatantly sell their products using these services. These companies have effectively found a following using various strategies, including posts of photos of recent events, employees, and customers using their products and even introducing creative and innovative ways to do something using their brands, products, or services.

The Upsurge in Visual Social Media

The trend toward incorporating visual has also been influenced by the uptick in mobile use. More and more people engage with one another using social media on their smartphones, tablets, and other portable devices. Research indicates that when people interact with brands on social networking sites, they are more likely to engage with those brands that post images over other forms of media.[11] The need for and rise in the incorporation of images will undoubtedly increase in the coming years. Consumers have emphatically shown that they would like to see what a company is made of. Whether it is a fashion house giving fans a peek behind the label or a chef welcoming you to his or her kitchen, photos are becoming a staple in social media campaigns.

#LRNSMPR

Learn More: Photo Sharing on the Social Web

- "5 Brands That Are Doing Great Things on Instagram": http://bit.ly/1eiU7GP
- "@Statigram and What It Can Do for Your Brand and @Instagram Account": http://bit.ly/18jwCXY
- "Here's How You Should Be Using Flickr to Boost Business": http://read.bi/19ucyBe

Notes

[1] L. Safko, *The Social Media Bible: Tactics, Tools and Strategies for Business Success* (New York: Wiley, 2010), chap. 9.

[2] C. Smith, "How Many People Use the Top Social Media, Apps and Services," *DMR Digital Marketing Ramblings*, September 15, 2013; C. Smith, "By the Numbers: 12 Interesting Instagram Stats," *DMR Digital Marketing Ramblings*, September 8, 2013.

[3] B. DiFeo, "Some Tactics to Consider When Planning an Instagram Campaign," SocialFresh, June 7, 2012, http://socialfresh.com/instagram-followers.

[4] M. Gingerich, "How to Use Instagram Video for Marketing," Social Media Examiner, July 8, 2013.

[5] G. Soskey, "10 Brands That Jumped on Instagram Video (and Rocked It)," HubSpot, July 12, 2013, http://blog.hubspot.com/brands-jumped-instagram-video-li.

[6] Gingerich, "How to Use Instagram Video for Marketing."

[7] DiFeo, "Some Tactics to Consider When Planning an Instagram Campaign."

[8] C. Parker, "How to Use Flickr to Grow Your Brand," Memeburn, August 4, 2010, http://memeburn.com/2010/08/how-to-use-flickr-to-grow-your-brand-%E2%80%93-part-1.

[9] "Brands on Flickr," *Supercollider*, July 12, 2008, http://geoffnorthcott.com/blog/2008/07/brands-on-flickr.

[10] Samir Balwani, "Presenting: 10 of the Smartest Big Brands in Social Media," *Mashable*, February 6, 2009, http://mashable.com/2009/02/06/social-media-smartest-brands.

[11] ROI Research Inc., "Performics," SlideShare, last modified July 25, 2012, accessed September 22, 2013, http://www.slideshare.net/performics_us/performics-life-on-demand-2012-summary-deck.

Video $\Large 8$

The introduction of video on the social web in 2003 created an area of substantial growth for public relations practitioners and social strategists alike. Approximately 200 million people, or roughly 76 percent of the online population, will be consistently viewing video using online platforms in just a few short years.[1] Companies can step into the spotlight and generate user-specific content that resonates with their customers through creative, high-impact, well-thought-out videos.

1.8 Million Words

According to Dr. James McQuivey of Forrester Research, video is worth 1.8 million words.[2] Imagine this: in a single frame, a video can deliver the same amount of information as three pages of text or an astonishing thirty-six hundred average webpages. In all, it would take a person 150 days of writing to achieve relatively the same impact that a single one-minute video has.[3]

Scientifically speaking, it is well understood that when people read, they convert text into images and emotions.[4] So it should not come as a surprise that when people receive information directly from images as opposed to text, the mind creates more connections intellectually and emotionally because the translation from word to image is not necessary. People are drawn to video for four simple reasons: we see the face as a point for gathering information and believability; the voice allows us to convert information into meaningful content; body language resonates; and movement grabs and holds our attention.[5] For public relations professionals and social strategists, this is great news.

Video is most effective when implemented with the total communications strategy in mind. Companies can increase outreach to influencers, build credibility, promote brand awareness, enhance SEO, and, more importantly, create a loyal following of brand ambassadors.

Idea to Implementation

Create content that is relevant. Keeping your audience in mind is essential to the success or failure of a video strategy. Videos can be shot in a variety of styles and formats. The first step for a public relations practitioner is to decide which format is right for the organization. Generally there are three overarching varieties of videos found on the web:

- *Product Demonstrations:* This type of video captures a product's best features and uniqueness while entertaining and engaging your audience. One of the most famous examples is the Blendtec blender.[6] To illustrate the amazing capabilities of the product, CEO Tom Dickson blends items like iPads, iPhones, golf balls, Justin Bieber CDs, and even his mother's dentures. The company posted these videos on its YouTube channel, and the "Will It Blend?" series exploded. The videos not only increased brand awareness but also made the Blendtec product a household name. In fact, shortly after the video series launched in 2006, sales increased over 1,000 percent. Today, the Blendtec videos receive hits, likes, and shares in the millions (http://www.youtube.com/user/Blendtec).

- *How-To/Educational Videos:* This video format shares best practices and builds trust with consumers. Ranking the highest among brands, Home Depot stands out because it publishes content about topics that are relevant to its brand without blatantly promoting or advertising the specific products it sells.[7] Home Depot strategists have established their brand as a trusted expert and resource for home renovation and repair projects while at the same time humanizing the company. Videos are hosted by and feature employees sharing a wealth of home-improvement information (http://www.youtube.com/user/homedepot).

- *Viral Videos:* Every brand wishes that its videos would go viral, but none can guarantee that particular outcome. Viral videos typically share two things in common: relatability and discussability.[8] People are drawn to content that affects them deeply. The videos can be serious in nature or comical. Either way, the content is emotionally stimulating and creates a connection with the viewer, so much so that the viewer wants to discuss it and share the video with others. In essence, it is the viewers who make videos "go viral," not the actual videos. Dove's Real Beauty Sketches (http://bit.ly/1hpZuRD), the Harlem Shake (http://bit.ly/1ccJNPU), and Pepsi's Test Drive prank with Jeff Gordon (http://bit.ly/22TyAJU) rank among the top viral videos—each garnering millions of views, likes, and shares.

Videos, like most forms of social media, should not "sell" anything. The most successful videos are the ones that resonate. Useful, smart, interesting, captivating, and entertaining videos tend to be the most popular. Social media strategists and public relations professionals need to decide why a video should be part of an overarching strategy and then ultimately what content should go into the video. Does the company want to drive traffic to a website or landing page? Perhaps growing the number of company YouTube subscribers is the ultimate goal. Increasing blog followers, heightening brand awareness, and setting up an RSS feed (which would allow users to subscribe to your channel) are all plausible objectives. These milestones will become important in measuring the video's overall level of success. Content within the videos can range from a simple interview to a complex story line, like Pepsi's Test Drive prank or Chipotle's mini animated movie about a lone scarecrow looking for ways to provide alternatives to the unsustainable processed-food world we live in.

Producing Quality Videos

Video has the potential to spread copious amounts of information to a broad audience. Every detail is critical, whether you are shooting a thirty-minute video or a six-second video. When a social strategist or public relations professional steps behind the camera, he or she becomes a video maker and thus is responsible for every image and message conveyed in each frame of the finalized product.

YouTube, Vine, and Instagram, all video-sharing social media sites, have their own sets of rules, time constraints, and uses. When using these platforms for filming videos, the following guidelines can be used:

1. *Audience and Platform:* This may seem obvious, but believe it or not, it often isn't. Knowing whether the video should be six seconds or sixty minutes means that you need to know your audience, which platform will work best for the content you plan to promote, and on which social media platform the video will make the most impact.

International Relations

Using Video in Europe and Succeeding

Walkers, a UK–based company best known for making "crisps," recently completed a successful campaign aimed at deciphering which retro flavor consumers wanted to bring back.[1] Walkers created an interactive campaign using a series of topical Vines, recording all customer votes in order to determine the most popular flavor.

Vloggers, also known as video bloggers, have become reality stars in Europe.[2] Felix Kjellberg, aka PewDiePie, a twenty-five-year-old Swedish comedian and the world's most popular YouTube star, is reported to have earned $8.5 million in 2014. UK superstar vloggers Zoella and Alfie Deyes have amassed 12 million YouTube subscribers, 6.8 million Instagram followers, and almost 6 million Twitter followers.

Marmite, a brand of spread that consumers around the world either love or hate, launched a worldwide social media campaign designed to engage passionate Marmite fans with the potential to win a free flight home.[3] The competition, developed by Ogilvy New Zealand, targeted expats throughout the world to share their love of this delicious spread. Nearly five thousand people took part in the competition, with many developing songs and videos as part of their entries. The campaign generated over $650,000 in free advertising and media and got the entire country and Kiwis all around the world excited about the brand again. Here is one of the most popular video entries: https://www.youtube.com/watch?v=Kxx7S5NKGls.

1 "Best Branded Videos on Vines and Instagram," *Reelseo*, http://www.reelseo.com/best-branded-vines-instagram-videos/#ixzz3rb1p0i6D.
2 Susan McLean and Dom Rothbarth, "How UK Brands That Use Vlogger Endorsements and Social Media for Marketing Can Stay on the Right Side of the Law," *Socially Aware Blog*, October 15, 2015, accessed November 15, 2015, http://www.sociallyawareblog.com/2015/10/05/how-uk-brands-that-use-vlogger-endorsements-social-media-for-marketing-can-stay-on-the-right-side-of-the-law.
3 Niall Harbison, "Brilliant Social Media Campaign for Marmite in New Zealand," Digital Marketing Institute, August 3, 2011, accessed November 15, 2015, http://digitalmarketinginstitute.com/blog/brilliant-social-media-campaign-for-marmite-in-new-zealand-video-case-study.

2. *Purpose and Storyboard:* Understanding the purpose and then taking the time to storyboard the idea are the first steps toward creating the framework for a company video. Even short videos, including those being considered for Vine and Instagram, need a purpose and a storyboard. Defining the purpose helps to deliver the core message. Creating a storyboard is a technique that maps out a video sequence prior to filming. Essentially it is a written plan for the content going into the video.

3. *Style and Tone:* The style of the video sets the stage. Videos can be serious, funny, cheerful, professional, or even whimsical. Regardless of the style, the message needs to fit the overall tone. Some professionals have created videos many times over. To these individuals, conveying a style and setting the tone may be simple. However, not all social strategists or public relations professionals are trained videographers. By taking a look at videos with similar messaging or formats on YouTube, Vine, and Instagram, professionals can catch a glimpse of how certain tones and feelings have previously been conveyed. Seeing the work of others may inspire you or give you an idea. Consider these tips:

   - *Tone:* Upbeat, carefree, serious minded, or staid
   - *Dialogue:* "Talking head" interview style or free-flowing conversation
   - *Production Quality:* In-house studio or on location
   - *Video Quality:* Simple, online, made-it-myself video or big-budget professional production

4. *Script Writing:* Once the purpose and tone have been decided, it is time to write the script. For longer YouTube interview-style videos, write out the list of questions so that you are prepared. For more conversational videos, use bulleted notes. Is it possible to pack a story into a six-second or a fifteen-second video? The answer is yes! The key here will be to weave in quick edits and multiple shot angles throughout.

5. *Angles and Shots:* How the video is made has a direct effect on whether the content will resonate. Remember that all videos need to be relatable, discussable, and shareable. When filming a video, you need to take into consideration the best angle and perspective for each sequence. For videos that require multiple frames, characters, or scenes, it is best to script out your video in detail. This includes notes related to the sets, stage actions, props, and dialogue.

6. *Images, Sound, and Lighting:* Graphics, music, and imagery also play a critical role in video. These elements support the tone, dialogue, and effectiveness of the messaging. When storyboarding the video, think about the types of still shots, b-roll footage, music, and background sounds that can be used. Lighting can make or break the quality of a video. Poor lighting creates dark, shadowy, discolored, or even gritty images. Never record a scene with a window in the background. The subjects will appear dark, and although some editing can happen, the quality of the shot is diminished. Viewers tend to accept ordinary, uninspiring graphics but have very little tolerance for poor sound. Invest in external microphones to ensure good sound quality.

7. *Editing to Final Product:* The three most commonly used desktop editing tools for YouTube videos are iMovie, Camtasia, and Windows Movie Maker. The websites associated with each of these tools provide in-depth instructions for how to use each editing product. Both iMovie and Windows Movie Maker are easy to use and have drag-and-drop tools, while Camtasia is an excellent tool for simple videos and screencasts.

8. *Sharing:* Once the video has achieved production-ready status, it is now time to publish the video for the world to see. Be sure that the original goals of the video are in line with the company's overarching social media goals. This can include calls to action, hashtags, clever captions, and tags. Since YouTube, Vine, and Instagram are embeddable, the potential for innovative storytelling is limitless.

Regardless of the route, there are many options supporting inclusion of a video into a social strategy. It was not that long ago that YouTube was the only outlet for video. Not anymore. Today videos also appear on Vine and Instagram, both of which facilitate easy video capabilities and are generating quite the stir in the video-creation sphere.

YouTube

The practicality of YouTube, for end users, is quite simple: it allows them to locate and watch videos. However, for social strategists and public relations practitioners, this platform is much more. Owned by Google, YouTube is a search engine, promotional platform, social network, and community site with a loyal viewership. One unique feature that YouTube boasts is the ability to create branded channels.

The YouTube branded channels allow for the creation of a specific space for all of the videos that pertain to that company. Users do not have to search to find the content they desire because these branded channels ultimately create a set destination for customers to locate the content they seek. YouTube channels afford the opportunity for companies to engage and further shape formidable relationships with their audiences using an environment that consumers know and trust.

Mind-Numbing YouTube Stats and Figures

YouTube has over a billion users—almost a third of all people on the Internet.

80 percent of YouTube's views are from outside the United States.

YouTube has launched local versions in more than 70 countries.

You can navigate YouTube in a total of seventy-six different languages, covering 95 percent of the Internet population.

The number of people watching YouTube each day has increased by 40 percent year over year since 2014.

Once users are on YouTube, they spend more time per session watching videos. On mobile, the average viewing session is now more than forty minutes. That's an increase of more than 50 percent year over year.

The number of hours people spend watching videos on mobile has increased by 100 percent.

More than half of YouTube views come from mobile devices.

The YouTube Spaces team is focused on helping creators make great content through strategic programs and workshops that are mostly administered at the YouTube Space production facilities in Los Angeles, New York, London, Tokyo, Sao Paulo, and Berlin.

As of March 2015, creators filming in YouTube Spaces have produced over ten thousand videos, which have generated over 1 billion views and 70+ million hours of watch time.

Source: "Statistics," YouTube, March 1, 2015, accessed November 15, 2015, https://www.youtube.com/yt/press/en-GB/statistics.html.

Channels should reflect the brand itself through the use of company images, graphics, and colors. YouTube does offer an upgrade to its channel services that help public relations and social strategists further maintain company branding. Users can benefit from this by accessing templates that can be customized and personalized to complement other social sites, the company website, and even printed collateral material. Using this functionality helps create and align content with key demographics and the company's goals, products, and mission.

It may not come as a surprise that Red Bull is one company that understands how to maximize YouTube's potential. Red Bull's overarching theme embedded throughout all of its communication strategies focuses on extreme sports and extreme athletes. Its Facebook page and twenty Pinterest boards feature spectacular images and videos of Red Bull–sponsored extreme sports and extreme sport athletes, while its Twitter feed is dedicated to various events and current projects. To keep its content fresh and new, Red Bull posts between one and three new videos per day—all of which are directed toward its key niche audience.

When Felix Baumgartner took his leap from the edge of space, Red Bull's live broadcast of the remarkable video pulled in more than 9 million streams of the actual dive. Aside from the historic feat, what made this video so successful was that Red Bull documented the days leading up to the jump by producing and posting more than fifteen videos that chronicled the journey. The project, Red Bull Stratos, drew millions of viewers to Red Bull's site. In all, Red Bull Stratos garnered over 366 million content views on YouTube alone.[9]

Vine

If a midge (a type of gnat) can beat its wings one thousand times in one second, a rattlesnake can shake its tail in warning sixty times in a mere second, and a fast human can spring thirty-nine feet in just one second,[10] imagine what social media strategists and public relations practitioners can do with six seconds! Creating lasting impressions on Vine, Twitter's mobile video app, is fast becoming prominent in the social sphere.

By fusing video content and static imagery and incorporating audio, Vine enables mobile users to capture and share miniature moments. The videos play on a loop, much like animated GIFs. "Posts on Vine are about abbreviation—the shortened

Theory into Practice

Skittles: "Smash the Rainbow. Taste the Rainbow."[1]

Skittles brand enlisted DDB Chicago, a public relations agency, to help create a promotional spot that might be considered quite different from your ordinary candy commercial. The completed commercial was released on YouTube as an interactive commercial that allowed viewers to "pick up" virtual figurines and smash them onto the ground, resulting in the figurine turning into a pile of rainbow-colored Skittles.[2] The Skittles brand tried to take a different approach in this advertisement in an effort to make its brand stand out and be more memorable. See the video at http://www.youtube.com/watch?v=ywTgLeb4458.

Target Audience

For this campaign, the Skittles brand target audience included teens and young adults. By incorporating an interactive element within the commercial, the Skittles brand was banking on the fact that teens and young adults are much more likely to search videos on YouTube and, thus, would also be much more likely to share and interact with a video commercial like this.[3]

Objectives/Goals

The overarching goal of this campaign was to make the Skittles advertisement stand out over those promotions from competing brands. The idea of airing a YouTube video that lets the viewer choose which figurines he or she wants to "smash" in order to get Skittles is very innovative. This promotion is very unique and unlike any other candy commercial in the market. By creating a much more personalized commercial and experience, Skittles is establishing a stronger connection between its consumers and the brand and also allowing consumers to feel as if they have become a part of the brand.

Strategies

By using such an unorthodox interactive advertisement, the Skittles brand drew a lot more attention than just an ordinary commercial traditionally might. Since many teens and young adults spend a lot of time on YouTube, they tend to share videos with their friends and family more often than adults do. The Skittles brand took advantage of this tendency and, by posting this commercial on YouTube, made it easier for people to share and interact, which makes people feel a closer connection to the brand.

Tactics

Using interactive advertising, Skittles can promote an interest in watching the commercial. Although figurines cannot actually be smashed and magically turned into Skittles, it makes the advertisement more personalized and builds a connection between the user and Skittles brand as a whole.

Evaluation

This commercial received two hundred thousand views on YouTube, and the Skittles Facebook page now has over 25 million "likes"; the brand has over 116,000 followers on Twitter.[4]

---

1 Rosemary Sheridan, Regina Luttrell, and Melissa Meyer, "Smash the Rainbow: Taste the Rainbow" (working paper, College of Saint Rose, 2013).

2 "Video Viral of the Week: Skittles Lets Viewers 'Smash the Rainbow' with Interactive YouTube Ad," Digital Strategy Consulting, accessed October 3, 2013, http://www.digitalstrategyconsulting.com/intelligence/2013/06/video_viral_of_the_week_skittles_lets_viewers_smash_the_rainbow_with_interactive_youtube_ad.php.

3 "Skittles' New Digital Marketing Campaign Showcases the Trend towards Interactive Videos," *Marketing Easy*, accessed October 3, 2013, http://marketingeasy.net/skittles-smash-the-rainbow-digital-marketing-campaign/2013-08-07.

4 "Help Tommy Smash Porcelain Figurines as He Hunts for Skittles," TrendHunter Marketing, July 1, 2013, accessed October 3, 2013, http://www.trendhunter.com/trends/porcelain-figurines.

form of something larger. They're little windows into the people, settings, ideas and objects that make up your life."[11]

The Vine app is an easy-to-use, easy-to-understand tool that can support the need for video within a company's overall social media strategy. Since the videos are only six seconds in length, companies can get creative and show off some of their personality. General Electric was one of the first brands to embrace Vine. With its #6SecondScience campaign, the company effectively created the world's first Internet science fair. The campaign challenged its audience by asking one question: "How much science can you fit into six seconds?" During the weeklong campaign, more than four hundred videos were submitted, covering a wide range of topics showcasing much of the magic behind science. Some Twitter followers received a special science kit that included a thank-you card, a bumper sticker, and a 4M Kitchen Science Kit to help in the creation of the videos. Each kit included experiments on how to power a clock using lemons or take fingerprints with flour. Within the first twenty-four hours of the campaign, more than one hundred Vine videos were created.[12] As the videos continued to roll in, GE shared them with its audience using its Facebook, Twitter, and #6SecondScience Tumblr pages, which acted as the center of the campaign. Those individuals seeking inspiration need only look to GE's Pinterest page for ideas. The company highlighted numerous Vines by retweeting, revining, and reblogging. The underlying idea of this campaign was to create a community for sharing ideas and participating in a fun, creative way.

Not every company is a science powerhouse like GE, but that doesn't mean creative campaigns are not possible to realize. The following three brands have also found success in generating creative Vine campaigns:

Oreo: Like fresh ground cookie on your ice cream? Then check out our latest Vine, #OreoSnackHacks (http://bit.ly/1e4k6iL).

Lowe's: Keep squirrels away from your plants with a dash of cayenne pepper, #LowesFixInSix #howto (https://vine.co/Lowes).

Ford: With *Back to the Future*–related content spreading throughout the social sphere on October 21, 2015, Ford was sure to refer back to a picture of a futuristic Ford car from *Back to the Future II* (http://bit.ly/1NyhhGg).

Instagram Video

Instagram video, part of the Instagram photo site, is an online video-sharing and social networking service that enables users to take videos, apply those crafty digital filters (fifteen in all), and share them on a variety of social networking sites. In contrast to Vine's six seconds, users can shoot a slightly longer video, fifteen seconds, using this service. That's a whopping nine extra seconds to capture a customer's attention and tell your story. Another great feature of this video service is the ability to go back and add or delete scenes after you have shot some additional video. Vine does not allow for this feature. The videos on Instagram generally have a defined beginning and end, which may also be preferable over the continual loop offered on Vine. This feature allows content creators to capture a story more completely. Burberry has successfully used Instagram video to build interest surrounding its upcoming 2014 men's clothing line, while Michael Kors has launched #instakors, which showcases the life of designer Michael Kors.

Video Apps Taking Center Stage

As companies continue to move toward proactive social media encounters with users, apps like Meerkat (http://meerkatapp.co), Periscope (http://www.periscope.tv),

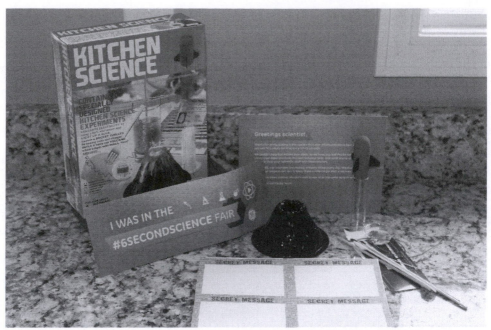

The Science Kit from GE that was sent to fans, encouraging participation in the world's first Internet science fair. *Source*: Regina Luttrell.

and Live from Facebook are not just cool new tools of the trade but rather platforms for rapid response and engagement around key issues.[13] Meerkat and Periscope are both live-streaming apps and platforms, having many similarities and differences at the same time. According to Michael Hay, head of creative services at LEWIS Pulse, "In 2015, livestreaming came to the fore, with mobile apps making it more accessible than ever. As livestreaming platforms are becoming increasingly popular, with brands using them for events and launches, in the future this technology will have to be more creative in its approach. Visual and unique creative solutions will be increasingly influential to generate engagement with key audiences and keep them entertained."

As previously mentioned, social media sites like Instagram and Vine allow users to record short video clips and then post them online. In contrast, Meerkat, Periscope, and Live take a much different approach. Users can record live video streams and share them with their networks. Periscope's founders said, "It may sound crazy, but we wanted to build the closest thing to teleportation. While there are many ways to discover events and places, we realized there is no better way to experience a place right now than through live video."[14] Live-streaming apps encourage engagement through likes and comments. This provides brands new opportunities to interact with their audiences in real time.

The following are examples of how brands are incorporating live streaming into their strategies:

Sneak-Peeks into Exclusive Events: Automaker Nissan streamed the unveiling of its 2016 Maxima model at the New York auto show using Periscope, which helped the automaker build buzz and extend its reach. Similarly, Target used Periscope to draw attention to its Lilly Pulitzer line, fueling such a huge consumer demand that 90 percent of the collection sold out in a few days.[15] Using Meerkat, Red Bull offered a backstage video of a Double Pipe competition to all viewers of the stream.[16]

Mobile and Video Are Making an Impact

Video is undoubtedly effective. Consider these two facts: (1) two-thirds of the world's mobile traffic is expected to comprise solely video by 2017; and (2) mobile makes up more than 25 percent of YouTube's total global watch time. Vine and Instagram are also mastering the mobile sphere; thus, paying attention to the results that companies are seeing on these platforms will help put their effectiveness into perspective.[1]

Vine Stats

Five tweets per second contain a Vine link.

A branded Vine video is four times more likely to be seen than a regular branded video.

The first day of Honda's #WantNewCar Vine campaign brought the car brand 1,020 new followers (compared to its six-month average of 242 new followers) and 2,292 mentions.

Over a single month, Vine videos got 0.0206 percent average engagement rate and an average of twenty retweets, while Instagram videos got 0.0111 percent average engagement rate and an average of seven retweets.

Between 10 a.m. and 11 a.m. is the most popular time of day to post Vine videos.

On April 15, 2013, the day of the Boston Marathon bombing, a record 19,667 Vines were made.

Historically speaking, three of the five most retweeted Vines were created by musicians.

Instagram Stats

Instagram has roughly 300 million active users.

Two-thirds of the top one hundred world brands were already on Instagram before it introduced video.

Since the launch of Instagram video, there has been a 37 percent increase in Instagram shares on Twitter.

Instagram videos are promoting two times more engagement than Instagram photos alone.

Lululemon, one of the first brands to use Instagram video, receives approximately seven times as many comments on its Instagram videos as it does on its photos.

Of the brands on Instagram, 62 percent have shared at least one Instagram video.

---

[1] S. Weissman, "15 Stats You Need to Know about Vine and Instagram Video," Digiday, September 9, 2013, http://digiday.com/brands/15-stats-vine-and-instagram-video.

Announcements of Products and Special Offers: Taco Bell hosted a mock press conference about its new breakfast menu item and the associated Breakfast Defector Day. The brand invited fans to stop by Taco Bell on Cinco de Mayo to enjoy a free Biscuit Taco. Starbucks used Meerkat to give a special tour of its facilities for coffee lovers.[17] Sony Masterworks set up a real-time chat on Facebook to promote a new album from artist Jackie Evancho, while MTV set up a Facebook chat with *Teen Mom 2* star Kailyn Lowry to talk about her show.

Celebrity Takeovers: In its first Periscope stream, retail chain JCPenney hosted Eva Longoria, who introduced fans to her new JCPenney bedding collection and answered questions from an exclusive launch event held in Los Angeles. Live streaming allows brands to create a sense of urgency in the content they are creating. To see what is happening, viewers must tune in "live," or they will miss the stream.

Live Q&As: San Francisco–based makeup brand Benefit Cosmetics frequently engages its community by hosting both Q&As and live makeup tutorials with its own experts and influencers on Periscope. With more than two thousand live viewers, on average, tuning in to a stream, its use of live streaming has been considered quite successful. In fact, the most recent Periscope live stream received over 19,700 hearts. Mashable, a successful Meerkat adopter, hosts a Meerkat almost daily, with interviews of its CEO Pete Cashmore, exclusive footage during conferences, or talk about tech news.[18] Jimmy Fallon uses Meerkat to guide his fans through a behind-the-scenes look at what happens on his show. Viewers watched live rehearsals, scenes from his desk, and even a little hair and makeup action.[19]

Inside Looks into a Brand's Culture: DKNY uses Periscope to take fans on "inside" tours, introducing them to the faces behind the brand. GE used drones equipped with Periscope on guided tours through remote facilities as a part of its #Droneweek social event.[20]

YouTube, Vine, Instagram, Meerkat, Periscope, or Live?

Social media strategists and public relations professionals are in a great position in that they have three integrateable video platforms to choose from. Knowing when to use the right platform is critical to the ultimate success of the project. Here are some general guidelines:

YouTube: Good for practical advice, guest speakers, case studies, conference events, and longer how-to videos.

Vine: A perfect platform for invitations to events, video teasers, new products, and how-tos.[21]

Instagram Video: Nice for promotional campaigns, layered stories, video series, and commercial-style videos.[22]

Meerkat: Great to connect with your Twitter following for longer than a few seconds. This video app allows content creators to stream live video from any mobile device to followers on Twitter.[23]

Periscope: Provides users the ability to catch a live stream and encourages engagement through likes. The app provides brands with new opportunities to interact with their audiences in real time.[24]

Livestream from Facebook: An excellent way to live broadcast what's happening in the newsfeed. Users can watch comments overlaid in real time on their streams and then make the recordings permanently available for viewing.[25]

As noted previously, any of these platforms can be used to showcase sneak peeks, promote an upcoming speaker or event, highlight a quick clip to demo a new product or feature, spotlight community-service initiatives, or provide a behind-the-scenes look at the office. The key to success is that the video idea should be creative in a personal yet professional way. Relatability and discussability should be at the forefront of the campaign.

Regardless of which platform is selected to support videos, the same manner in which a company promotes its other social media strategies should be followed. This strategy typically lends itself to cross promotion over multiple social platforms for maximum exposure. Whether embedding the video in a company blog post, tweeting the link, including links to websites or microsites, sharing the video on the company Facebook or Pinterest pages, posting it straight to the company website, or sharing the video on Vine and Instagram, one can see that there are many options for sharing content. Cross promotion also lends itself to opportunities for further engaging in and encouraging conversations by listening and reacting to what is being said about

Meerkat v Periscope

Comparison of the features of these two live streaming apps

Meerkat	Periscope
Web version **available** to view streams online	Web version **available** to view streams online
Streams **can be emailed** to friends using a web link	Streams **can be emailed** to friends using a web link
Posting to Twitter is **compulsory**	Posting to Twitter is **optional**
Streams can be saved and re-shared later	Streams can be re-watched afterwards for 24h
No private streams available	Private streams **can be setup**
Host account **can interact with viewers** via comments	Host account **cannot add their own comments**
Comments **cannot be turned off**	Comments **can be turned off**
Available on iOS and Android	Available on iOS and Android
Video can be recorded in **landscape mode**	Video can be recorded in **landscape mode**
Streams can be scheduled	Scheduling streams is not an option

Ray Stone
from the top
3 now watching

@MarkJ Nice views
@HelenFS
@Alb3rt That looks amazing

Updated version. December 2015. Information correct at time of print.

lewispulse.com

Infographic made by

LEWIS PULSE

Video Newcomers

Two players newer to the video scene are Keek and Magisto. Both of these platforms possess a number of unique characteristics that differentiate them from YouTube, Vine, and Instagram. Although small in scale, the features provided by Keek and Magisto may give some of the more veteran video platforms a run for their money.

Keek: Keek, meaning a "short look," "glimpse," or "peek," is a relatively new app and budding social networking site that allows users to create and instantly watch quick, short video updates using any smartphone, tablet, or laptop—and then share these with their friends.[1] This platform has been described as a "new wave" in technology and even a "mini version" of YouTube. Functions of the app are similar to those seen in Vine and Instagram, with other elements of YouTube interspersed within as well. Users, also referred to as "Keekers," create and post short videos—up to thirty-six seconds in length—and then share with the Keek social community. As with many other social networking sites, users upload their videos from the mobile app or from the users' desktop webcam. Keekers can follow other Keekers, like their videos, share them, and, of course, comment on them. Although relatively new to the social scene, Keek has already amassed 75 million users. With 250,000 new users signing up to the site each day, Keek is already the top video app in eighteen countries around the world.[2] Available for iOS, Blackberry, and Android, Keek operates via a hashtag system where users can utilize the "#" sign to unite conversations or create campaigns. Businesses can share their Keeks on other social media platforms, allowing them to incorporate their existing campaigns and magnify the results. Uses of Keek include showcasing everything from live demonstrations to even a "Keek" behind the scenes of a company.

Magisto: Some in the social arena are calling Magisto a fresh spin on personal video that has started to set the stage for social sharing and brand curation.[3] Magisto is an automated online video editor. "Using artificial intelligence algorithms, the software takes 3 to 20 minutes of video and up to 20 photos, analyzes the content and condenses it down to a 1 to 3 minute narrative arc."[4] Using the Magisto app, users create unique and one-of-a-kind videos using photos right from a digital camera roll or computer.[5] Users choose from a variety of themes and can also incorporate music from a selection offered by Magisto or from the user's personal playlist.

Brands have already taken notice of Keek and Magisto and started using both in promoting their messages. Currently, the top users of Keek are the social media mavens Kim, Khloe, and Kourtney Kardashian and British Olympic swimmer Tom Daley. Since Keek plays on the strengths of quick interactions in real time, celebrities and brands that take chances will thrive on this social networking site.

A company quick to adopt the Magisto utility is Sierra Trading Post. This company recently ran a promotion involving Magisto, encouraging consumers to create and post a fun outdoor adventure movie. During the two-week promotion, two hundred Magisto videos were posted, generating fifty-four thousand views.[6] As a point of reference, over a four-year period, videos on Sierra's YouTube channel have garnered a total of four hundred thousand views. Sporting goods maker Rawlings has also embraced the widespread appeal of video-sharing sites and recently invited baseball fans to create movies about their love for America's favorite pastime.[7] Ten winners were selected from the fifty most liked videos in the Rawlings-branded album on Magisto.

---

1 Regina Luttrell, "Keek: What's That?," Gina Luttrell PhD (blog), August 13, 2013, http://ginaluttrellphd.com/2013/08/13/keek-whats-that.
2 Luttrell, "Keek."
3 "A Fresh Spin on Personal Video," Adweek, October 21, 2013, http://www.adweek.com/sa-article/fresh-spin-personal-video-153211.
4 "A Fresh Spin on Personal Video."
5 Regina Luttrell and Laura Jackson, "Magisto—You Heard It Here First!," Gina Luttrell PhD, October 10, 2013, http://ginaluttrellphd.com/2013/10/10/magisto-you-heard-it-here-first.
6 "A Fresh Spin on Personal Video."
7 "A Fresh Spin on Personal Video."

the videos. Finally, you cannot overlook the metrics aspect. Tracking video viewership will help a company understand its audience and how its members interact.

With the advent of multiple video-supporting platforms within the social sphere, one can see that video is growing expeditiously. Social strategists and public relations professionals can thank smartphones, tablets, and laptops for this advance in the profession. As access to these handheld devices expands, so does the opportunity to reach your intended audience.

#LRNSMPR

Learn More: Video on the Social Web

- "Why You Need a Branded YouTube Channel and How-To Tips That Attract Viewers": http://bit.ly/1fdAXCA
- "Beautiful Chipotle Promo Video Goes Viral": http://ti.me/GCPfyA
- "Five Video Projects You Can Do in 25 Minutes or Less": http://bit.ly/1dZyvg8
- "10 Editing Tips for Making Killer Instagram Videos": http://bit.ly/16OsNhN
- "5 Ways Brands Are Using Periscope": http://bit.ly/1N5pTd1
- "Periscope vs. Meerkat: Which Has the edge?": http://trib.in/1LgQmg9
- "20 Best Branded Vines from February 2015": http://bit.ly/1ML3wYr

Notes

[1] Claudio Pannunzio, "SMK: Social Media Knowledge," i-Impact Group, last modified April 18, 2012, accessed September 30, 2013, http://www.i-impactgroup.com/A Video Is Worth_041812.pdf.

[2] Pannunzio, "SMK: Social Media Knowledge."

[3] A. Follett, "18 Big Video Marketing Statistics and What They Mean for Your Business," *Video Brewery*, April 11, 2013, http://www.videobrewery.com/blog/18-video-marketing-statistics.

[4] Kobus Barnard et al., "Matching Words and Pictures," *Journal of Machine Learning Research* 3 (2003): 1107–35.

[5] S. Rosensteel, "Why Online Video Is Vital for Your 2013 Content Marketing Objectives," *Forbes*, January 28, 2013, http://www.forbes.com/sites/seanrosensteel/2013/01/28/why-online-video-is-vital-for-your-2013-content-marketing-objectives.

[6] R. Parker, "Content Marketing Shoutout: Blendtec," Resonance Content Marketing, January 8, 2013, http://www.resonancecontent.com/blog/bid/169002.

[7] G. Reinhard, "YouTube Brands: 5 Outstanding Leaders in YouTube Marketing," *Mashable*, June 1, 2009, http://mashable.com/2009/06/01/youtube-brands/.

[8] S. Fiegerman, "Here's Why These 6 Videos Went Viral," *Mashable*, May 15, 2013, http://mashable.com/2013/05/15/viral-video-factors/.

[9] G. Abramovich, "The Best YouTube Brand Channels of 2012," Digiday, December 11, 2012, http://digiday.com/brands/the-best-youtube-brand-channels-of-2012.

[10] Steve Jenkins, *Just a Second* (Boston: HMH Books for Young Readers, 2011).

[11] Dom Hoffman, "Introducing Vine," *Vine Blog*, January 24, 2013, http://blog.vine.co/post/55514427556/introducing-vine.

[12] L. Lacy, "GE Hosts World's First Science Fair on Vine," *ClickZ*, August 13, 2013, http://www.clickz.com/clickz/news/2288357/ge-hosts-worlds-first-science-fair-on-vine.

[13] Peter Rush, "Social Media Impact Study for Associations 2015," 2015, Kellen, accessed November 15, 2015, http://kellencompany.com/wp-content/uploads/Kellen-Social-Media-Impact-Report-for-Associations-2015-digital.pdf.

[14] "About Us," Periscope, accessed November 15, 2015, https://www.periscope.tv/about.

[15] Tanya Dua, "5 Ways Brands Are Using Periscope," Digiday, August 17, 2015, accessed November 15, 2015, http://digiday.com/brands/5-ways-brands-using-periscope.

[16] Audrey Liberge, "Four Ways to Use Meerkat for PR," *LEWIS Blog*, March 30, 2015, accessed November 16, 2015, http://blog.lewispr.com/2015/03/four-ways-to-use-meerkat-for-pr.html.

[17] Liberge, "Four Ways to Use Meerkat for PR."

18 Liberge, "Four Ways to Use Meerkat for PR."

19 Philip Michaels, "Meerkat FAQ: Everything You Need to Know," Tom's Guide, accessed November 15, 2015, http://www.tomsguide.com/us/meerkat-faq,news-20663.html.

20 Michaels, "Meerkat FAQ."

21 A. Patel, "When to Use Vine and When to Use Instagram," *Venture Beat*, August 12, 2013, http://venturebeat.com/2013/08/12/when-to-use-vine-and-when-to-use-instagram.

22 Patel, "When to Use Vine and When to Use Instagram."

23 Michaels, "Meerkat FAQ."

24 Dua, "5 Ways Brands Are Using Periscope."

25 Josh Constine, "Facebook Launches 'Live' Streaming Video Feature, but Only for Celebrities," *Tech-Crunch*, August 5, 2015, accessed December 7, 2015, http://techcrunch.com/2015/08/05/face-scope/#.h7mcbdc:88lu.

"Sticky" Social Media 9

Thus far, we have discussed how to create and publish interesting content to social media channels as a way to engage with fans and followers. However, the idea of developing highly targeted social content to drive unique online experiences is becoming a larger part of today's public relations practitioner's job. This chapter focuses on specific elements needed to create content that is shareable.

Creating Shareable Social Content

For some practitioners, the holy grail and ultimate goal of a good social media campaign is to achieve "viral" status. The challenge here is that increased brand awareness using social media channels grows progressively more difficult every day. When users are uploading one hundred hours of video to YouTube every sixty seconds, sharing more than 4.75 billion pieces of content on Facebook every twenty-four hours, and sending 500 million new tweets daily, the chances of breaking through the noise can seem practically nonexistent.[1]

Luckily, there are numerous savvy companies that are utilizing creative tactics to explode into the mainstream by executing fresh, catchy campaigns that encourage consumers to share content within their social spheres. We know this type of content as either "viral," "contagious," or "sticky." What's the difference?

Viral: This includes any public relations, marketing, or social media technique that induces users to pass messages on to other users, potentially creating exponential growth in the messages' visibility and effect.[2]

Contagious: This involves users' spreading or tending to spread messages from one to another through social media, public relations, and marketing mechanisms. The idea is to get people talking, sharing, and telling others using word of mouth.[3]

Sticky: This is content that is developed in order to gain the user's attention and increase the possibility that he or she will share the content with others.[4]

Regardless of the definition, the end result is the same—professionals need to create content that is shareable. This raises the question, Are there existing steps that companies can take to ensure that their brands, images, and content will grab the attention of the intended audience? Most people identify viral content as something that just "happens." Viral videos are often considered flukes that only happen once; however, that's not necessarily the case.

Jonah Berger and Malcolm Gladwell are two influential thought leaders who are researching this exact topic. Berger believes that all successful viral campaigns contain triggers that get people talking.[5] Similarly, Gladwell believes that there are forces that cause social phenomena to "tip," or make the leap from small groups to big groups.[6] Gladwell calls one of those factors "stickiness." An idea, concept, or product is considered sticky when it is remembered, repeated, and acted upon by many people.

In essence, Berger's research reveals six main factors that help explain social pandemics, while Gladwell identifies three. There is overlap in the findings of both researchers. So who is right? Is content contagious or sticky? Can it be both? Logic would tell us that both researchers are right, and, yes, there are steps that companies can take to create shareable, sticky, contagious content. Between Berger's six factors on social pandemics and Gladwell's three, we can identify four overarching areas of importance when developing shareable content:

1. Storytelling
2. Social Currency
3. Influencers
4. Sharability

Storytelling

Stories have been and continue to be the most useful and persuasive tools when communicating with others. A successful public relations professional must be able to describe something in a compelling way. Great storytellers can find unique, emotion-filled angles to capture the interests of their intended audiences. Savvy public relations integrates language and visual cues to engage targeted publics, leading them to discover something new about a brand, product, or service. With the onset and universal adoption of the digital age, PR professionals have new tools and opportunities to express their brands. Today, an organization can share its brand's story using a variety of social media platforms, including Facebook, Twitter, Instagram, YouTube, Snapchat, and many others.

Although pulling together coherent narratives may seem challenging, it is certainly not impossible. A practitioner is responsible for developing custom content that communicates a particular angle or story, provides some level of engagement and value, and identifies the company as a brand that can be considered the go-to source for related information in the future.[7] Stories must be told in a way that consumers deem relatable and trigger an emotion that resonates with them. What experience do you desire for your customers to share within their social spheres? The information that you are trying to convey about your organization or brand should be included in this story. Remember, stories are a quick and easy way for audiences to consume information in a meaningful way. Many of the most effective stories often originate from sound research and have a particular audience or perspective in mind. Prior to launching any campaign, practitioners should devote considerable time to planning its execution and associated content.

ESSENTIAL ELEMENTS OF STICKY SOCIAL MEDIA

SOCIAL MEDIA

STORYTELLING
Tap into emotions. Tell a story that helps consumers understand & care about the idea behind it.

Idea!

01

SOCIAL CURRENCY
How we look to others matters. Create stories that are remarkable & unusual.

02

03

INFLUENCERS
Maximize people "in-the-know" who have impact over others.

SHARABLE
Produce content that is so extraordinary people willingly share it with others. Make it easy to share by including sharing buttons.

Share

04

Twitter @genelailhall
Follow the conversation #UPSSMPR
Connect - www.genelailhallphd.com

The #LikeAGirl Rocks campaign created and executed by the Always brand of Procter & Gamble is an exceptional example of storytelling. This campaign examined the emotional side of what it means to do something "like a girl." According to A&AD, the creative agency tasked with developing the campaign, the Always brand has been committed to empowering girls and educating them about puberty-related topics for decades. However, the brand's purpose was not immediately apparent to the newest generation of consumers: Millennials. The challenge that Always faced was to develop a new, fresh, and meaningful message about "confidence" that would resonate with the next generation of consumers. Always was interested in creating a campaign that not only leveraged the brand's legacy but also reinforced why the brand was "relevant to me" today.[8] Research revealed that more than half of women claimed that they experienced a decline in confidence at puberty. The opportunity was clear—empowering girls during this time of their lives, when confidence is most susceptible to influence, would provide a powerful, relevant, and purposeful role.

The campaign's "story" was to turn a phrase widely accepted as an insult into an empowering message—#LikeAGirl. The idea quickly snowballed into a global initiative. The creative team set out to redefine confidence in a way that was much more relevant, yet remain true to the brand and turn the phrase "like a girl" from insult into empowerment.[9] The campaign was built around a social experiment to show the impact that the phrase "like a girl" had on society—especially on pre- and postpubescent girls. The centerpiece of the campaign was a video (http://bit.ly/1PKkvfW) that recorded the interpretation of the phrase "like a girl" from people of all ages.

As a secondary strategy supporting the video element of the campaign, the hashtag #LikeAGirl was introduced as a rallying cry.

The #LikeAGirl video was launched simultaneously at a PR event on June 26, 2014, and on YouTube. The public relations practitioner played a huge part in amplifying the impact and reaching the appropriate media outlets and influencers.[10] Ultimately, the Always #LikeAGirl initiative generated considerable global awareness and influenced the way that people interpreted the phrase "like a girl"—achieving more than 85 million global views on YouTube from more than 150 countries. Prior to the video, only 19 percent of women between the ages of sixteen and twenty-four held a positive association with the phrase "like a girl." Following the video, an astonishing 76 percent of this population said that they no longer perceived the phrase negatively.[11] Furthermore, two out of three men who watched the video noted that they would now think twice before using the phrase "like a girl" in a derogatory manner. Six months after the campaign was initiated, Always ran a sixty-second television spot highlighting the initiative during sporting events, including the Super Bowl and the World Cup. The video realized a total of 53 million views during a World Cup year when many ads were dominated by high-profile athletes.[12] This brand-defining moment helped Always further solidify the company as one of the preeminent thought leaders in empowering women and also as a true innovator.

There is incredible value that great storytelling can bring to a campaign or news story. Successful initiatives tend to all contain similar elements, including an amazing storyline, emotional appeal, and context, which together trigger experiences that stay at the forefront of the consumer's mind. Now that we have a better understanding of the components necessary to create and develop good stories, we need to investigate the mechanisms behind why people share them with others.

Social Currency

Being "in the know" makes people feel special, influential, and admired. In general, people like to discuss topics that make them look intelligent in the eyes of their peers and want to be thought of highly by those around them—a fact that often finds its way into what we talk about.[13] Think about it: we tell funny jokes because we want others to see that we are witty or share our intimate knowledge about the latest celebrity scandal because it makes us seem cool. Not surprisingly, "people prefer sharing things that make them seem entertaining rather than boring, clever rather than dumb, and hip rather than dull."[14]

When we possess information related to a unique topic that others may not be aware of, we have what is termed "social currency." Social currency allows an individual to enhance his or her own identity, status, or recognition. Therefore, people tend to share things that make them look good. Research has shown that more than 40 percent of online topics are about personal experiences or relationships.[15] As public relations professionals, it is our job to create that fantastic experience that inspires a sense of importance, thereby providing consumers with the opportunity to share with others.

Let's take a look at another example. Nearly all women purchase and wear bras. This item is considered a staple in most women's daily wardrobe. You can imagine that competing for the attention and loyalty of women all over the world is priority number one for companies playing in this space. So how does an established brand like Victoria's Secret break through the clutter and get people talking?

Add diamonds, of course!

The price of an average bra is approximately $65 at the traditional higher-end retailers, while the price plummets to around $13.90 at the major mass retailers.[16] Back in 1996, when Victoria's Secret began creating bras with million-dollar price tags, consumers began to talk, and, well, they haven't stopped. As a result, the Victoria's Secret Fantasy Bra has since become the centerpiece of the annual Victoria's Secret fashion show. Designed by renowned jewelers such as Damiani and advertised as the "ultimate" holiday gift, the bras are available for purchase for only one year following their debut. The most expensive Fantasy Bra was valued at $15 million and holds the Guinness World Record for the most expensive lingerie ever created. Modeled by Gisele Bündchen in 2000, the luxury item was made of red satin decorated with more than three hundred carats of Thai rubies.[17]

In this initiative, Victoria's Secret focused on a specific piece of clothing and, by adding diamonds and gemstones, created something that was newsworthy. The response over the years has been nothing less than extraordinary. The brand now makes an annual announcement identifying the next Victoria's Secret "Angel" who will don the expensive, sparkly undergarment. The bra, as well as the coveted role of "Angel," has become iconic with loyal patrons of the brand. The Victoria's Secret Fantasy Bras are recognized as some of the most show-stopping lingerie in history. The ornate designs have served as the dazzling finale of almost every highly anticipated fashion show since 2001.[18]

Even if you never purchase one of these bras, you will most likely talk about them and share what you know with others. Countless media outlets pick up the story annually in order to discuss the price tag, the jewels, and the girl who will be wearing the piece. And let's be honest—it is only a bra after all. This is a "sticky" story oozing with social currency, and that is what entices us to share it. Victoria's Secret found a way to make a more or less mundane object remarkable. It uses scarcity (the bra is only available for a limited time) and exclusivity to make people feel like insiders who are receiving information that others do not necessarily have access to.

Now, not all brands can simply take a piece of clothing, add diamonds, and garner similar reactions; however, any brand can utilize exclusivity and scarcity as a tactic. Let's look at Coach Outlet and Bath & Body Works.

Coach Outlet often runs periodic sales lasting from twenty-four to forty-eight hours that offer deep discounts on the normal cost of Coach merchandise. The exclusivity element here is that consumers need a personal invite to capitalize on the deals.

And an email address that is on Coach's exclusive list.

The website that Coach utilizes for this promotion is unlike a traditional shopping website where anyone has access to purchase. Invited consumers can only purchase items during a specific period using the link contained within a special email. Consumers are not allowed to share or forward the email; otherwise it will deactivate. It only works for shoppers "on the list." A few years ago, the company provided an opportunity to those customers already "in the know" and "on the list" to invite others to become part of this specialized community. When friends shop, the original member receives $10 to shop. These incentives can add up quickly, especially if you are receiving 50 percent off Coach bags, jewelry, and accessories.

Garnering an equal level of buzz and exclusivity, Bath & Body Works initiated a First Look promotional email campaign that invites customers to provide their email addresses in order to join the company's First Look mailing list. This allows subscribers to receive exclusive glimpses of upcoming items, exclusive offers, and fun surprises. Only those individuals lucky enough to receive these special email notifications are aware of secret sales or new fragrances before they hit the mainstream.

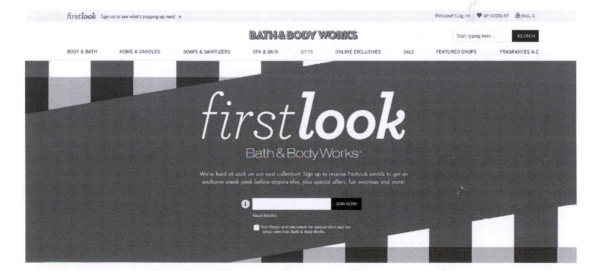

Victoria's Secret, Coach, and Bath & Body Works are a few brands that know how to make their customers feel special. Select consumers are provided with an exclusive benefit to share with others—something so unique that it is sticky, thus providing the consumer with social currency.

Influencers

In order for stories to catch the attention of media outlets, there needs to be a catalyst that broadens the appeal to a larger audience. This is where influencers play a critical role. If an idea were solely contagious, it would only depend on a particular channel to spread the story. Something that is sticky factors in not only the channel but also the specific audience necessary to disperse the message to the masses. These influencers circulate the message by communicating, influencing, and persuading other individuals or groups to act.

Influencers are people who possess extensive social networks. They are often successful business executives, politicians, celebrities, or folks who are simply connected to an "in crowd." These individuals are integral to the process of spreading ideas because their influence stems from a particular expertise, level of popularity, or reputation. Within their pervasive group of friends and acquaintances, influencers can communicate a message rapidly to a readily available, receptive audience.

On the entertainment front, celebrities are often considered influencers due to their high visibility. Think about it: when a celebrity uses a product, the maker of that product gains enormous exposure. Bloggers should also be considered important influencers because they are seen as authentic and have loyal followings. As with a celebrity, when an influential blogger recommends a product, it seems more trustworthy than traditional advertising efforts.[19] Not surprisingly, entire companies now exist that help promote this connection of messaging and influencers. IZEA, a company that specializes in influencer relations, connects brands with influential content creators and publishers in order to spread messages.

In order to educate consumers about the benefits of grass-fed beef, La Cense Beef used the influence of foodie bloggers to spread the message about its brand. In support of this activity, the company developed a website containing information about the grass-fed movement and sustainable agriculture specifically to target and provide information to influential bloggers.[20] The selected bloggers tended to have significant authority among gourmet meat buyers. The website made it easy for these prominent bloggers not only to research the movement but also to write about the benefits of La Cense Beef and distribute the message to the appropriate audience.

Another brand, Barilla Pasta, utilized influencers to promote its products by providing them with "Test Kitchen" packages containing Barilla products necessary to pull off a successful dinner party.[21] Influencers were challenged to prepare and serve the meal to their friends, snap photos of the gathering, and share their experiences with Barilla regarding the food. The submitted photos were then used to create authentic-looking advertising featuring real Barilla customers.

General Motors is another company that successfully utilized exclusivity as a promotional tool. Like other organizations, GM developed an exclusive, limited-access website, this one for "GM Insiders." The "insiders" were customers who not only had a deep knowledge of and history with the brand but also belonged to an influential network to share the information with.[22] GM Insiders were given access to exclusive news, offers, and sneak peeks available only to this special group of individuals. By catering to this passionate and influential segment of its customer base, GM was able to encourage the GM Insiders to share what they learned with friends and family.[23]

The common thread in each of the preceding examples is that the influencers were all encouraged to tell a unique story and provided the social currency and particular channel to share the message. People communicate information in a virtual, online environment for many of the same reasons that they share in real life. We are driven by our personal desire to create or strengthen relationships with other people by sharing information with others—especially if we believe that the knowledge we have is new or unfamiliar.

Shareable

As President Barack Obama was confirming the polling results of his reelection bid, he also cemented his place in social media history at the same time. Once the election results were announced, President Obama posted a photo of himself hugging his wife, Michelle, to his official Facebook and Twitter accounts.[24] The photo, titled "Four More Years," has since become the most frequently tweeted and most liked in Twitter and Facebook history.

International Relations

Sharing in the European Twittersphere

In 2015, the European Twittersphere was abuzz with new hashtags like #SocksBattle4DS, #Fishface, #EUPickupLines, #BrusselsBikeJungle and #EarthHour. European commissioners, managers, and employees have been enthusiastically sharing, retweeting, and posting photos from a variety of advocacy campaigns. Here are a couple:

The #SocksBattle4DS campaign for World Down Syndrome Day requested the public to wear different socks on each foot, snap a picture, and then post it on social networks using the hashtag #SocksBattle4DS. The idea was not only fun but also simple, making it easy to share for such a great cause.

Similarly, the World Widelife Fund launched a challenge for people to share a #Fishface photo on social media to support sustainable fishing and healthy oceans. #Fishface was a fun way to show support for sustainable fishing standards.

Source: Antoine Mellado, Bastien De Zutter, and Alba Màlaga Homs, "Four Tips to Create Social Media Buzz for Your EU Campaign," 3 Communications, May 11, 2015, accessed November 25, 2015, http://3communications.com/wp-content/uploads/2015/05/socksbattle4DS.jpg.

In a completely unrelated but relevant episode, a man named Nolan Daniels shared a different type of Facebook photo weeks after Obama's unprecedented photo share. Daniels's photo nearly quadrupled the number of shares that the president's photo garnered.[25] His image, in the tumult of a $588 million Powerball jackpot lottery drawing, showed him allegedly holding the winning numbers and declaring that he was indeed one of the lucky winners. But what made this photo so shareable was the message attached to the image: "Share this photo and I will give a random person 1 million dollars!" You might imagine that the response from this post was rapid and widespread, resulting in over 2 million shares.[26] Ultimately, Daniels's post ended up being a hoax.

Theory into Practice

Dove and Kmart

Social media can be an equalizer. Any company can cut through the noise, regardless of brand awareness or financial constraints. It merely takes a clever story with social currency, a couple of influencers, and the ability to easily share.

Using the principles described in the chapter, identify how each of the following campaigns positioned itself as sticky. Specifically, include the storytelling elements that provoked emotion, the social currency that created something remarkable or unusual, what type of influencers were utilized, and the ways in which consumers could share the message.

Dove: The aim of the Real Beauty Sketches video campaign was to highlight the drastic contrast between how women view themselves and how they are viewed by others. According to Dove, 54 percent of women worldwide confess to being their own worst critic of how they look. Dove hired Gil Zamora, an FBI-trained forensic artist, to draw a series of women from behind a curtain, completing the sketches based on each woman's verbal description of her appearance. Zamora was then tasked with creating a second sketch based on strangers' accounts of the same women. The resulting sketches from the strangers' perspectives tended to correspond more accurately with reality and were more flattering depictions than those based on the women's own self-effacing descriptions. The video generated record-breaking online interest, with more than 114 million views during the first month alone. Dove spread the message everywhere. The company uploaded the video to thirty-three of its official YouTube channels in twenty-five different languages, reaching consumers in more than 110 countries. The campaign struck a chord, generating close to 3.8 million shares in its first month online and adding fifteen thousand new subscribers to Dove's YouTube channel over the ensuing two months. The impact of the campaign spread across traditional media as well, resulting in extensive print features, broadcast news segments, and online discussions. Watch the video: http://bit.ly/1hpZuRD.

Kmart: With revenue trending downward, Kmart needed to do something to get customers talking—and shopping. Teaming with creative agency FCB, it created the Ship My Pants online video campaign. Embracing juvenile wordplay, this message was a clever way to inform customers that out-of-stock items in Kmart stores may now be shipped directly to a consumer's home for free. Enthusiastically, one elderly shopper proclaims, "I just shipped my pants, and it's very convenient!"; another announces, "I just shipped my bed!" Some viewers called it "gross" and "vulgar," but the video triggered 20 million YouTube views, at one point realizing one share for every nine views. Kmart and FCB followed Ship My Pants with the equally funny Big Gas Savings campaign. Watch the videos: Ship my Pants: http://bit.ly/1QskW9f; Big Gas Savings: http://bit.ly/1ppjcre.

Source: Ankeny, "How These 10 Marketing Campaigns Became Viral Hits."

These two examples clearly highlight that there exists a direct connection between shareable content and high social engagement—which is apparent when something achieves "viral" status.[27] The more compelling and provocative the content, the more likely it is to be embraced and distributed across multiple networks.

Simply stated, experiences prompt people to communicate with others. Brands can tap into this urge to share by creating content that starts the conversation. The New York Times Customer Insight Group published a study that highlights four key factors that cause people to share content. These key motivations include[28]

- defining ourselves to others;
- bringing valuable and entertaining content to others;
- growing and nourishing relationships;
- getting the word out about causes and brands that we care about.

In order to motivate consumers to share, practitioners need to make it easy to share the content. Sharing buttons enable visitors and content viewers to easily communicate your company's content with their social media connections and networks. Adding these buttons to content pieces allows a company to expand its reach to new audiences and generate new visitors.[29] PR practitioners should get into the habit of adding social media sharing links and buttons to every piece of content created, including landing pages, web pages, individual blog articles, and email efforts.[30]

Go Forth and Create Sticky Content

With the numerous avenues available for the distribution of messaging, there is an equal number of ways to create socially shareable, sticky, and contagious content in support of these communications. As you apply the best practices within this chapter to your next campaign, be sure to measure engagement rates in order to understand how consumers are talking about your company or brand. Remember, measurement allows companies to evaluate what is and is not working and to continue to improve the quality of its content.[31] We discuss metrics more in depth in chapter 14.

#LRNSMPR

Learn More: Sticky, Contagious, and Viral

- "6 Elements of a 'Sticky' Pinterest Campaign": http://bit.ly/1POD2rm
- "The Ultimate Cheat Sheet for Creating Social Media Buttons": http://bit.ly/1Os00RU
- "The 7 Factors That Make for Viral Content": http://entm.ag/1XfmzRj
- "Which Brands Create the Most Contagious Content on Social?": http://bit.ly/1Qlc7O8

Notes

1. Jason Ankeny, "How These 10 Marketing Campaigns Became Viral Hits," *Entrepreneur*, April 23, 2014, accessed November 22, 2015, http://www.entrepreneur.com/article/233207.
2. "What Is Viral Marketing?—Definition from WhatIs.com," SearchCRM, 2015, accessed November 22, 2015, http://searchcrm.techtarget.com/definition/viral-marketing.
3. Jonah Berger, *Contagious: Why Things Catch On* (New York: Simon & Schuster, 2013).
4. Berger, *Contagious*.
5. Berger, *Contagious*.
6. Malcolm Gladwell, *The Tipping Point: How Little Things Can Make a Big Difference* (Boston: Little, Brown, 2000).

[7] Steve Armenti, "6 Principles for Creating Contagious Social Content," *Content Standard*, November 11, 2013, accessed November 23, 2015, http://www.skyword.com/contentstandard/enterprise-marketing/6-principles-for-creating-contagious-social-content.

[8] "Case Study: Always #LikeAGirl," D&AD, June 26, 2014, accessed November 23, 2015, http://www.dandad.org/en/case-study-always-likeagirl.

[9] "Case Study: Always #LikeAGirl."

[10] "Case Study: Always #LikeAGirl."

[11] "Case Study: Always #LikeAGirl."

[12] "The 30 Most Brilliant Social Media Campaigns of the Last Half of 2014," Salesforce Blog, December 31, 2014, accessed November 23, 2015, https://www.salesforce.com/blog/2014/12/the-30-most-brilliant-social-media-campaigns-of-the-last-half-of-2014-152015.html.

[13] Berger, *Contagious*.

[14] Berger, *Contagious*.

[15] "Online Dating & Relationships," Pew Research Center Internet Science Tech RSS, October 20, 2013, accessed November 23, 2015, http://www.pewinternet.org/2013/10/21/online-dating-relationships.

[16] Elizabeth Olson, "Finding the Right Fit, with Technology's Help," *New York Times*, August 16, 2012, accessed November 24, 2015, http://www.nytimes.com/2012/08/17/business/media/finding-the-best-fitting-bra-with-technologys-help.html?_r=0.

[17] Charlie Lankinston, "As Victoria's Secret Unveils Two Fantasy Bras, FEMAIL Takes a Look Back at the History of the World's Most Expensive Lingerie," *Mail Online*, November 4, 2014, accessed November 24, 2015, http://www.dailymail.co.uk/femail/article-2819365/A-Victoria-s-Secret-unveils-two-Fantasy-Bras-FEMAIL-takes-look-history-world-s-expensive-lingerie.html.

[18] Lankinston, "As Victoria's Secret Unveils Two Fantasy Bras."

[19] "Influencer Marketing," Marketing-Schools.org, 2012, accessed November 25, 2015, http://www.marketing-schools.org/types-of-marketing/influencer-marketing.html.

[20] "Influencer Marketing | What Is Influencer Marketing?"

[21] "Influencer Marketing | What Is Influencer Marketing?"

[22] "Influencer Marketing | What Is Influencer Marketing?"

[23] "Influencer Marketing | What Is Influencer Marketing?"

[24] "Shareable Content—the Key to Social Media Engagement Success," Cision, May 2, 2015, accessed November 25, 2015, http://www.cision.com/us/resources/white-papers/shareable-content-the-key-to-social-media-engagement-success.

[25] "Shareable Content."

[26] "Shareable Content."

[27] "Shareable Content."

[28] Jeff Bullass, "10 Ways to Create Contagious Content for Your Social Media Marketing," Jeffbullass.com, October 20, 2014, accessed November 25, 2015, http://www.jeffbullas.com/2014/10/21/10-ways-to-create-contagious-content-for-your-social-media-marketing.

[29] Pamela Vaughen, "The Ultimate Cheat Sheet for Creating Social Media Buttons," HubSpot, October 30, 2014, accessed November 25, 2015, http://blog.hubspot.com/blog/tabid/6307/bid/29544/The-Ultimate-Cheat-Sheet-for-Creating-Social-Media-Buttons.aspx.

[30] Vaughen, "The Ultimate Cheat Sheet for Creating Social Media Buttons."

[31] Bullass, "10 Ways To Create Contagious Content for Your Social Media Marketing."

Crisis Management on the Social Sphere

10

Social networks create significant opportunities for brands, but they also become platforms on which crises can develop and perpetuate at an unprecedented rate. In dealing with a rogue tweet, a product recall, an employee acting badly on YouTube, a disparaging review on Yelp, or a spokesperson who has tarnished the brand, preparing for a crisis situation in a digital age requires a fresh perspective.

Millennial-Era Crises

In the age of social media, the potential for a crisis scenario to arise has increased exponentially. From lewd photos of a C-suite executive appearing on Facebook or Instagram to proprietary information being leaked and posted to Twitter and LinkedIn, crises happen in real time and only take minutes to spread to the masses.[1]

A recent survey revealed that more than 28 percent of reported crises spread internationally within an hour, and over two-thirds spread within the first twenty-four hours.[2] Despite having traditional crisis plans in place, organizations often find that they are not prepared to manage the crisis on the social sphere. In fact, 50 percent of communications professionals believe companies are not adequately prepared to handle such situations, and 94 percent think that the failure to effectively define how to handle online issues leaves an organization open to "trial by Twitter."[3] These statistics illustrate the impact that social media has on crisis management. Governments, educational institutions, nonprofit organizations, corporations, and even private citizens are not immune. The following examples highlight this exact point:

Governments: During the Arab Spring movement, social media–savvy activists across the Middle East and North Africa contributed to the downfall of two dictators, causing widespread disruption. "We use Facebook to schedule the protests, Twitter to coordinate, and YouTube to tell the world," an Arab Spring activist told a reporter during the riots.[4] These types of demonstrations force countries and governments to move into a crisis-response mode.

Educational Institutions: Penn State University remained silent amid allegations of sexual abuse, years of coverups, and acts of misuse and exploitation, while the larger community took to Twitter, Facebook, and hundreds of other online news and media sites to voice their opinions and blast the Penn State brand.

Nonprofit Organizations: After admitting to doping and using performance-enhancing drugs to win seven Tour de France titles, Lance Armstrong stepped down as chairman of the Livestrong Foundation. The public lambasted Armstrong on several social sites, tarnishing the reputation of both his charity and his personal image. In the aftermath of this crisis, the Livestrong Foundation amped up efforts to detach itself from the cyclist.

Corporations: The BP oil spill in the Gulf of Mexico spawned an oil disaster so large that the complete ramifications are still unknown more than half a decade later. In response to the crisis, CEO Tony Hayward demonstrated an argumentative approach, landing him in hot water with the public and throughout the social sphere. During the crisis Hayward was quoted as saying, "Well, it wasn't our accident, but we are absolutely responsible for the oil, for cleaning up" (May 3, 2010); "The Gulf of Mexico is a very big ocean. The amount of volume of oil and dispersant we are putting into it is tiny in relation to the water volume" (May 14, 2010); and "The environmental impact of this disaster is likely to have been very, very modest" (May 18, 2010).[5] Hayward's attempt to apologize and mitigate the crisis led to further outrage: "I'm sorry—we're sorry—for the massive disruption this has caused their lives. And there's no one who wants this over more than I do. You know, I want my life back" (May 30, 2010). Hayward, and as a result BP, became fodder on numerous blogs, and the topic continues to retain genuine staying power within the Twitterverse.[6]

Private Individuals: Chelsea Welch, an angry Applebee's waitress, catapulted Pastor Alois Bell from private citizen to evil villainess after the pastor left an ungenerous note on the waitress's receipt. The social sphere reacted swiftly, harshly, and without mercy to the Applebee's response in the matter and to the pastor herself.

These five examples represent modern-day crises that spread on social media as the events unfolded in real time. The reputation of a brand can easily be tarnished in mere moments because an active public now has the ability to take a stance, make a statement, and judge that brand based on how the company chooses to address (or not address) the crisis at hand.

Social media is immediate, pervasive, and widely available, and it appeals to hundreds of millions of people. However, for many of those same reasons, social media can also be dangerous for brands, especially during a time of crisis, requiring the addition of entirely new components in crisis communication. The days of "textbook" crisis situations (think of the Johnson & Johnson Tylenol and *Exxon Valdez* oil spill cases) are long gone. Today, public relations practitioners employ an amalgam of tactics, strategies, and responses during a time of crisis via the social web. A fresh perspective is necessary to effectively respond to today's crisis situations.

Five Stages of Crisis Management in the Digital Age

Konrad Palubicki (@konradpalubicki), from Edelman Digital in Seattle, Washington, developed what he considers the five most important stages of crisis management in the digital age:[7]

Prepare in advance.
Isolate the origin.
Evaluate the impact.
Mitigate the crisis.
Learn from the crisis.

Prepare in Advance

We all love watching viral videos just as much as the next person. The Harlem Shake, Conversations with My Two-Year-Old, and "What Does the Fox Say?" are all funny, shareable, and lighthearted videos. But when a viral video is about your company, brand, or products, it may not be as funny.[8] It is unrealistic to believe that brands can prepare for every potential crisis, but precrisis planning is essential. Author and crisis communication professional Kathleen Fearn-Banks suggests creating a crisis communication plan.[9] The plan should list the individuals on the crisis-management team, generate a crisis audit, and develop key messages, objectives, procedures, and specific guidelines. Some companies take the added step of developing a "dark" website that only goes live in the event of an emergency.[10] Prewritten messaging and critical information can be created ahead of the crisis, uploaded to the site, and launched if a crisis ever breaks.

Preparing in advance also means that companies must pay attention to the conversations occurring on their social channels. The task of perusing the company Twitter feed or browsing the company Facebook posts should not be considered truly listening. Organizations need to use specific social media–monitoring software such as Meltwater Buzz, Crimson Hexagon, Sysomos, Lithium, Viralheat, and Social Mention to understand the messages that pertain to their company or brand. These software systems help companies monitor who is participating in conversations and what is being said across multiple social media platforms, blogs, and website comments. Monitoring also aids in identifying where a crisis originated.

CRISIS ON THE SOCIAL SPHERE

1 Prepare in Advance
- Create a plan
- Set up monitoring tools

2 Isolate the Origin
- Identify where the crisis originated and on which social channels
- Don't fight back - with journalists or consumers

3 Evaluate the Impact
- Take inventory of the situation
- Establish a clear chain of command

4 Mitigate the Crisis
- Respond quickly and with empathy
- Take appropriate action

5 Learn from the Crisis
- When it's over go back and review

Isolate the Origin

Being able to identify where a crisis initiates and on what social channels the conversations fueling the crisis are happening is paramount in controlling the crisis situation.[11] When brands understand the cause of the crisis, they can better assess how to respond. Proper identification helps a company determine whether a full social media crisis is present and is also invaluable in helping a company decide the next steps in formulating a proper response.

Evaluate the Impact

Take inventory of the situation. Create a log to determine which stakeholders require attention first—and fast. There are two primary audiences during a crisis: those directly affected and those whose attitudes about the company could be influenced.[12] Determine whether one group is being impacted more than another and evaluate the immediate impacts of the situation, which could include the following:[13]

Uptick in calls to the customer service hotline
Rise in media inquiries
Flurry of comments on social channels
Interest from government regulators
Inquiries from the board of directors
Disaffection toward brands or products
Drop in sales
Potential lawsuits
Vulnerability to personal, societal, and economic conditions

Social Media Crisis or Not?

Would you know if your company was in the midst of a social media crisis? These three characteristics can help determine whether a company is in a true social media crisis mode:

1. *Definite change from the norm:* Companies should watch for sudden changes in tone and sentiment in discussion and comments on social media sites.

2. *Information separation:* The company is not aware of the situation any more than the public.

3. *Widespread impact throughout the company:* The scope and scale are so large and incomprehensible during the initial stage when the crisis breaks that it has ramifications at every level.

Source: Jay Baer, *Youtility* (New York: Penguin, 2013).

If a company waits too long to acknowledge and respond while a crisis breaks, it can quickly lose credibility. Social media crises will not disappear after a few days. On the contrary, without proper management, a crisis will continue to build momentum and accelerate to a tipping point. Twenty-four hours on the social web is too long to wait to acknowledge and respond. Heck—four hours could be too long!

Mitigate the Crisis

The more rapid the response time, the better a company's chance of limiting the total time the crisis lasts. The first rule in crisis management is "Stop the bleeding." Acting fast and responding to the situation is paramount. Once the crisis team establishes an initial response, focus should then shift toward ensuring a continuity of messages across all traditional and social channels.

It is important to sustain real-time updates by including details that are honest and straightforward. Remember the "dark" website suggestion from earlier in the chapter? Bring that to life. A website dedicated to the crisis serves two purposes. First, the website can minimize the conversations happening on social sites. Second, the website illustrates that the company is proactive in resolving the issue at hand. A website of this nature can provide companies with a platform for providing regular updates, contact information, video or photo updates, current actions related to the crisis, and plans to ensure the incident will not happen again.

Continue listening using the monitoring tools set in place prior to the crisis. Establish an in-house crisis command center so that the crisis team can collaborate in real time.[14] Companies can track the crisis using all traditional media channels and social platforms simultaneously. Companies can use Twitter and Facebook to proactively post statements such as "We are aware of the issue. Live updates are here: [provide URL]." The URLs will drive traffic back to the company-dedicated website that contains the most relevant information.

Learn from the Crisis

All crises are learning opportunities. Crises may not necessarily be the type of lessons we love, but they are opportunities to gain valuable insights. Companies should conduct a postcrisis meeting to determine how the organization performed during the crisis. An analysis of emails sent, offline media coverage garnered, company statements, and all social mentions, including tweets, blog comments, pins, videos,

Trouble for TalkTalk

The UK-based telecom giant faced fierce criticism after a delay in communicating that the company was the victim of a "significant and sustained" cyberattack that led to the theft of credit card and bank details for up to 4 million customers.[1]

In recent years, global customers have seen an increase in hackers' accessing private information from numerous organizations. It should not be a surprise that TalkTalk customers were outraged to learn that the company had not tightened security, especially since the most recent incident was the third cyberattack to directly affect TalkTalk. In August 2015, hackers breached the personal data of customers on its mobile site. This security lapse occurred less than six months after scammers previously accessed thousands of account numbers and names from the company's computers.[2] The thefts were only discovered when TalkTalk began to look into a spike in complaints from customers about scam calls between October and December 2014.[3]

Rather than being open and honest with its customers, TalkTalk responded with panic and shared very little information with its customers. In its initial response to the crisis, the company waited approximately thirty-six hours before notifying customers of the most recent breach, arguing that it would have been difficult to communicate any earlier. TalkTalk also completely shut down its website and did not inform customers about what they should be doing to protect their information.[4]

According to Jacques de Cock, a faculty member at the London School of Marketing, "TalkTalk needs to invest much more in its client communication and social media management if it is to succeed in the modern hyperlinked and interactive world. It has a long way to go."[5]

1 Nadia Khomami, "TalkTalk Hacking Crisis Deepens as More Details Emerge," *Guardian*, October 23, 2015, accessed November 16, 2015, http://www.theguardian.com/business/2015/oct/23/talktalk-hacking-crisis-deepens-as-more-details-emerge.
2 Khomami, "TalkTalk Hacking Crisis Deepens as More Details Emerge."
3 Jacques de Cock, "TalkTalk's Crisis PR: Its Hack Response Is 'Mirroring the Incredulity and Panic of the Public,'" *The Drum*, October 23, 2015, accessed November 16, 2015, http://www.thedrum.com/opinion/2015/10/23/talktalks-crisis-pr-its-hack-response-mirroring-incredulity-and-panic-public.
4 de Cock, "TalkTalk's Crisis PR."
5 de Cock, "TalkTalk's Crisis PR."

Facebook updates, and any other online media mentions, should be conducted. The process of analysis is evaluative and designed to bring about change that helps prevent similar future crises.[15]

Smart Companies, Unfortunate Crises

Some organizations are better equipped to handle a crisis than others. Regardless of how prepared a company believes it is to handle a crisis, there is always something to learn from the experience. Companies can learn how to strengthen their own social media crisis-management strategies by examining how other organizations, including media company IAC, Oreo, JCPenney, Burger King, KitchenAid, Applebee's, Paula Deen, and British Airways, dealt with crises in the social sphere.

Offensive Tweet Not a Match Made in Heaven[16]

Justine Sacco, former corporate communications director for the prominent New York–based Internet media company IAC, lost her job after she tweeted "Going to Africa. Hope I don't get AIDS. Just Kidding. I'm White!" IAC owns and operates more than a dozen websites, including the news websites The Daily Beast and CollegeHumor; dating websites such as Match.com, BlackPeopleMeet.com, and OKCupid; and other well-known brands like Vimeo. IAC acted swiftly, which illustrated just how seriously the company took the incident. In a public statement, company spokespeople were quoted as saying, "The offensive comment does not reflect the views and values of IAC. We take this issue very seriously, and we have parted ways with the employee in question." Sacco herself apologized in a written statement "for being insensitive to this crisis—which does not discriminate by race, gender or sexual orientation, but which terrifies us all uniformly—and to the millions of people living with the virus, I am ashamed."[17] This incident is an excellent reminder for corporations as well as individuals that each opinion expressed on the Internet can be heard by the millions of active users who are listening, following, and sharing. Sentiments that individuals or corporations tweet, like, or share can have grave consequences.

Colorful Cookie

Kraft Foods, the brand behind Oreo cookies, found itself in some trouble after it posted a rainbow-stuffed cookie with the caption "Proudly support love!" in honor of Gay Pride Month.[18] The backlash to this initiative came from some consumers who felt that the brand should not support gay rights. Consumers voiced their opinions on both Twitter and the Oreo Facebook page. Kraft Foods was facing a possible boycott from the public over this initiative. Basil Maglaris, a spokeswoman for Kraft Foods, responded by saying, "We are excited to illustrate what is making history today in a fun and playful way. As a company, Kraft Foods has a proud history of celebrating diversity and inclusiveness. We feel the OREO ad is a fun reflection of our values."[19]

On the flip side, there were also numerous fans who supported the campaign. Loyal Oreo cookie supporters from across the globe defended the issue on the company's Facebook page and Twitter feed. Talk about devotion! Fans who are willing to help in a time of crisis are just the kind of fans a brand wants to attract. This example illustrates how much trust consumers have in Oreo and the type of genuine relationship that Oreo has built with its customer base. The tone and consistency with which Kraft Foods responded to the public contributed greatly to the success of its response. From email to social media, Kraft Foods consistently stood by its company values and stopped the crisis from igniting into a maelstrom of negativity.

Teapot Debacle

JCPenney came under fire after a number of reddit users noted that the company's newest teapot design closely resembled the former German dictator Adolf Hitler.[20] An innocent mistake on behalf of the designer, yes, and some might even argue that the interpretation is a matter of personal perception. In this instance, however, perception did not seem to matter much. JCPenney now had a potential firestorm brewing and needed to respond quickly before the situation could escalate into a full-blown social media crisis. JCPenney's approach involved addressing the situation quickly and acknowledging the social references. Using Twitter, the crisis team developed and delivered a tweet response for each instance in which the teapot's likeness to Adolf Hitler was mentioned: "Certainly unintentionally. If we had designed the kettle to look like something, we would have gone with a snowman or something fun." The tweet illustrated good intentions, acknowledged what consumers were chatting about on the social web, noted that the act was unintentional, and attempted to keep the response respectful yet humorous. JCPenney had the wherewithal to discern the difference between a social media issue, which this was, and a social media crisis. The company handled the situation well by staying calm, responding promptly, and providing the public with the right amount of information.

Hacked Burger

In February 2013, the Burger King Twitter account was hacked.[21] The pranksters changed Burger King's company avatar and name to that of its rival McDonald's. The hackers then proceeded to tweet numerous questionable and offensive tweets from this account. Within the first thirty minutes of the attack, the Burger King Twitter account attracted five thousand new followers. By the time Burger King had regained control of its account and issued an apology, the brand had gained more than thirty thousand new followers. In this instance the response was rapid, and information was proactively shared with the public during the crisis. Burger King took the proper steps to "stop the bleeding" and ended up with an increased following due to this event.

Messy Mix-Up

What happens when an employee tweets from the company account rather than his or her own personal Twitter account? KitchenAid knows all too well the ramifications of a crisis like this.[22] A member of the KitchenAid social media team posted an insensitive tweet about President Barack Obama's grandmother during Obama's first presidential campaign. Rather than using a personal Twitter account, the employee

Theory into Practice

Burger King's Damaging Lettuce Debacle

Burger King is no stranger to crises involving employees participating in disgusting acts and then alerting the public to these incidents. In 2008, a Burger King employee posted a Myspace video of himself bathing in a restaurant sink. The company handled the crisis well and with swift action.[1]

More recently, Burger King faced another crisis after an employee posted a picture to 4chan depicting himself standing in two containers of lettuce.[2] The caption read, "This is the lettuce you eat at Burger King." Some 4chan users were so outraged that they took it upon themselves to take action. Using GPS data attached to the image, 4chan users traced the photo and were able to pinpoint the location of the Burger King restaurant where the photograph had been taken. Once the offending employees were identified, Burger King promptly fired them, and the company released the following statement:

> Burger King Corp. has recently been made aware of a photo posted on a social networking site that allegedly shows a Burger King restaurant employee violating the company's stringent food handling procedures. Food safety is a top priority at all Burger King restaurants, and the company maintains a zero-tolerance policy against any violations such as the one in question.

Read the full story and watch the following video: article: http://huff.to/18x5RBE; video: http://bit.ly/1gtAttl.

Discussion Questions

Could Burger King have prevented the employee from taking and posting the image of himself on the Internet?

What can Burger King do to prevent a crisis like this from occurring in the future?

How shareable was this story?

Was the brand hurt in any way?

Was Burger King's response sufficient?

Were you surprised that consumers took action to locate where the photo was taken?

Would you have handled this social media crisis differently? If yes, how so? If no, what was exemplary about how Burger King handled it?

---

1 "Burger King Workers Fired over Video of Teen Bathing in Sink," Fox News, August 13, 2008, http://www.foxnews.com/story/2008/08/13/burger-king-workers-fired-over-video-teen-bathing-in-sink.html.

2 Andres Jauregui, "Burger King Employee Posts *Photo* of Himself Stepping in Lettuce, Gets Busted by 4chan Users [Updated]," *Huffington Post*, last modified July 17, 2013, accessed October 19, 2013, http://www.huffingtonpost.com/2012/07/17/burger-king-employee-steps-in-lettuce-busted-4chan_n_1679793.html.

Amy Neumann on Crisis Communication

Amy Neumann (@CharityIdeas), a digital media and technology expert, recommends incorporating the following actions during a crisis:

- Stay on top of conversations about your company with simple tools.
- Watch for sudden changes in tone and sentiment from positive or neutral to negative.
- Set up and monitor keywords related to your business.
- Monitor who is talking to you across all social media platforms and website comments.
- Respond, both individually and more broadly.
- Provide updates on the same platforms users talk on and invite them to email you if deeper interaction is needed.

- Acknowledge there is a situation.
- Keep real-time updates flowing.
- Be honest and straightforward with details.
- Make sure customers feel heard by replying, directing them to resources for updates.
- Answer questions directly.
- Thank them for their feedback, and do not delete negative comments.
- Update social media platforms with outcomes; update websites.
- Notify the media for additional outreach.
- Outline the resolution, what was learned, and how similar situations will be prevented in the future.

Source: Neumann, "5 Steps for Crisis Management Using Social Media."

posted the message to the KitchenAid Twitter account. The outrageous tweet read, "Obamas gma even knew it was going 2 b bad! She died 3 days b4 he became president." The tweet was deleted from the KitchenAid account within fifteen minutes of its original post, but countless people had already seen it, shared it, and commented on it. It only took fifteen minutes to damage the KitchenAid brand. Cynthia Soledad, the head of the KitchenAid brand, immediately apologized to both President Obama and the public. In a series of 140-character tweets and a full apology on the company website, Soledad issued the following apology: "During the debate tonight, a member of our Twitter team mistakenly posted an offensive tweet from the KitchenAid handle instead of a personal handle. The tasteless joke in no way represents our values at KitchenAid, and that person won't be tweeting for us anymore. That said, I lead the KitchenAid brand, and I take responsibility for the whole team. I am deeply sorry to President Obama, his family, and the Twitter community for this careless error. Thanks for hearing me out."[23]

Several actions on the part of the brand manager deserve applause in this time of crisis. Soledad's response was quick and sincere; she confronted the situation head on, showing empathy, compassion, and transparency; and she humanized the brand through her words. She also stated what the company was going to do to address the situation so that it did not happen in the future. There are many takeaways from this social crisis, but stressing the importance of keeping personal and company accounts separate is an imperative lesson for businesses and employees alike. Many social strategists use tools like HootSuite to manage their personal and client accounts, but this social media crisis keenly illustrates the ramifications of not paying attention. If a mistake like this does occur, it should be addressed immediately. What saved KitchenAid was Soledad's candid, authentic explanation and personal tone of regret. By regaining control quickly, the company ensured that the apology was well received, minimizing any long-term damage to the brand's reputation.

Oreo, JCPenney, Burger King, and KitchenAid are all examples of what should be done during a social media crisis. Not all brands understand the power and magnitude of consumers on the Internet. Just as a quick and well-timed reaction or sincere apology can prevent a potential crisis from forming, the opposite response can have an equally rapid, disastrous consequence for a brand. With that in mind, let us examine what happened when Volkswagen, Applebee's, Paula Deen, and British Airways faced their own social media crises.

Under a Haze of Smog

It took some time, but Volkswagen finally admitted that it had distorted the results of vehicle emission tests for years in order to pass requirements set by the U.S. Environmental Protection Agency (EPA). The company said that more than 11 million diesel engine vehicles had software installed that manipulated the emissions tests results to make sure that emissions levels met EPA standards.[24] The company issued several statements admitting that Volkswagen had "totally screwed up," apologized for what had happened, and noted that it was working to find a solution to the problem. Chief Executive Martin Winterkorn and other senior-level executives issued apologies using both statements and videos, but the corporate response was lackluster at best. The company's initial statement confirmed that it had received notice of an EPA investigation and that the company "takes the matter very seriously and is cooperating with the investigation."[25] This is a meaningless comment that lacks any personal, human response. Ira Kalb, assistant professor of clinical marketing at the University of Southern California's Marshall School of Business, noted that the vilest part of this crisis was that "Volkswagen evaded regulators and deceived the public regarding the emissions of its diesel vehicles by employing a 'defeat device.'" Because this was a deliberate deception that endangered public health and violated Volkswagen's "clean diesel" branding, the company seriously compromised its integrity. Even worse, the company did not disclose the deception.[26] Volkswagen will need to put forth a great deal of effort to change public opinion and win back customers. It remains to be determined if Volkswagen will survive this crisis.

What's Good for the Goose Isn't Always Good for the Gander

A seemingly innocent note incited fury on the social web and set a series of bad events in motion for the Applebee's restaurant chain.[27] Pastor Alois Bell had eaten at an Applebee's restaurant and, upon paying her bill, crossed out the automatic 18 percent tip charged for parties of more than eight people and left the following message on the receipt above her signature: "I give God 10% why do you get 18?" The waitress, Chelsea Welch, was so upset that she took a photo of the receipt and posted it on the social news and entertainment website reddit. Subsequently, the waitress was fired for "violating customer privacy." Actions related to violating this policy would have been completely understandable if Applebee's had not posted a similar receipt that was *complimenting* the company only two weeks prior. As news of this incident spread and enraged people across virtually every social media platform, Applebee's responded with this short post defending its actions on its Facebook page: "We wish this situation hadn't happened. Our Guests' personal information—including their meal check—is private, and neither Applebee's nor its franchisees have a right to share this information publicly. We value our Guests' trust above all else. Our franchisee has apologized to the Guest and has taken disciplinary action with the Team Member for violating their Guest's right to privacy."[28] Almost instantaneously, the Applebee's statement precipitated more than ten thousand comments—most of which were negative in nature. At this point, Applebee's was knee deep in a social media crisis that it did not appear prepared to manage. Applebee's began posting the same message in its response to comments on multiple social media platforms. The repetitive response only garnered additional negative feedback. Applebee's then deleted all negative messages and started to block fans. The downward spiral of contempt continued as Applebee's persisted in defending its actions and arguing with—even criticizing—its fans during the crisis. Another questionable move by Applebee's involved a decision to hide the original post. Not surprisingly, this action spawned even more public fury and annoyance.

In retrospect, it may be easy to see that Applebee's broke many rules regarding crisis communication. Companies must remember that it is not about winning an argument; rather, it is about responding with empathy, honesty, patience, authenticity, and transparency. During a period in which a crisis exists, people are angry. In some instances, anger is at such an elevated level that any company response may incite added rage. Make sure that employees know not to go "tit for tat" with upset consumers. Applebee's also failed to observe the "rule of three": never, ever, send a third reply.[29] A third reply is an argument and no longer an answer. If a company feels that it must explain its actions a third time, then it is time to take the conversation offline. In this case, Applebee's was well past having a conversation; instead, it was engaged in a full-blown argument with fans. The defensive and confrontational approach amplified the disastrous crisis situation. Intentionally hiding comments or criticisms should never be a consideration because these actions can only make the crisis worse. Simply put, arguing with Facebook fans is always wrong and never appropriate. This crisis, including the Applebee's response in handling it, may be remembered as one of the most ill-thought-out social media crisis communication strategies to date.

Now in Session: The Court of Public Opinion

June 2013 was a very bad month for Paula Deen, the "Queen of Butter" and a celebrity personality on the Food Network.[30] After allegations surfaced that Deen had testified under oath to using the N-word, mistreating and harassing employees, and demonstrating a dubious level of awareness as to what it means to have racist tendencies and intolerance, she found herself watching her career careen out of control. Deen failed to obey the golden rule of crisis management: acknowledge, say sorry, and truly mean it. A company, brand, or (in this case) individual has only one opportunity to apologize. After posting three insincere video apologies *days after the crisis broke*, and following an in-person appearance on the *Today Show* in which she displayed a defensive attitude, the Food Network, Walmart, Sears, Kmart, JCPenney, Walgreens, and a laundry list of other high-profile sponsors all ended their long-term relationships with Deen. And sponsors were not the only ones who'd had enough. Many of Deen's loyal followers had also thrown in the towel. The Paula Deen Facebook page and Twitter feed were littered with comments from outraged fans. Deen had very quickly lost control of the crisis, and the court of public opinion had taken over.

The challenge here is that Deen had never fully recovered from her first crisis when a second crisis occurred in July 2015. An image posted on her social media accounts showed Deen and her son Bobby dressed as Lucy and Ricky Ricardo from the classic 1950s TV comedy show *I Love Lucy*. Many on social media were quick to call out Bobby's look as "brownface." In a statement issued by a spokeswoman, Deen apologized "to all who were offended" and blamed a social media manager for posting the image from a Halloween episode of *Paula's Best Dishes* that had aired in 2011.[31] "As such, Paula Deen Ventures has terminated their relationship with this Social Media Manager," noted the statement.[32]

Flying the Not-So-Friendly Skies

Promoted tweets are all the rage for celebrities and businesses alike, but when an angry customer buys a promoted tweet, you can imagine that a social media crisis is quick to ensue. In September 2013 an unhappy customer of British Airways purchased a promoted tweet to complain about the lack of customer service provided by the airline. In response to a lack of information regarding his missing luggage, British Airways passenger Hasan Syed had this to say: "Don't fly @BritishAirways. Their customer service is horrendous."[33] After what could be deemed a lifetime on social media—ten hours!—British Airways finally responded with an apathetic tweet of its own: "Sorry for the delay in responding, our twitter feed is open 09:00–17:00 GMT. Please DM your baggage ref and we'll look into this."[34] Today's consumers are more empowered than ever before. Social networks give people immediate platforms from which they can broadcast their messages. As in the case of Syed's lost luggage, consumers are now even taking the added step of buying their messages in an effort to communicate with companies. On a business level, there is really no excuse for not providing a real-time response to any type of social media issue. If a company is going to have a presence on social networking sites, it must also have a well-thought-out, online, strategic customer service policy in place. This plan should instruct employees in how to respond to disgruntled customers, provide examples of messaging, and include an action plan for escalated incidents deemed potential crises for the company or brand. The takeaway here is that with any crisis situation, it is vital to respond with humility. The response from British Airways lacked any degree of understanding, empathy, or compassion. Social customer service teams should be empowered to engage in a timely, personalized manner that illustrates to customers that the brand is listening and cares about what the customer is saying.

Today's Reality

Public relations practitioners should expect that within the first seconds or minutes after a crisis arises targeting a company, brand, or organization, conversations related to the crisis will be mentioned, shared, and talked about online. In the highly interconnected environment in which we conduct business today, the chance that a crisis can go viral has become extremely high. Knowing how to communicate with fans on the correct social networking platforms is critical to being able to properly manage a social media crisis.

#LRNSMPR

Learn More: Crisis Communication

- "Watch: What 2015's 'Big Six' PR Crises Can Teach Us about Crisis Communications": http://bit.ly/1UoLtly
- "6 Social Media 'Musts' for Crisis Communication": http://bit.ly/1O40eN4
- "Bombers Doping Scandal Is PR Disaster of the Decade!": http://bit.ly/1NYTOAY
- "What a Marketing Firm Did When a Former Client Killed Cecil the Lion": http://bit.ly/1StQTn0
- "Miss Puerto Rico Suspended after anti-Muslim Tweets": http://bit.ly/22FFrJw

Notes

[1] "Crisis Management in the Social Media Age," PR Council, 2014, accessed November 16, 2015, http://prcouncil.net/wp-content/uploads/2011/03/Affect_Social_Media_Crisis_Management_White_Paper.pdf.

[2] Freshfields, "Half of Businesses Unprepared to Handle 'Digital Age' Crises," Freshfields Bruckhaus Deringer, November 13, 2013, http://www.freshfields.com/en/news/Half_of_businesses_unprepared_to_handle_%E2%80%98digital_age%E2%80%99_crises.

[3] Freshfields, "Half of Businesses Unprepared to Handle 'Digital Age' Crises."

[4] Philip Howard, "The Arab Spring's Cascading Effects," *Pacific Standard*, February 11, 2011, accessed November 13, 2013, http://www.psmag.com/politics/the-cascading-effects-of-the-arab-spring-28575.

[5] Julian Hoffmann, "BP Oil Spill: Failed Crisis Communication," *My PR Master*, January 17, 2013, http://myprmaster.wordpress.com/2013/01/17/bp-oil-spill-failed-crisis-communication.

[6] Ian Capstick, "5 Digital PR Lessons from BP's Oil Spill Response," *Media Shift*, July 12, 2010, http://www.pbs.org/mediashift/2010/07/5-digital-pr-lessons-from-bps-oil-spill-response193.

[7] Konrad Palubicki, "Friday Five: Crisis Management in a Digital Age," Edelman Digital, June 14, 2013, http://www.edelmandigital.com/2013/06/14/friday-five-crisis-management-in-a-digital-age.

[8] Amy Neumann, "5 Steps for Crisis Management Using Social Media," *Huffington Post*, August 20, 2012, accessed October 16, 2013, http://www.huffingtonpost.com/amy-neumann/5-steps-for-crisis-manage_b_1791673.html.

[9] Kathleen Fearn-Banks, *Crisis Communication: A Casebook Approach*, 4th ed. (New York: Routledge, 2011).

[10] Palubicki, "Friday Five: Crisis Management in a Digital Age."

[11] Palubicki, "Friday Five: Crisis Management in a Digital Age."

[12] Fearn-Banks, *Crisis Communication*.

[13] Palubicki, "Friday Five: Crisis Management in a Digital Age."

[14] Palubicki, "Friday Five: Crisis Management in a Digital Age."

[15] Neumann, "5 Steps for Crisis Management Using Social Media."

[16] Ashley Southhall, "A Twitter Message about AIDS, Followed by a Firing and an Apology," *The Lede* (blog), *New York Times*, December 20, 2013, http://thelede.blogs.nytimes.com/2013/12/20/a-twitter-message-about-aids-africa-and-race/?_r=1; Rob Beschizza, "The Tweet Heard Round the World," *Boing Boing*, December 20, 2013, http://boingboing.net/2013/12/20/the-tweet-heard-round-the-worl.html.

[17] Kami Dimitrova, Shahriar Rahmanzadeh, and Jane Lipman, "Justine Sacco, Fired after Tweet on AIDS in Africa, Issues Apology," *ABC News*, December 22, 2013, http://abcnews.go.com/International/justine-sacco-fired-tweet-aids-africa-issues-apology/story?id=21301833.

[18] Leslie Poston, "Shining Examples of Excellent Social Media Crisis Management," Salesforce Marketing Cloud, September 21, 2012, http://www.salesforcemarketingcloud.com/blog/2012/09/shining-examples-of-excellent-social-media-crisis-management.

[19] Amy Bingham, "Oreo Pride: Rainbow-Stuffed Cookie Sparks Threats of Boycott," *ABC News*, June 26, 2012, accessed October 19, 2013, http://abcnews.go.com/blogs/politics/2012/06/oreo-pride-rainbow-stuffed-cookie-sparks-boycott.

[20] M. Agnes, "JC Penney Handled Their Hitler Teapot Debacle like a Pro," Melissa Agnes Crisis Management, May 29, 2013, http://www.melissaagnescrisismanagement.com/jc-penney-handled-their-hitler-teapot-debacle-like-a-pro.

[21] Alana Horowitz, "Burger King Twitter Account Hacked," *Huffington Post*, February 18, 2012, accessed October 19, 2013, http://www.huffingtonpost.com/2013/02/18/burger-king-twitter-hacked_n_2711661.html.

[22] Kristen Lee, "What a Twit! KitchenAid Takes a Beating over Tasteless Rogue Tweet about Obama's Dead Grandmother," *Huffington Post*, October 4, 2012, accessed October 19, 2013, http://www.huffingtonpost.com/2013/02/18/burger-king-twitter-hacked_n_2711661.html.

[23] Brian Anthony Hernandez, "KitchenAid Tweets Joke about Obama's Dead Grandma [Updated]," *Mashable*, October 3, 2012, http://mashable.com/2012/10/03/kitchen-aid-obama-dead-grandma.

[24] Ben Dipierto, "Crisis of the Week: Volkswagen Scandal Pollutes Carmaker's Reputation," *Risk Compliance* (blog), *Wall Street Journal*, September 28, 2015, accessed November 16, 2015, http://blogs.wsj.com/riskandcompliance/2015/09/28/crisis-of-the-week-volkswagen-scandal-pollutes-carmakers-reputation.

[25] Dipierto, "Crisis of the Week."

[26] Dipierto, "Crisis of the Week."

[27] R. L. Stollar, "Applebee's Overnight Social Media Meltdown: A Photo Essay," *Overturning Tables*, February 2, 2013, http://rlstollar.wordpress.com/2013/02/02/applebees-overnight-social-media-meltdown-a-photo-essay.

28 Dean Spencer, "Social Media Storm Hits Applebee's Hard," *American Citizen's Daily*, February 8, 2013, http://tacdnews.com/2013/02/08/social-media-storm-hits-applebees-hard.

29 Baer, *Youtility*.

30 Melissa Agnes, "Lessons to Learn from Paula Deen's Three Crappy Apologies," Melissa Agnes Crisis Management, June 24, 2013, http://www.melissaagnescrisismanagement.com/lessons-to-learn-from-paula-deens-three-crappy-apologies.

31 Emanuella Grinberg, "Paula Deen under Fire for Photo of Son in Brownface," CNN, July 7, 2015, accessed November 16, 2015, http://www.cnn.com/2015/07/07/living/paula-deen-brownface-feat.

32 Grinberg, "Paula Deen under Fire for Photo of Son in Brownface."

33 Todd Wasserman, "Man Buys Promoted Tweet to Complain about British Airways," *Mashable*, September 2, 2013, http://mashable.com/2013/09/02/man-promoted-tweet-british-airways.

34 Katy Ryan Schamberger, "British Airways Sponsored Tweet: Customer Service Is Critical," *Business 2 Community*, September 9, 2013, http://www.business2community.com/customer-experience/british-airways-sponsored-tweet-customer-service-critical-0609554.

Social Media Ethics

Todays public relations professionals are faced with a variety of ethical dilemmas, many of which result from the introduction and use of social media. Due to their interactive nature beyond traditional media forms, social media possess unique characteristics that present unforeseen ethical dilemmas for working professionals.

Doing What's Right

The social sphere can be considered as an evolutionary entity, neither static in nature nor fixed. As in any developing system, there are a variety of challenges and moral opportunities that present themselves over time. If we consider the first generation of the web, while important in the advancement of technology for companies, it simply did not represent a major variation in how businesses and ethical situations were handled. In contrast, the most recent version of the web has in fact changed the way technology is used, and therefore it presents unique challenges to professionals.[1]

Ethics has been defined as "standards of conduct that indicate how one should behave based on moral duties and virtues."[2] These values provide the framework for determining the difference between behaviors that are considered correct and those that are not. In principle, this may seem like a simple exercise; however, the line between conveying the truth, playing fair, telling a lie, and purposefully hurting others is oftentimes blurred. Each of us has our own litmus for what's right and wrong. A person's ethical beliefs and approach to decision making depend on a variety of factors, including culture, education, economics, and religion, among others.[3] It may be that one individual believes that it is inappropriate to write a ghost blog on behalf of a client, while a colleague feels that it is just part of his or her job. The process of making ethics-based decisions can be murky at best.

As rapidly as business is conducted today, decisions are often made quickly, leaving much room for error. Many of the more severe, yet common, ethical dilemmas faced by practitioners include lying for a client, engaging in deceptive practices by gathering information about another practitioner's client, helping to conceal illegal acts, or presenting true but slightly misleading information in an interview.[4] Consider what you would do if a client asked you to tweet on his or her behalf, write a positive review on a forum, repin a post on Pinterest, or, better yet, friend the competition on Facebook. Would you judge these requests as unethical? The Public Relations Society of America (PRSA) has developed ethical standards for use in the profession to help answer such questions. Because social media have not yet adopted a set of standardized guidelines to use when faced with ethical situations, PR practitioners should refer to the PRSA code of ethics as their guide.

Public relations practitioners serve as advocates for the organizations that they assist, their clients, and various other stakeholders. Ethical situations are bound to arise with such a multitude of external factors. The PRSA standards help practitioners by providing guidance when making difficult decisions. The following six values provide the foundation for the PRSA member code of ethics and set the industry standard for the professional practice of public relations:[5]

ADVOCACY: We serve the public interest by acting as responsible advocates for those we represent. We provide a voice in the marketplace of ideas, facts, and viewpoints to aid informed public debate.

HONESTY: We adhere to the highest standards of accuracy and truth in advancing the interests of those we represent and in communicating with the public.

EXPERTISE: We acquire and responsibly use specialized knowledge and experience. We advance the profession through continued expert-level development, research, and education. We build mutual understanding, credibility, and relationships among a wide array of institutions and audiences.

INDEPENDENCE: We provide objective counsel to those we represent. We are accountable for our actions.

LOYALTY: We are faithful to those we represent, while also honoring our obligation to serve the public interest.

FAIRNESS: We deal fairly with clients, employers, competitors, peers, vendors, the media, and the general public. We respect all opinions and support the right of free expression.

For public relations professionals, ethical dilemmas arise when responsibilities and loyalties conflict and a resulting decision must be made regarding the appropriate ethical course of action. The following guide, which has been adapted to meet the specific needs of public relations professionals, is offered as one approach for practitioners to reference when addressing ethical dilemmas:[6]

* Identify the specific ethical issue or conflict.
* Identify internal/external factors (e.g., legal, political, social, economic) that may influence the decision.
* Identify the key values associated with the PRSA code of ethics that may be under violation.
* Identify the parties who will be affected by the decision and understand the professional obligation to each that the practitioner possesses.
* Select the ethical principle to guide the PR practitioner through the decision-making process.
* Make a decision and justify it.

PRSA has been a leader in the effort to foster a strong sense of professionalism among its membership. The principles included in the PRSA code of ethics indicate that the practice of public relations is built on trust, transparency, and the protection of the public interest by providing honest and accurate information. It is important that public relations professionals, who are responsible for managing social media outlets, be well versed in workplace and business ethics.

Practicing Good Ethics within Social Media

The ability to make the appropriate ethical decisions can promote an increase in trust, loyalty, and friendship. As for poor ethical choices, well, we've seen where those lead far too often. There are several common ethical dilemmas that occur on social media that can result in challenging situations if not identified and dealt with appropriately.

International Relations

CIPR Code of Ethics

According to the Chartered Institute of Public Relations (CIPR), "Reputation has a direct and major impact on the corporate well-being of every organization. That is why the professionalism of public relations practitioners is so important. As the voice of the PR profession, we play a key role in setting and maintaining standards. We do this through a code of conduct which we encourage all our members to follow."

The CIPR provides a series of seven videos on its website that not only explain the code of ethics but also give real-world examples and provide solutions. See http://www.cipr.co.uk/content/about-us/our-organisation/professionalism-and-ethics.

Source: "Professionalism and Ethics," CIPR, 2015, accessed November 20, 2015, http://www.cipr.co.uk/content/about-us/our-organisation/professionalism-and-ethics.

Spamming

Companies are continuously promoting their products and services; however, there is a big difference between reaching out, connecting, and engaging with consumers and spamming them by way of posting links and promotional messages. If you recall from earlier in the book, the Pareto principle comes into play here: 80 percent of the time you should be providing valuable information to consumers, with the remaining 20 percent devoted specifically to your company. Answer questions, give sneak peeks, and talk about what's happening in the industry. Share what's going on beyond the events that are occurring within your organization. Spam is never received well.

Public Feuds

With consumer relations at an all-time high as a result of social platforms, it can be easy to allow for an argument to go public on your social channels. Fans not only follow brands but are also loyal to the people who promote those brands. As practitioners it is important to remember that you represent your company *all of the time*, not just during work hours. Even when you are on the soccer field, at the grocery store, or enjoying that nice Sunday morning latte at the local cafe, you are still representing your company and your clients. Social media is about helping others, not about putting them down. Public feuds are far more likely to damage your personal or organizational reputation than help it.

Lying

As we have seen on multiple occasions throughout the book, transparency is a fundamental principle of social media. There is simply no place for lying within a transparent environment. The act of lying to your consumer base tarnishes the company's brand image and results in a substantial breach of trust.

Eric Schwartzman, founder, Comply Socially

Did you know it's illegal to buy fake reviews on social networks and plenty of companies have been fined upwards of $250,000 for this sort of skullduggery?

Misrepresentation

This act should also be guided by the "Be transparent" rule. While you may not necessarily be lying to your desired public by liking and sharing a new product that your client has launched, you are also being dishonest when you do not inform the social community of your association with that company. Be forthcoming.

As a rule, if you are being compensated by a client or organization to provide a product review or contribute to its digital footprint, the guidelines set forth by the U.S. Federal Trade Commission require that this information be officially recorded and disclosed. It is important to keep in mind that endorsements and reviews are intended to depict the views and feelings from actual consumers regarding a specific product or service. If you fail to reveal that you have been compensated for your review, one could consider this an act of wrongfully influencing a customer base.

Eric Schwartzman, founder, Comply Socially

Did you know that if employees tweet on behalf of their employer without disclosing their employee status, their employer can be fined up to $11,000 per incident?

Disclosing Sensitive Company or Client Information

Most public relations practitioners typically have access to sensitive company information, including proprietary software; details about a planned product or service launch, event, or media release; or even a "secret ingredient." This information must always be protected.

As organizations become more sophisticated in their engagement with stakeholders, challenges surrounding ethical decisions and the subsequent legal implications of those actions are bound to frame some of the discussion. Social networking platforms are sometimes referred to by lawyers as the "Wild West" because social media still seem to operate outside normal laws and regulations.

Social Media and the Law

According to Eric Schwartzman, founder of Comply Socially, "Technology advances faster than government can adapt, so laws that were enacted before social media existed often determine its lawful use."[7] Unethical decisions often provide the potential for malpractice because they fail to conform to fundamental obligations of the professional communicator to foster informed decision making in a democratic society.[8] PRSA has identified three areas of concern.

Deceptive Online Practices

Defined under the PRSA code of ethics, the source of editorial material must be clearly identified. Any attempts to mislead or deceive an uninformed audience are considered malpractice. The PRSA code calls for truth and transparency and full disclosure of the causes and interests represented. The goal should be responsible advocacy on behalf of clients, building and sustaining credibility with all audiences, and strengthening the public's trust in the information that it receives. Deceptive practices lead to unethical advocacy. Within the code, Professional Standards Advisory PS-8 specifically targets deceptive online practices by individuals or organizations using blogs, viral marketing, and anonymous Internet posting.[9]

Front Groups

Third-party groups, commonly referred to as "front groups," are established to foster misrepresentation and unethical advocacy by deceiving or misleading an audience about a particular position on a topic, as well as its source. In Professional Standards Advisory PS-7, the PRSA code of ethics details the unethical nature of engaging in or assisting such groups' deceptive descriptions of goals, causes, tactics, sponsors, intentions, or participants. The ethical communicator

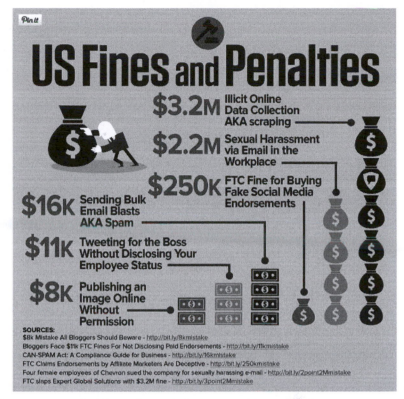

US Fines and Penalties

$3.2M Illicit Online Data Collection AKA scraping

$2.2M Sexual Harassment via Email in the Workplace

$250K FTC Fine for Buying Fake Social Media Endorsements

$16K Sending Bulk Email Blasts AKA Spam

$11K Tweeting for the Boss Without Disclosing Your Employee Status

$8K Publishing an Image Online Without Permission

SOURCES:
$8k Mistake All Bloggers Should Beware - http://bit.ly/8kmistake
Bloggers Face $11k FTC Fines For Not Disclosing Paid Endorsements - http://bit.ly/11kmistake
CAN-SPAM Act: A Compliance Guide for Business - http://bit.ly/16kmistake
FTC Claims Endorsements by Affiliate Marketers Are Deceptive - http://bit.ly/250kmistake
Four female employees of Chevron sued the company for sexually harassing e-mail - http://bit.ly/2point2Mmistake
FTC slaps Expert Global Solutions with $3.2M fine - http://bit.ly/3point2Mmistake

is obligated to reveal all information needed for informed decision making, thereby maintaining the public trust. Purposefully withholding or disingenuously concealing sources or sponsors of information, including their intentions or motivations, fails to satisfy the principles of truth in advancing the interest of clients and serving the public interest as responsible advocates.[10]

Pay for Play

Providing payment to generate or influence editorial coverage, regardless of the channel, is unethical and constitutes malpractice under the PRSA code. This should be obvious because such exchanges of value are hidden from the reader, viewer, or listener. The PRSA code defends the values of honesty, fairness, transparency, and objective counsel to clients. "Pay for play" directly contrasts with the code's warning to avoid any conflict of interest that impedes the trust of clients, employers, or the public. Under Professional Standards Advisory PS-9, professionals are told to disclose any exchange of compensation so that readers, viewers, or listeners have the opportunity to make up their own minds about the value, bias, accuracy, and usefulness of information provided by others.[11]

Should Ethics Combine with Social Media Policies?

Both ethics and social media are undeniably essential and interrelated within the practice of public relations. The question that arises is, What is the best way to manage these two aspects simultaneously?[12] Should they be treated as separate and distinct conversations? Should ethics be specifically addressed within a company's social media policy?

Ultimately, the conversations resulting from an employee's online presence are a direct reflection of the business. When creating a policy governing ethics and social

> ## Theory into Practice

Deceptive Practices

The Public Relations Society of America (PRSA) issued a statement that condemned instances of promotional tactics that were unethical in the field of public relations. It reads, "PRSA states categorically that misrepresenting the nature of editorial content or intentionally failing to clearly reveal the source of message contents is unethical."[1]

PRSA lists the following as examples of unethical practices:

- A public relations firm's engaging its interns to write positive product reviews for online message boards
- A lobbying firm's sending letters using another organizations' letterhead
- Bloggers posting positive reviews of products and services while receiving products for free, as well as being paid by the sponsor for such positive reviews
- A marketing firm's creating a program to match clients with influencers for positive mentions
- Special interest groups setting up and funding front groups to disseminate information without disclosing the true source

While examples vary in method and execution, each scenario shares a common, unethical behavior. Each practice illustrates a failure to conform to fundamental obligations of the professional communicator to protect and advance the free flow of accurate and truthful information and foster informed decision making in a democratic society.

Using the PRSA code of ethics as your guide, rationalize whether or not the following scenarios would be considered unethical, and then discuss how you would respond to your boss or client.

Tweeting on Behalf of a Client[2]

You work at a PR agency and your client is speaking at an international conference. The client is a well-known influencer in her field and one of the few C-Suite executives that "get" social media. In fact, this individual has a loyal and active following on Twitter, posting regularly, often several times per day.

Your client would prefer that her Twitter feed reflect her activity at the conference and highlight what else is happening. She's concerned that she will not be able to support everything with all of her obligations to the conference.

This client trusts your agency implicitly and asks you to "take over" her Twitter account during the conference. What do you do?

Commenting to Consumers[3]

Your client is an absolute giant in the sports industry. It has deep pockets and an even bigger following on the social sphere but only one internal staff member responsible for managing its social media outlets. Admittedly, when one person must both monitor and engage directly with fans through multiple online channels, this can be overwhelming. This client has asked your agency to be its eyes and voice when engaging with its sports fans. It trusts you and feels that you know its audience just as much as an internal staff member. What do you do?

Posting Positive Reviews

Your agency just took on a new client, a small restaurant serving burgers and craft beer. Eager to get good reviews on Yelp, it asks you to post positive reviews of the restaurant and the food. This is an obvious violation of the PRSA code of ethics, so you decline. However, a few days later you notice that the restaurant has fifteen positive reviews and is not slated to open for another three weeks. You are an agency of record, with a reputation to protect. It is known within the community that your agency is working with this restaurant, conducting its public relations efforts. What do you say to the client?

---

1 "PRSA Condemns the Growing Use of Disingenuous Editorial Content, Deceptive Commentary on Blogs and Other Venues."
2 Todd Defren, "Real-World Ethical Dilemmas in Social Media," PRSquared Social Media Marketing and Public Relations RSS, January 25, 2010, accessed November 20, 2015, http://www.pr-squared.com/index.php/2010/01/real-world-ethical-dilemmas-in-social-media-upcoming-series.
3 Defren, "Real-World Ethical Dilemmas in Social Media."

media, it is imperative to address employee expectations and behavior. Expectations of a business online, and even offline, should be included in order to create an identity. Conversations on the social sphere are different from in-person conversations or even printed communication pieces. Be aware of the ways in which social media can be used: Which audiences are receiving your message, who is sharing messages, and what are they sharing? Take responsibility for any online behaviors—positive and negative—and understand the logic behind having an online presence. Whether a company chooses to incorporate ethics into its social media policy or deal with the two topics independently, setting expectations, conducting training, and enforcing accountable behavior is essential. The book delves more deeply into creating solid social media policies in a separate chapter.

#LRNSMPR

Learn More: Ethics in Social Media

- "Ethical Practice of Social Media in Public Relations": http://bit.ly/1SQun9R
- "#Ethics in the Age of Social Media and Public Conversations": http://bit.ly/1PCeNdJ
- "Ethics and the Five Deadly Sins of Social Media": http://onforb.es/1RJiq45
- "The Ethical Challenges of Social Media": http://bit.ly/1TlhbYF
- "The Ethics of Social Media Accuracy": http://huff.to/1R672ND

Notes

1. David Gunkel, "Social Media: Changing the Rules of Business Ethics," *NIU Newsroom*, March 15, 2015, accessed November 20, 2015, http://newsroom.niu.edu/2015/03/17/social-media-changing-the-rules-of-business-ethics.
2. Michael Josephson, "Making Ethical Decisions: The Six Pillars of Character," Josephson Institute, accessed November 20, 2015, http://josephsoninstitute.org/med/med-2sixpillars.
3. Fraser P. Seitel, *The Practice of Public Relations*, 8th ed. (Upper Saddle River, NJ: Prentice Hall, 2014).
4. Patricia Swann, *Cases in Public Relations Management* (Boston: McGraw Hill, 2014).
5. "Public Relations Society of America (PRSA) Member Code of Ethics," PRSA, 2015, accessed November 20, 2015, https://www.prsa.org/aboutprsa/ethics/codeenglish/#.Vk8_enarS70.
6. Kathy Fitzpatrick, "Ethical Decision-Making Guide Helps Resolve Ethical Dilemmas," PRSA, accessed November 21, 2015, http://www.prsa.org/AboutPRSA/Ethics/documents/decisionguide.pdf.
7. Eric Schwartzman, "How to Prevent a Social Media Crisis," *PRNewser*, June 25, 2015, accessed November 21, 2015, http://www.adweek.com/prnewser/how-to-prevent-a-social-media-crisis/115650.
8. "PRSA Condemns the Growing Use of Disingenuous Editorial Content, Deceptive Commentary on Blogs and Other Venues," PRSA, August 27, 2009, accessed November 20, 2015, http://media.prsa.org/article_print.cfm?article_id=1370.
9. "PRSA Condemns the Growing Use of Disingenuous Editorial Content."
10. "PRSA Condemns the Growing Use of Disingenuous Editorial Content."
11. "PRSA Condemns the Growing Use of Disingenuous Editorial Content."
12. Sharlyn Lauby, "Ethics and Social Media: Where Should You Draw the Line?," *Mashable*, March 17, 2012, accessed November 20, 2015, http://mashable.com/2012/03/17/social-media-ethics/#C0O.TcSaZqqG.

Rules of Engagement 12

Organizations that conduct business in today's on-demand media environment should possess a social media policy; yet, surprisingly, very few do. Social media policies provide a framework for carrying out social strategies and implementing tactics.

Establishing the Groundwork

Like traditional public relations and social media planning, social media policies are part of a larger, more encompassing strategy. As a company establishes the groundwork for its public relations and social media efforts, instituting clear objectives and a strategy to achieve them is paramount. Development of such a strategy fosters cross-departmental coordination and encourages synergistic cooperation throughout the organization. It also requires strategic input from the individuals tasked with drafting the document and those intending to engage in social media communications on behalf of the organization. The most successful strategies result from the combined opinions and recommendations of many individuals, and regardless of job title or level, all contribute to the larger cause.

Companies face various forms and levels of risk when engaging in social media strategies. However, the necessary steps to mitigate risks tend to all be fairly similar. Often referred to as social media policies or social media guidelines, these parameters provide a framework for when employees interact online. Some companies may choose to implement rigid policies that spell out exactly what is permissible on company-sponsored social media channels, while others may develop policies that serve as a reference point for staff but allow them flexibility in making decisions on their own.

All companies are unique; as a result, their social media policies are also unique. Social media policies tend to reflect the personality of the company. While a single template or set of standards applicable to all businesses or organizations has yet to be developed, most social media policies share the following characteristics:[1]

Trust and Respect: Good policies stem from mutual trust. The policy should foster a positive atmosphere in which employees are free to share personal opinions while respecting the opinions of others without living in fear of retribution. Effective policies outline acceptable online employee behavior rather than listing the actions that are forbidden.

Values: Companies should reflect upon their core values and overarching company culture when drafting their social media policies.[2] This will provide the correct foundation to build a policy that is central to the work that the company does. These values might include integrity, respect, humility, teamwork, and accountability. Respect is a core value often found within many organizations. It might then make sense to include a point within the social media policy related to respecting others' opinions and valuing all contributions. A policy addressing respect may read as follows: "It's OK to be yourself and say what is on your mind, but do so respectfully. We want you to connect with colleagues and engage with the larger community. We just ask that when you do, you provide value, share content, ask questions, and

Social Media Policy

52%

52% of online adults use multiple social media sites

Setting the right expectations at work is paramount

Policies

- Provide clear expectations
- Protect the reputation clients & the business

Qualities every policy should include:
- Trust & Respect
- Values Driven
- Fluid
- Jargon Free
- No Zero Tolerance
- Sensible
- Friendly
- Consistent
- Clear Consequences

Quality

80%

80% of employers have official social media policies

70% have disciplined an employee for social media misuse

Less than one-third offer training on how to use social media responsibly

Sources:

Cision. "Developing Social Media Policies," last modified 2009, accessed November 8, 2013.

"Social Media Update 2014." Pew Research Center Internet Science Tech RSS. January 9, 2015. Accessed November 21, 2015. http://www.pewinternet.org/2015/01/09/social-media-update-2014/.

Schwartzman, Eric. "How to Prevent a Social Media Crisis." PRNewser. June 25, 2015. Accessed November 21, 2015. http://www.adweek.com/prnewser/how-to-prevent-a-social-media-crisis/115650.

participate in meaningful conversations politely, considerately, and without malice toward others."

Fluidity: Companies should be open to adjusting and incorporating changes into their policies over time. Just as social media sites change over time, policies should be fluid enough to accommodate future modifications. If policies and guidelines are narrowly focused, they may become outdated rather quickly.[3] Successful social media policies tend to capture the big picture, are not overly complicated, and are easy to understand.

Avoidance of Zero Tolerance: Stay away from using words such as "always," "must," "shall," and "never."[4] A "zero-tolerance policy" can be extremely tough to implement and problematic to enforce. The legal restrictions within this area are currently evolving at an unprecedented rate. Consider it a best practice to consult the legal and human resources departments for guidance during severe or ongoing circumstances.[5]

Lack of Jargon: Eliminate highly technical language or legalese. Develop a policy that can be understood across departments. This will encourage participation and become more meaningful to employees.

Sensibleness: The policy should not be so complicated that employees need a reference book to understand what to do when they need to interact on social media channels. Provide practical examples and easy-to-understand points. Encourage employees to reference the policy when they are faced with a new or unfamiliar situation.

Friendliness: Policies should be written in such a way that encourages participation. This should include all acceptable actions and employee empowerments.

Consistency: The best policy is one that is consistent with regard to participation and enforcement throughout the organization. Consistency helps organizations keep their social media efforts on course while also avoiding accusations of favoritism or discrimination.[6]

Clear Consequences: Employees should know what actions the company will take if they violate any part of the social media policy. Should the company need to take action, make certain that the employees are afforded due process and are allowed to present their side of the story.[7] If the transgression requires serious disciplinary consequences, including termination, due process will become even more important.

Social media policies are "living" documents. This means that once the policy is created, it should not simply be put away and forgotten. Organizations should review and modify their policies on a recurring basis—perhaps quarterly or biannually. A company might consider some of the following questions when revising its social media policy or guidelines:

Is the policy still relevant?
Have any social media sites changed? If so, do the changes impact our policy?
Has the online environment changed? If so, what should we consider revising?
Are there legal updates that need to be addressed?
Does anything new need to be added? If so, what?
Are there any gaps?
Does a guideline require any clarification? Are examples necessary?

As these policies are revised, seek employee feedback. Keeping the line of communication open and free will maintain continued interest among staff.

Rolling Out the Policy

Once the social media policy is finalized and ready for implementation, take the time to communicate to employees the importance of every aspect of the policy. An organization's human resources, legal, and public relations departments can serve as hosts for various events to roll out the new social media policy. As with any other company initiative, create a buzz and drive excitement. Make a big deal out of the new policy.

Consider starting with a number of informal "brown bag lunch" sessions. Invite staff to attend several planned luncheons at which the policy is presented and explained and employees have the opportunity to ask questions. For smaller businesses, one session may be sufficient, but in larger organizations with multiple sites, it may be necessary to schedule multiple sessions. Employees are more likely to participate if they are given flexibility regarding attendance at an informational meeting.

Once the in-person, educational sessions are completed, companies can create and post a video outlining the guidelines, allowing employees to access the information at will. This material can be posted to the company website or Intranet. A series of blog posts can also be written to illustrate examples, best practices, and case studies.[8] Employees tend to respond with the same enthusiasm that is exhibited by the company. If a company shows a low level of interest regarding the social media policy, it should expect that employees will mimic that same behavior.

Key Sections

Social media policies have three main sections: an introduction, the main policy points, and a conclusion. The following list highlights five examples of corporate social media policies that you can review, analyze, and consider as you draft your own set of guidelines. Make note of the key sections as you read these policies.

> *Best Buy:* Under the premise of "Be smart. Be respectful. Be human," Best Buy clearly presents its dos and don'ts for all company employees engaging in social media activities (http://bit.ly/HJee3k).
>
> *Oracle:* Oracle provides a stricter approach to its social media policy. This set of guidelines includes a higher degree of specificity and also provides pertinent examples (http://bit.ly/HNDs0y).
>
> *Walmart:* Walmart's social media policies speak to almost every area of online engagement, from intellectual property to disgruntled employees to social media engagement (http://bit.ly/18mihJn).

International Relations

Advice for Employers from the CIPR

According to the UK-based Chartered Institute of Public Relations (CIPR), European businesses are also debating the boundaries companies should set for their employees' use of social media. While there is no definitive answer, the CIPR advises that both the employer and employee take responsibility for understanding and adhering to social media best practices. CIPR suggests that employers should support their employees and ensure that employees know what defines good practice and clear company policies.

Source: "Public Relations Social Media Panel" (lecture, Chartered Institute of Public Relations, London, December 1, 2013).

National Labor Relations Board

As the presence of social media expands within business, the court systems throughout the United States are experiencing an influx of employee lawsuits against their employers.[1] Numerous court cases regarding social media within business arenas that focus on labor relations issues and related violations by employers continue to appear. For this reason, in May 2012 the National Labor Relations Board (NLRB) created a sample of a lawful social media policy for employers to use as a guideline. Take a moment to read the policy from the NLRB and then choose a social media policy presented within the chapter or one found on the Social Media Governance website (http://bit.ly/18cWVOl). Compare the two.

What are the differences?

Are the guidelines too broad?

Are there any guidelines that might be considered open to interpretation?

How might you need to amend these guidelines in order to apply them to your organization?

Are there any guidelines that are not clear or that could be misinterpreted by an employee?

A Sample Social Media Policy from the NLRB[2]

At [Employer], we understand that social media can be a fun and rewarding way to share your experiences and opinions with family, friends, and coworkers around the world. However, the use of social media also presents certain risks and carries with it certain responsibilities. To assist you in making responsible decisions about your use of social media, we have established these guidelines for appropriate use of social media.

This policy applies to all associates who work for [Employer], or one of its subsidiary companies in the United States ([Employer]). Managers and supervisors should use the supplemental Social Media Management Guidelines for additional guidance in administering the policy.

Guidelines

In the rapidly expanding world of electronic communication, *social media* can mean many things. *Social media* includes all means of communicating or posting information or content of any sort on the Internet, including to your own or someone else's web log or blog, journal or diary, personal website, social networking or affinity website, web bulletin board or a chat room, whether or not associated or affiliated with [Employer], as well as any other form of electronic communication.

The same principles and guidelines found in [Employer] policies and three basic beliefs apply to your activities online. Ultimately, you are solely responsible for what you post online. Before creating online content, consider some of the risks and rewards that are involved. Keep in mind that any aspect of your conduct that adversely affects your job performance, the performance of fellow associates, or otherwise adversely affects members, customers, suppliers, people who work on behalf of [Employer] or [Employer's] legitimate business interests may result in disciplinary action up to and including termination.

Know and Follow the Rules

Carefully read these guidelines, the [Employer] Statement of Ethics Policy, the [Employer] Information Policy, and the Discrimination and Harassment Prevention Policy, and ensure your postings are consistent with these policies. Inappropriate postings that may include discriminatory remarks, harassment, and threats of violence or similar inappropriate or unlawful conduct will not be tolerated and may subject you to disciplinary action up to and including termination.

Be Respectful

Always be fair and courteous to fellow associates, customers, members, suppliers, or people who work on behalf of [Employer]. Also, keep in mind that you are more likely to resolve work-related complaints by speaking directly with your coworkers or by utilizing our Open Door Policy than by posting complaints to a social media outlet. Nevertheless, if you decide to post complaints or criticism, avoid using statements, photographs, video, or audio that reasonably could be viewed as malicious, obscene, threatening, or intimidating; that disparage customers, members, associates, or suppliers; or that might constitute harassment or bullying. Examples of such conduct might include offensive posts meant to intentionally harm someone's reputation or posts that could contribute to a hostile work environment on the basis of race, sex, disability, religion, or any other status protected by law or company policy.

Be Honest and Accurate

Make sure you are always honest and accurate when posting information or news, and if you make a mistake, correct it quickly. Be open about any previous posts you have altered. Remember that the Internet archives almost everything; therefore, even deleted postings can be searched. Never post any information or rumors that you know to be false about [Employer], fellow associates, members, customers, suppliers, people working on behalf of [Employer], or competitors.

Post Only Appropriate and Respectful Content

Maintain the confidentiality of [Employer] trade secrets and private or confidential information. Trade secrets may include information regarding the development of systems, processes, products, know-how, and technology. Do not post internal reports, policies, procedures, or other internal business-related confidential communications.

Respect financial disclosure laws. It is illegal to communicate or give a "tip" on inside information to others so that they may buy or sell stocks or securities. Such online conduct may also violate the Insider Trading Policy.

Do not create a link from your blog, website, or other social networking site to a [Employer] website without identifying yourself as a [Employer] associate.

Express only your personal opinions. Never represent yourself as a spokesperson for [Employer]. If [Employer] is a subject of the content you are creating, be clear and open about the fact that you are an associate and make it clear that your views do not represent those of [Employer], fellow associates, members, customers, suppliers, or people

working on behalf of [Employer]. If you do publish a blog or post online related to the work you do or subjects associated with [Employer], make it clear that you are not speaking on behalf of [Employer]. It is best to include a disclaimer, such as "The postings on this site are my own and do not necessarily reflect the views of [Employer]."

Using Social Media at Work

Refrain from using social media while on work time or on equipment we provide, unless it is work related as authorized by your manager or consistent with the Company Equipment Policy.

Do not use [Employer] email addresses to register on social networks, blogs, or other online tools utilized for personal use.

Retaliation Is Prohibited

[Employer] prohibits taking negative action against any associate for reporting a possible deviation from this policy or for cooperating in an investigation. Any associate who retaliates against another associate for reporting a possible deviation from this policy or for cooperating in an investigation will be subject to disciplinary action, up to and including termination.

Media Contacts

Associates should not speak to the media on [Employer's] behalf without contacting the Corporate Affairs Department. All media inquiries should be directed to them.

For More Information

If you have questions or need further guidance, please contact your human resources representative.

---

1 Gardner, "Two Great Social Media Law Cases Involving Facebook and LinkedIn."
2 "The NLRB and Social Media," National Labor Relations Board, http://www.nlrb.gov/news-outreach/fact-sheets/nlrb-and-social-media.

IBM: This clear-cut social media policy is specific enough to avoid mistakes created by a lack of common sense demonstrated by employees (http://ibm.co/1gDnS6i).

Shippensburg University (Shippensburg, Pennsylvania): This set of social media guidelines is specific to official university social media accounts. What is great about these guidelines is that they provide employees with numerous outside links that assist with everything from privacy to graphics standards (http://bit.ly/1iZyv0i).

Ubiquitous Sphere

A social media policy is one of the most important sets of guidelines that an organization can develop and execute. A well-thought-out policy will encourage employee participation and interaction with customers, build relationships, foster transparency, and minimize risks. It is unrealistic to think that any company can foresee or protect against what may happen on social media platforms used by employees. A proactive and thoughtful approach to creating social media policies can help avoid many of the pitfalls before they are realized. As long as a company has the appropriate team in place, asks the right questions, revisits the guidelines every now and again, and acknowledges that the culture within the social sphere values transparency, trust, empowerment, and creativity, it is well on its way to creating a policy that fits its needs.

#LRNSMPR

Learn More: Social Media Guidelines

- "NLRB Outlines Employers' Social Media Policy Dos and Don'ts": http://bit.ly/1azPO3p
- "Best Practices for Developing a Social Media Policy": http://bit.ly/1a7tN0Y
- "Six Recent NLRB Cases Provide Further Insight on Structuring Employers' Social Media Policies: http://bit.ly/1MN7dPF
- Southwest Airlines "Social Media Guidelines": http://bit.ly/1iRHNLy
- "Social Media Employee Policy Examples from Over 100 Organizations": http://bit.ly/1cOaRX3

Notes

[1] "Developing Social Media Policies," Cision, last modified 2009, accessed November 8, 2013.

[2] Andrea Berry and Ben Stuart, "Create a Social Media Policy for Your Nonprofit Elines to Cover All of Your Social Media Bases," *Social Brite*, February 5, 2013, http://www.socialbrite.org/2013/02/05/create-a-social-media-policy-for-your-nonprofit.

[3] Berry and Stuart, "Create a Social Media Policy."

[4] Berry and Stuart, "Create a Social Media Policy."

[5] Alyesha Asghar Dotson, "NLRB Outlines Employers' Social Media Policy Dos and Don'ts," Spilman Thomas & Battle, April 29, 2013, http://www.spilmanlaw.com/Resources/Attorney-Authored-Articles/Labor---Employment/NLRB-Outlines-Employers--Social-Media-Policy-Dos-a.

[6] Lindy Dwyear, Maddie Grand, and Leslie White, "Social Media, Risk, and Policies," SocialFish, last modified 2009, accessed November 18, 2013, http://www.socialfish.org/wp-content/downloads/socialfish-policies-whitepaper.pdf.

[7] Dwyear, Grand, and White, "Social Media, Risk, and Policies."

[8] Sean Gardner, "Two Great Social Media Law Cases Involving Facebook and Linked-In," *The 2morrowknight*, September 28, 2013, http://www.2morrowknight.com/two-great-social-media-law-cases-involving-facebook-and-linkedin.

Online Media Centers in a Connected World 13

The online media center is among the highest-ranked webpages on a company website and is an integral part of a successful media relations strategy. If implemented correctly, journalists will flock to this area of a company website, potentially leading to an increase in media coverage.

Make a Good First Impression

Research indicates that reporters continue to take on more work with fewer resources.[1] Public relations professionals can make the job of any media representative easier by creating online media centers allowing journalists a quick and efficient way to find key information necessary to pull together a story. If a reporter has to dig too deep to find information on a company or to determine whether the story has any merit, he or she will simply leave the website.[2] An online media center helps tell a company's story. It is our job as public relations professionals to make it easy for journalists. Developing a compelling online media center, with relevant information, is fairly straightforward. The content should be accessible, easy to share, and easy to find.[3]

Accessible

Flashy is not necessarily better. Too often companies choose appearance over content. Grandiose images, varied logos, flash technology, video intros, and just about every social media technology out there lack true value if journalists cannot find the information they need to complete a story. If you recall, "content is king." Well, the same rule applies here. Content is the driving force behind long-standing, trusting relationships between public relations professionals and journalists. Content such as social media–generated press releases, executive bios, white papers, company logos, and photographs are all essential elements within a company's media center. These elements will be explored in more depth in this chapter.

An important aspect of accessibility to a journalist is the ability to be "found." Make sure to take the appropriate steps to maximize the company's SEO strategy and confirm that the online media center is easily located using major search engines. If this is done properly, web searches using Google, Bing, and Yahoo! should locate the company media center at the top of the results. Journalists should find a prominently featured tab dedicated to the online media center on the website's main home page.[4] Allow journalists to subscribe to categorized RSS feeds or receive email updates when new content becomes available.[5] RSS feeds, email updates, and e-newsletters will draw journalists to the website over and over. Journalists who subscribe to the company's content are demonstrating that they are interested in the company and that the content the company is generating is relevant to them. Moreover, they see the company as a resource for future stories.

International Relations

Accessibility in France

Did you know that in contrast to the United States, France is a high-context culture where nonverbal communication is more important than words? This means that if you are a public relations practitioner in France, building relationships is even more important. In France, the well-being of one's family, the community, or the region is stressed over that of the individual. Moral of this story: get to know the journalist beyond the online press release!

Source: Betty J. Pritchard, Catherine B. Ashles, and Nathalie Bardin, "Public Relations Practice in France Compared to the United States" (lecture, 8th International Public Relations Research Conference, Best Western, South Miami, March 10, 2013).

Easy to Share

Make content easy to share and bookmark—assign each page a unique URL for easy linking, and add social media tags to allow your audience to spread the content for you. You can also embed supplemental video and photos within the media center to make your site more compelling.

Easy to Find

Frequently journalists complain that they are unable to find necessary information. This might include a photo, an old press release, or the contact information of the media relations department for the company. In general, company websites are designed for customers looking for products, services, or information about a company. This makes it critically important to prominently feature the online media center on the home page of the website to make it easier for journalists to contact a company representative. Companies may also refer to the online media center as a "press center" or "newsroom." Regardless of the name, the focus and purpose remain the same: companies have the ability to present themselves to an expansive audience with the intent to motivate more significant participation and openness while potentially boosting organic website SEO.[6]

Business Wire Media Survey

Reporters need specific content and look to online newsrooms to find it. When they research a company, the first place they look is the company's own websites (92 percent), online newsroom (77 percent), and social media channels (42 percent). Reporters prefer websites with a range of usable content, in easy-to-find, easy-to-use formats.

Components of an Ideal Online Media Center

Online media centers should be viewed as a press kit in digital format.[7] They contain similar elements as found within a physical press kit but are clickable and shareable—both of which are essential elements of media relations in our connected world.

> *Press Releases:* Ideal media centers incorporate the most recent press releases and feature them prominently. The media center home page should list three to five of the company's most recent press releases and also link to a separate

SHIFT Communications developed the first template that companies could use as a guide to evolve their online newsrooms for the "social media" age. *Source*: SHIFT Communications.

archive section. Press releases should be listed in reverse chronological order, with the most recent press release listed first. For press releases that garner media coverage, include links to the articles near the press release. McDonald's separates its press releases into corporate news and financial news and makes it easy for journalists to quickly and efficiently locate the information that they need.[8]

Contact Information: Media contacts are one of the most important elements in an online media center. Journalists often complain that they cannot quickly locate the public relations contact information on a media center webpage without clicking at least five times.[9] This can potentially lead to missing out on media coverage for the company. The contact information for the public relations person should be prominently displayed. For the benefit of journalists who are working on tight deadlines and need to reach someone immediately, list the best telephone number, email address, and any social media channels that they can quickly utilize. If a company representative is not directly available to the reporter, or if the reporter cannot easily find a phone number, the journalist will move on to another source. Including a tab titled "Media Inquiries" with the phone number and email addresses of the persons responsible

Business Wire Media Survey

With online publishing moving faster than ever, journalists rely heavily on press releases to meet reporting deadlines. Eighty-nine percent of journalists who responded to the Media Survey from Business Wire said they used press releases.

for responding to journalists is simple and effective. Southwest Airlines, Lands' End, and Dick's Sporting Goods have all adopted this strategy.[10]

Company Background/Statements: Include information that explains the history of the company or product(s). As the name implies, this tab should provide background information on the company: how it began, milestones the company has reached, and the mission, vision, and goals of the company. Starbucks, for example, includes a tab titled "Views."[11] Within the Starbucks "Views" tab, consumers can read about the company's stance on topics like fostering a culture of responsible self-government, comprehensive health care, the Earth's changing climate, and more.

Leadership Team: Within this tab, integrate short biographies of the company owners or founders as well as the top leadership team. Often the name of the individual, the individual's professional title, and a photograph are included. Make the images clickable so that a journalist can select the person they wish to learn more about. The Campbell's Soup Company provides a list of its executive team members,[12] while Hewlett-Packard uses a yearbook-style format (http://bit.ly/1cgZPn5) that provides the journalists with the option of immediately downloading a high-resolution image of the individuals comprising the executive team, since their photos are provided as part of the biographies. Again, this tactic makes reporters' work easier because they now have an image to include in their article.

Multimedia: The multimedia tab should include photographs of essential personnel, special events, products, and logos, as well as infographics and video snippets. White papers, reports, webcasts, presentations, and b-roll round out a well-apportioned multimedia area. Some companies create separate tabs or provide a drop-down menu related to multimedia. One of the most comprehensive multimedia centers can be found on the Coca-Cola Company's website (http://bit.ly/1ch1V6b).

Products: Include a list of products or services, with a brief description of each. Include copy that illustrates why the products or services are significant in the marketplace.[13]

FAQs/Fact Sheets: Many companies have a list comprised of the FAQs from media representatives. Use this portion of the online media center to answer those questions. It is also a best practice to include a fact sheet or sheets depending on the business. Starbucks provides a general company fact sheet, company timeline, and a series of fact sheets on its products (http://bit.ly/1bOJwD2).

Speakers or Interview Topics: Perform the legwork for a journalist by providing a list of topics that company spokespeople can speak to. Consider this tab the company's "expert's directory," an online resource typically developed by the public relations department for use by members of local, regional, and national media who are seeking sources for interviews, inquiries, news,

Theory into Practice

Online Newsrooms

Planning is the key to designing an effective online media center and developing a social media press release. Company webpages can be great resources and highlight many of the aspects that are mentioned in this chapter. Visit an online newsroom from the list provided:

FedEx: http://about.van.fedex.com/newsroom/ global-english

Hershey: http://www.thehersheycompany.com

IBM: http://www-03.ibm.com

After exploring the media centers, provide answers to the following questions:

How easy is it to find the online media center from the home page of the website?

Once in the online media center:

Is the contact information prominently displayed?

Are there clearly marked tabs devoted to specific information?

Are there links to rich content like infographics, webcasts, podcasts, audio files, and Slide-Share presentations?

How many quotes are available?

Are there avenues to share the information?

Does the company provide contact info, names of press contacts (including contact info), RSS links, and social media platforms?

Is the information accessible on a mobile device?

Is a Creative Commons License in place, or is the information strictly for journalists?

---

and feature stories. Directories like this incorporate members from various departments and areas of expertise. In providing an avenue for a company's experts to converse with members of the media, the company not only gains media exposure but also enhances its public image and illustrates the wealth of expertise that the company possesses.

Additional items to consider for the company media center include an AddThis or ShareThis solution that allows the media to share content more easily.[14] It is also a good idea to incorporate a calendar of events, highlighting upcoming events or trade shows, speaking engagements, and community appearances. Providing links to the company newsletter can also be beneficial and provides journalists with insights not available through press releases, fact sheets, white papers, images, or b-roll footage.

Navigating the Online Media Center

The design of the online media center is almost as important as the content itself. A website designer can help develop the best layout, navigation, and features based on specific requirements. However, the online media center should have its own navigation tab featured on the home page of the company website. Information presented within the online media center should be partitioned into separate tabs. This will make it easy for a journalist to navigate from one tab to the next without ever having to leave the online media center.

The "Press Info" section within Apple's online media center (http://bit.ly/1eX-EZwa) prominently features the company's media contacts, followed by the latest news, media resources, and product images and the leadership team. The Hershey Company's media center (http://bit.ly/1jxNOQL) contains tabs that feature its newsroom, historical press releases, a calendar of events, financial press releases, media contact information, and the latest featured story. Starbucks (http://bit.ly/1kmXYkX) has seven tabs in its media center—"Featured," "News," "Fast Facts," "Views," "Leadership Team," "Multimedia," and "Contact"—all with drop-down menus in each tab that provide further details.

As technology and communication channels continue to evolve, the development of online media resources is now a business essential. Online media centers are vital for the modern journalist—equally as important as a traditional or social media press release. Beyond journalists, a much larger, more demanding audience is showing interest in accessing the information found within a press release, including bloggers, citizen journalists, content creators, the general public, and various other stakeholders. As a result of this trend toward companies providing more online content, the required elements within a press release have also changed. Not only do audiences desire substantial content that communicates an overarching story, but they also expect to see video, pictures, infographics, stats, and quotes. The public in general now yearns to experience the news, not just read about it. With this in mind, it is essential that practitioners understand how an online (social) press release differs from a traditional press release with respect to content and format.

Business Wire Media Survey

Text-only press releases are slowly being phased out. While an overwhelming majority of journalists want press releases to include photos (73 percent), a significant number also prefer graphics (43 percent), infographics (32 percent), logos (29 percent), and videos (27 percent) to round out their reporting.

Modern Press Releases

One of the most noteworthy events in the history of public relations occurred on October 28, 1906. A tragic accident led to the advent of the first press release. Public relations expert Ivy Lee was working with the Pennsylvania Railroad when the tragic accident occurred. The lives of fifty passengers were taken when a three-car train of the Pennsylvania Railroad's new electric service jumped a trestle in Atlantic City, New Jersey, and plummeted into the Thoroughfare Creek.[15]

It is reported that Ivy Lee convinced the railroad company to release a statement about what had occurred. In doing so, Lee set in motion what is now considered the first press release. Ivy Lee created a public statement and presented it to journalists at the location of the train accident.[16] The *New York Times* was said to have been so utterly impressed with Lee's information that the newspaper printed the press release word for word on October 30, 1906.[17] Although it is rare for media outlets to use them verbatim these days, press releases do still often act as a starting point for journalists, bloggers, and content creators to compose a story.

Despite some backlash and criticism of the viability of the press release in more recent years, it still remains one of the most important tools for attracting the attention of journalists more than one hundred years after its inception. A press release that is newsworthy, specifically targeted, and well written is always appreciated by media professionals. In printed form, the structure of the traditional press release has not evolved considerably in format. However, press releases communicated via social media are vastly different.

In the broadest terms, a social media press release, also referred to as a social media news release, can be defined as "a single page of web content designed to enable the content to be removed and used on blogs, wikis and other social channels."[18] SHIFT Communications developed the world's first social media press release template in 2006. Shortly thereafter, Edelman launched StoryCrafter, and

The Blog Post Heard around the World[1]

Influential Silicon Valley journalist and blogger Tom Foremski's now famous blog post, "Die! Press Release! Die! Die! Die!" sparked a revolution in the public relations industry. The way public relations professionals announced news to the media had not changed since 1906. Our tactics were stale.

When Formeski wrote this post, the year was 2006, and the public relations industry was experiencing vast changes. Blogs, bloggers, citizen journalists, and social networking sites began to flood the scene. The long-standing rules between journalists and public relations professionals were in a state of flux. Bloggers were "rogue" and played by different rules. For the first time bloggers like Chris Anderson were "outing" bad public relations professionals,[2] and the industry began its transformation. Journalists needed more from PR professionals, and Foremski's blog post announced what was necessary—loud and clear!

To Foremski's credit, he did not just condemn and criticize the press release; he deconstructed what the problem was and suggested alternatives. Essentially he put the framework together for what we now know as the social media press release. He suggested that public relations professionals should deconstruct the press release into specific sections and tag the information so that media personnel could compile and connect useful information to aspects of the story. It was also suggested

to include a larger number of links within the press release body and other relevant links to news articles and references. Foremski also proposed that a specific section of the social media press release include a brief description of the announcement, various quotes from C-suite executives, and financial information in varied formats.

Today's press releases need to adhere to the requirements of a modern-day audience in response to the way that information is obtained. Press releases that are interesting, informative, and entertaining need to be nimble and fit into multiple formats in order to resonate.[3] Captivating visuals, tweetable headlines, interesting factoids, keyword-friendly text, and easy-to-share pages provide the user with an enhanced experience over a traditional press release. Take the time to examine the overall outcomes and the actions that you want to inspire with a press release hosted within the social sphere.

---

1 Tom Foremski, "Die! Press Release! Die! Die! Die!," *Silicon Valley Watcher*, February 27, 2006, http://www.silicon-valleywatcher.com/mt/archives/2006/02/die_press_relea.php.
2 C. Anderson, "Sorry PR People: You're Blocked," *The Long Tail*, October 29, 2007, http://bit.ly/1bRpBRy.
3 Magdalena Georgieva, "3 Characteristics of Successful Modern-Day Press Releases," HubSpot, October 21, 2011, http://blog.hubspot.com/blog/tabid/6307/bid/27623/3-Characteristics-of-Successful-Modern-Day-Press-Releases.aspx.

---

the emergence of varied configurations of the social media press release soon followed. The format of the social media press release has gone through many iterations and revisions over the years; however, there are some elements that have remained constant.[19]

Contact Information: Prominently feature the media relations personnel contact information at the top. In addition to traditional details like an email address and office and mobile telephone numbers, include other pertinent contact information, such as other social media platforms that the company uses. Keep in mind that you should only list the outlets that you would want a media representative to use to contact you. It's OK if you want bloggers and journalists to simply call or email you, but do not list a Twitter handle if you do not intend to respond via Twitter.

The Headline: A good headline has always been integral to entice a journalist to read your press release. You want the headline to immediately gain readers' attention so that they will continue to read further. Write captivating copy and include specific keywords that are likely to be picked up by search engines.

Length: Headlines should fall between 60 and 120 characters in length. Shorter headlines are easier to share on social networking sites like Twitter and Facebook and are more easily read via subject lines in an email inbox. Additionally, many of the top search engines have specific headline character limits. Google displays headlines that are 60 characters in length, Bing allows for 71 characters, and Yahoo! displays 120 characters.

Format: Bold the headline, and capitalize each word except for prepositions and words three characters or less. For example, "Consumers Find Social Media Increasingly Trustworthy."[20]

The Introductory Paragraph: Using the standard inverted pyramid—who, why, what, when, and where—tell the whole story. Provide a synopsis of the information contained within the press release. A succinct introductory paragraph is critical since many distribution channels only display the headline, a short summary, and a link to the news release.

Length: One to four sentences.

Format: Title case—use capital letters at the start of the principal words.

Example: "In line with ING's ambition to be at the forefront of developments in social media, ING is today presenting the study 'Impact of Social Media 2012 (#SMING12)' based on a survey among 1,500 Dutch consumers. The survey shows that consumers find social media increasingly trustworthy. 65% said they find the information posted on online media to be trustworthy. 40% of consumers find posts made on social media to be trustworthy."[21]

Supporting Paragraphs/Details: Develop a well-written message that resonates with your audience by capitalizing on traditional public relations writing styles and incorporating bulleted points. The information provided within this section should tell your story. Stay away from advertising or marketing speak. Integrate details that support the main points, add interest, or reinforce a message. In traditional press releases, the use of multiple quotes can be frowned upon, but multiple quotes from staff, customers, or experts in the field can help round out the story in social media press releases. Bloggers and journalists like to have many quotes to choose from. Statistics and charts can provide additional research and numbers often appreciated by journalists. Be sure to include links throughout the body copy.

Length: Three hundred to eight hundred words.

Format: Title case, which uses capital letters at the start of the principal words.

Example: The following release was written and released by ING and is an excellent example of the critical elements used in social media press releases: http://bit.ly/1jAYgHo.

Anchor Text Links: Social media press releases incorporate many anchor text links. Anchor text links are keyword-rich phrases that are linked to a relevant page on the Internet, which then provides additional details related to the phrase. For example, when the American Humane Society announced the release of its documentary *Red Star™ Rescue in Oklahoma*, the organization linked the text "legendary red star" back to a webpage detailing the history of American Red Star Animal Relief. This tactic not only provided the reader with access to additional information on the program but also helped to improve the SEO of the press release itself. You can read the social media press release here: http://prn.to/1ckCBMG.

Facts and Stats: Create a space where bloggers and journalists can find links to the facts, stats, research, and statements highlighted within the press release.

Multimedia: Provide a variety of videos, photos, and sound bites that can be used to write the story. For example, if a new partnership is being announced, include a video interview with the CEO. If a new product is being launched, give bloggers and journalists an inside peek at the product by sharing multiple images or even a short video of the product.

Mobile Friendly Audio: When including audio sound bites, use a service such as SoundCloud. This service is mobile compatible and allows readers to see and hear all aspects of your social media press release even when they are on the go.

Video: Videos can be created on any platform, but recent research has shown that YouTube is one of the best video options.[22] YouTube is fully mobile and provides one of the largest audiences available. Videos can play on a variety of devices, allowing journalists, bloggers, and content creators to view your video no matter where they are. It is also important to note that nearly all social networks recognize YouTube URLs and allow videos coming from the site to be played instantly.

Infographics: Infographics have exploded in popularity across social media and mainstream media outlets. They are an excellent way to highlight research, focus group results, survey outcomes, or insights from the company's latest white paper.

SHIFT Communications Social Media Press Release Live Example

How to Make a Social Media Press Release [tweet this]

Making a social media press release is relatively straightforward. It's nothing more than a variable width table with the shareable social content in it. Remember that the goal of a social media press release is to make every piece of it shareable.

Everything you see on this page has a sharing mechanism of some kind, from the title itself to the story to the individual pieces of content. This way, everything is separable and divisible. If a media influencer just wants to use the video on their site, they can. If a podcaster just wants to grab the audio for inclusion in their show, they can. There's no requirement that you ship the entire thing lock, stock, and barrel.

The SMPR was created entirely in a plain vanilla HTML editor like Adobe Dreamweaver or BlueGriffon, using various social networks and content networks to provide the individual pieces.

There's a third hidden piece that's not immediately obvious. This social media press release is being hosted not on our corporate web site, but by our marketing automation system. As a result, it can detect when people who are already in our marketing database are looking at it, clicking on things, and sharing stuff, so we know if it resonates or not.

Like this? Let us know in the comments:

Video

Audio

SHIFT Communications pioneered the first social media press release. *Source:* SHIFT Communications.

Social Bookmarking: Incorporate buttons allowing readers to share and save webpages of interest. Digg, Delicious, and StumbleUpon are examples of frequently used social bookmarking tools.

Sharing Tools: Social media is all about sharing information, and so it is important for readers to have the option to digg your story, pin it, tweet it, like it on Facebook, share it on LinkedIn, and email it to friends. Many of these sharing buttons can be set up to share specific content or are text enabled so that your message is disseminated in the way that you intend.[23]

Social Commenting: Conversations are paramount on social media. Encourage conversations by integrating common plugins such as Facebook comments, WordPress, Livefyre, Realtidbits, Disqus, or other platforms that foster discussions.

Creative Commons License: Dissemination of news in a connected world requires new policies. Too often bloggers and other content creators will see warnings like "media use only" when visiting online media centers. This type of messaging can often dissuade these reporters from covering a company. A Creative Commons license is an online copyright release that clearly articulates how the content can be used and shared and should be considered as part of any media center's content-related policies. Removing any barriers or concerns about copyright that may cause your audience to hesitate is a best practice.[24]

The takeaway here is that a company should want its social media press releases to be shareable. Unlike traditional press releases that were deliberately sent specifically to journalists, social media press releases can be found, shared, and circulated through the social sphere. Prezly (http://www.prezly.com), Market-Wired (http://www.marketwired.com), PRESSfeed (http://www.press-feed.com), CNW (http://www.newswire.ca/en/index), and Pitch Engine (http://new.pitchengine.com) offer services to help with creating social media press releases and online media centers, as well as with distributing the finalized content.

Fostering Online Media Centers and Social Media Press Releases

Social media news releases achieve three times as much coverage as traditional news releases.[25] Today's public relations practitioners need to understand that company media centers and social media–based press releases are only effective if they incorporate the right content using the right platform. The advent of new "modernized" media relations requires practitioners to embrace new methodologies and technologies and learn how to best communicate and interact with journalists, bloggers, and content creators. Incorporating interactive and multimedia content is now considered the norm and should be done to enhance a story in ways that traditional media could not.

(Readers can find an interview with leaders at the College of Saint Rose regarding their campaign to promote the school using a combination of traditional public relations and social media efforts at http://ginaluttrellphd.com/videos.)

Learn More: Online Media Centers & Social Media Press Releases

- "Die! Press Release! Die! Die! Die!": http://bit.ly/18w8XGt
- "Social Media Release Must Evolve to Replace Press Release": http://to.pbs.org/1aObzMH
- "How to Write a Social Media Press Release": http://bit.ly/19bYpgt
- "What Is a 'Social Media Newsroom'?": http://bit.ly/1ckGgdv
- "20+ Free Press Release Distribution Sites": http://on.mash.to/1ksuVwj

Notes

1. "Online Newsroom Best Practices," PR Newswire, last modified 2013, accessed November 26, 2013, http://www.prnewswire.com/knowledge-center/online-public-relations/Online-Newsroom-Best-Practices.html.
2. Elena Verlee, "How to Create a Good Online Media Center," PR in Your Pajamas, http://prinyourpajamas.com/online-media-center.
3. "Online Newsroom Best Practices."
4. "Online Newsroom Best Practices."
5. David Meerman Scott, "Online Media Room Best Practices," Web in Know, 2005, http://www.davidmeermanscott.com/documents/online_media_room_best_practices.pdf.
6. Christopher Penn, "Social Media Press Release 2.0," SHIFT Communications, December 2013, http://www.shiftcomm.com/2012/12/social-media-press-release-2-0.
7. Verlee, "How to Create a Good Online Media Center."
8. For the McDonald's Newsroom's press releases, visit http://news.mcdonalds.com/Corporate/Press-Releases.
9. "Online Newsroom Best Practices."
10. For Southwest Airlines' "Media Inquiries" page, see http://www.swamedia.com/pages/contacts; for the Lands' End's media contacts, see http://www.landsend.com/newsroom/media_contacts; for the Dick's Sporting Goods "Press Room" page, visit http://www.dickssportinggoods.com/corp/index.jsp?page=pressRoom&ab=Footer_Know_PressRoom.
11. For the Starbucks Newsroom "Views" page, visit http://news.starbucks.com/views.
12. "Executive Team," Campbell's Soup Company, http://www.campbellsoupcompany.com/about-campbell/executive-team.
13. Verlee, "How to Create a Good Online Media Center."
14. Joel Kessel, "The Online Media Room: Why It Needs to Be Part of Our Communications Strategy," Kessel Communications, http://kesselcommunications.com/the-online-media-room-why-it-needs-to-be-part-of-our-communications-strategy.
15. Mary Belles, "How to Write a Press Release—Invention of the First Press Release," About.com, last modified 2013, accessed December 7, 2013, http://inventors.about.com/od/pstartinventions/a/press_release.htm.
16. Belles, "How to Write a Press Release."
17. Mickie Kennedy, "The History of the Press Release," eReleases, March 29, 2010, http://www.ereleases.com/prfuel/history-of-the-press-release.
18. Ian Capstick, "Social Media Release Must Evolve to Replace Press Release," Media Shift, April 23, 2010, http://www.pbs.org/mediashift/2010/04/social-media-release-must-evolve-to-replace-press-release113.
19. Penn, "Social Media Press Release 2.0"; "Writing Great Online News Releases," PRWeb, last modified December 2013, accessed December 8, 2013, http://lp.prweb.com/Global/FileLib/Guides/PRWEB_-_Writing_Great_Online_News_Releases.pdf; S. Bruce, Share This: The Social Media Handbook for PR Professionals (West Sussex: Wiley, 2012), chap. 16.
20. "Writing Great Online News Releases."
21. "Consumers Find Social Media Increasingly Trustworthy," ING, last modified November 15, 2012, accessed December 8, 2013, http://ing-group.pr.co/34147-consumers-find-social-media-increasingly-trustworthy.
22. Capstick, "Social Media Release Must Evolve to Replace Press Release."

23 Capstick, "Social Media Release Must Evolve to Replace Press Release."

24 Georgieva, "3 Characteristics of Successful Modern-Day Press Releases."

25 Adam Parker, "Social Media News Releases Achieve Three Times the Pickup," Show-MeNumb3R5, March 22, 2011, http://www.showmenumbers.com/news-release-distribution/social-media-news-releases-achieve-three-times-the-pickup.

Measuring Social Media's Impact and Value

14

The success that social media has achieved within mainstream business activities highlights the importance of measuring the outcomes of these campaigns. Traditionally, up to 5 percent of a typical public relations budget is allocated to the measurement and interpretation of campaign-related metrics. Today, companies expect their public relations and social media professionals to quantify the impact and value.

We've Listened, Now What?

Listening, as we have learned throughout the book, is a vital component of social media. When a company actively listens to its respective audiences, it can assess what is being said about the company, an individual, a brand, or a product in the social sphere. These conversations produce copious amounts of unstructured data, which can seem somewhat uninterpretable and overwhelming. Just ask the individuals who spend their time trolling through Twitter feeds, Facebook comments, pins, and posts, reading comments from blogs, and examining message boards or forums. Phew! It's exhausting just thinking about that! It is difficult enough to closely follow these conversations, let alone interpret the content and make sense of the information as an origin for action. Listening to and monitoring social media–driven conversations allows a company to gather data, create metric-driven reports, and identify important action items. As a company collects this data, direct correlations can be made based on the results of its campaigns or initiatives. However, this does not mean that this task is easy by any stretch of the imagination.

Measuring the success and impact of social media initiatives is not as simple as adding up the number of "likes" or "shares." In fact, measuring the effectiveness of a social media campaign and overall strategy can be extremely daunting. Experts like Bernadette Coleman have developed a series of equations to calculate everything from user lifetime value to impression value and social media expenditures in order to valuate social media efforts. For example, companies that would like to calculate their social media expenditure might use the following formula:

Expenditures (E) = hard costs + cost / time spent + sunk cost

Those companies interested in calculating their lifetime user value, however, might instead use

User lifetime value (U) = (gross distribution per customer) × Σ (yearly retention rate)^i / (1+ yearly discount rate)^i – (retention cost per customer per year) × Σ (yearly retention rate)^p / (1 + yearly discount rate)^p + 0.5[1]

While the formulaic approach can be confusing, other models and frameworks are more straightforward. Don Bartholomew (@Donbart), senior vice president of digital and social media research at Ketchum, is largely considered one of the industry's "resident experts" on measurement. His work[2] and the efforts of both the International Association for Measurement and Evaluation of Communications (AMEC) and the Conclave, a volunteer group representing different associations, organizations, and academia, are contributing to the development of a set of generally accepted standards within the communications industry.[3] In June 2013 the Conclave released the "Complete Social Media Measurement Standards" in an attempt to provide a framework around some generally accepted measurement principles. The full report can be found using the following link: http://bit.ly/1cKw9l4. Themes addressed in this report include the following:

Content and Sourcing: This area of the report attempts to capture information regarding content sources in order to provide transparency and ease of comparison across analyses.[4] This section highlights an analysis of content from multiple sources (channels), including Twitter, Facebook, Instagram, YouTube, forums, and monitoring services such as Radian6, Sysomos, and so on, along with methods of data collection and analysis. Key metrics that are calculated to understand reach, engagement, influence, and opinion/advocacy are also examined in this section. Even the coding for understanding sentiment is addressed.

Reach and Impressions: This section serves as a basis for defining data collection in social media so that subsequent metrics and other standards can be calculated consistently. In-depth definitions and explanations of "item," "mention," "impressions," and "reach" are provided.

Engagement and Conversation: "Engagement" and "conversation" are words commonly used by social media professionals; yet they are rarely defined with any type of consistency to guide sound measurement. Within this section of the report, definitions and differentiations between engagement and conversations are provided. For example, the report states, "Engagement counts for such actions as: likes, comments, shares, votes, +1s, links, retweets, video views, content embeds, etc. Engagement types and levels are unique to specific channels, but can be aggregated for cross-channel comparison."[5] Conversation, on the other hand, measures items such as blog posts, comments, tweets, Facebook posts/comments, video posts, replies, and so on.[6]

Opinion and Advocacy: Since not all practitioners are experts in market research, robust parameters and comprehensive examples regarding measuring sentiment, opinion, and advocacy are provided within this section of the report.

Influence: Buzz words like "influencers" and "influential" are regularly used in social media planning. However, consistent definitions of these words have not yet been adopted within the industry. Therefore, a common language

International Relations

Measurement

In a survey conducted by Adobe Omniture, more than five hundred marketing directors in the United Kingdom, France, Germany, Italy, and the Nordic countries stated that social media measurement was a top priority for their business. More than half, 55 percent, are looking to measure the impact their social media efforts are producing, while 40 percent of European businesses have purchased specific software to analyze their social efforts.

Source: "Measuring Social Media Success Is 'Top Priority' for European Marketers," Media Measurement, accessed December 2, 2015, http://development.mediameasurement.com/measuring-social-media-success-is-'top-priority'-for-european-marketers.

and conceptual framework have been developed to aid practitioners in being able to quantify "influencers."

Impact and Value: It is widely accepted that both "impact" and "value" represent the ultimate outcome of any social media or campaign effort.[7] Too often, these terms are interchanged and confused with return on investment (ROI). Descriptions and metrics related to "impact" and "value" provided within this section of the report enable practitioners to understand the difference between the three terms (ROI included) and how they relate to measuring outcomes.

The New Frontier: Social Media Models and Framework

For decades, communication models have been linear and almost formulaic in nature. There are countless examples that support this claim; we will look at three of the more widely adopted models. John Marston's R-A-C-E Four-Step Model for Public Relations is considered very straightforward.[8] The components include *r*esearch, *a*ction, *c*ommunication, and *e*valuation. Practitioners commonly begin with the research phase, continue to the action and communication phases, and then ultimately end with the evaluation phase in a linear fashion. R-O-P-E, another commonly adopted model used in communication planning, follows the same blueprint—practitioners start with *r*esearch, create *o*bjectives, *p*lan, and finally *e*valuate the outcomes. Schramm's Communication Model is the final example we will examine. Again, this model follows a linear process. Wilber Schramm is a pioneer in communication theory. He developed the one-way linear model of communication, which sought to explain how meaning was transferred between both individuals and organizations. Meaning, in the context of this model, includes five basic elements: source, encoder, signal, decoder, and destination.[9] Schramm's model emphasized that the source and receiver continually encode, interpret, decode, transmit, and receive information while also filtering out noise.

Schramm's model revolutionized how individuals thought about communication between senders and receivers.[10] These three models continue to be taught in universities across the globe and are still widely used in public relations planning and practice today. However, in today's digital age of communication, these models continue to provide challenges when tasked with measuring outcomes. There simply are no standards.

Since public relations activities are regarded as a series of actions, changes, and functions that generate results, the same can also apply to social media and social strategies. Social media impacts the way that content is created, distributed, and consumed. It should not come as a shock that measuring these efforts takes great change.[11]

Source	Encoder	Signal	Decoder	Destination

Noise

Wilber Schramm proposed the model of communication in the 1950s.

> ## Theory into Practice

Understanding Media Platforms:
Paid, Earned, Shared, Owned

Seasoned public relations professionals can have difficulty distinguishing between various forms of media in the digital age. An easy way to remember and understand the differences in the media landscape is by using the acronym PESO, which stands for "paid, earned, shared, and owned."

Paid refers to the social channels a company pays to leverage its message. For example, promoted tweets, banner ads, Facebook or LinkedIn advertisements, pay-per-click search ads, sponsorships, and ads in magazines or on radio are all considered paid media. The company has not *earned* the coverage; rather, it has *paid* for it.

Earned is where the customers become the channel for a company through word of mouth or achievement of viral status. Think of traditional public relations efforts. The resident public relations manager writes a narrative around the company's latest product launch and then pitches that story to both new and traditional media channels, including blogs. The resulting news coverage, broadcast hits, and blog posts are deemed "earned" media,

since the company did not pay the news writers, bloggers, or other media outlets for coverage. Therefore, the coverage was earned and resulted from the efforts of the public relations practitioners to gain coverage in both online and offline media channels.

Shared refers to the instances wherein consumers are working in conjunction with a brand to create, share, and promote the brand's content. This occurs only when a brand cultivates passionate and loyal followers who want to engage not only with the brand but also with a larger audience as well.

Owned is a term for channels that a company owns and controls. These include the company website, a Facebook brand page, blogs, e-books, infographics, an official Instagram account, Pinboards specifically maintained by the company, and Twitter accounts.

Source: Lee Odden, "Paid, Earned, Owned and Shared Media—What's Your Online Marketing Media Mix?," *Top Rank Marketing* (blog), 2011, http://www.toprankblog.com/2011/07/online-marketing-media-mix.

Social Media Metrics Model

Googling "how to measure social media" will result in hundreds of pages of advice. In this text you are presented with the framework for what one day may be generally accepted practices. Referencing the Conclave report and approximately fifteen other social media and communications models, Don Bartholomew and members of AMEC set out to develop a social media metrics model that takes into account the different stages of social media measurement.[12]

The social media metrics model presented can be considered a recommended approach that strives to create standard metrics for measuring social media. Incorporating models and developing intuitive frameworks is integral to properly conducting any measurement. A five-step social media measurement process accompanies this model to integrate all aspects.[13]

1. Step one of the social media measurement process begins with practitioners establishing measurable objectives that are aligned with desired business outcomes and key performance indicators.
2. Step two digs deeper and further defines the specific metrics required to assess performance against any and all measurable social media objectives. Performance targets should be set for each metric during this step.
3. Step three requires populating the selected social media model with the metrics specified and defined in the previous step.

Suggested Social Media Metrics Model

EXPOSURE	ENGAGEMENT	INFLUENCE	IMPACT	ADVOCACY
Create potential audience exposure to content & message.	Interaction that occurs in response to content on an owned channel **'engaging *with* you'**. Also *earned* social conversation **'talking about you'**.	Ability to cause or contribute to a change in opinion or behavior.	Effect of a social media campaign, program or effort on the target audience. Also Value - the financial impact.	Act of pleading or making the case for something. Includes positive sentiment and one of the following: • A recommendation • A call to action to purchase • Suggested usage or suggested change to opinion.

AMEC, the global trade body and professional institute for agencies and practitioners who provide media evaluation and communication research, and Don Bartholomew of Ketchum developed the suggested social media metrics model. *Source*: AMEC and Don Bartholomew, Ketchum.

4. With the measurement approach having been defined earlier in the planning process, step four focuses on the gathering and analysis of data. Practitioners should always strive to evaluate the performance against the objectives and targets.
5. Finally, report the results to stakeholders and interested parties as step five.

Social Media Valid Frameworks

Throughout the process of developing a set of accepted metrics and consistent definitions to aid in measuring the success of a social media initiative, Bartholomew and others have proposed a less complicated arrangement that captures social media metrics from three specific areas: programmatic, channel specific, and business. Bartholomew explains that "programmatic metrics directly tie to social media objectives while channel-specific metrics are the unique metrics associated with specific social media channels—tweets, RTs, MTs, Followers, Likes, Diggs, Talking About This, Pins, and Re-Pins, and finally, business metrics illustrate the business impact of the campaign or initiative."[14] Additionally, "paid, earned, owned" and "paid, earned, shared, owned" media metrics were also considered and enable businesses to measure integrated programs containing a variety of differing elements.

One can now see why the creators of social media–based measurement models have abandoned the one-size-fits-all framework that could be instituted across differing business platforms. Business goals and objectives vary; therefore a flexible and easily adaptable, one-size-fits-most approach is appropriate.[15] This approach allows for companies to focus the framework to their specific business objectives. Within the fifteen-plus models that were studied by Bartholomew and AMEC, the ideas related to postpurchase engagement and advocacy were repeatedly identified. As a result, these elements are also included in this recommended approach. Finally, engagement and influence have always been key concepts in social marketing and measurement; consequently, these elements are explicitly used in this mode.

The following images illustrate the two routes of metrics used.[16]

The methodologies and guidelines surrounding social media measurement are still evolving. When attempting to establish a measurement strategy for your company's social media efforts, expect moments of trial and error. But do not panic. Over time you will begin to see correlations between your social media strategies and the company's key performance indicators. Use the models presented within this chapter to help your organization develop a powerful measurement strategy that meets the specific needs and provides the necessary metrics.

	EXPOSURE	ENGAGEMENT	INFLUENCE	IMPACT	ADVOCACY
PROGRAM METRICS	**Total OTS for program content**	**Number of interactions with content** Interaction rate **Hashtag usage**	**Increase % association with key attributes** Change in issue sentiment	**New subscribers** Referral traffic to website **White paper downloads**	**Recommendation/ Total Mentions %**
CHANNEL METRICS	**Number of items** Mentions **Reach** Impressions CPM	**Post Likes** Comments **Shares** Views **RTs/1000 Followers**	**Net promoter % by channel**	**Unique visitors to website referred from each channel**	**Organic posts by advocates** Ratings/Reviews
BUSINESS METRICS			**Purchase consideration %** Likelihood to recommend % **Association with brand attributes**	**Sales** Repeat sales **Purchase frequency** Cost savings **Number leads**	**Employee ambassadors** Brand fans/advocates

The AMEC Social Media Valid Framework: Program, Channel, Business. *Source*: AMEC and Don Bartholomew, Ketchum.

	EXPOSURE	ENGAGEMENT	INFLUENCE	IMPACT	ADVOCACY
PAID	**Impressions** Reach **CPM** Active GRPs	**Interaction rate** Click-thrus **Time viewing** Completed plays	**Purchase consideration** Change in opinion	**Visit website** Attend event **Sales** Download coupon	**Mentions in Earned channel**
OWNED	**Unique visitors** Page views **Reach** Impressions **CPM**	**Return visits** Interaction rate **Duration** Subscriptions **Links**	**Tell a friend** Change in opinion **Association with key attributes**	**Download paper** Download app **Sales** Request info **Cost savings**	**Recommendations** Ratings
EARNED	**Number of items** Number of mentions **Number of Followers** OTS	**Comments/post** Shares **RTs/1000 Followers** Number of inbound links	**Purchase consideration** Tell a friend **Likelihood to Recommend**	**Visit store** Attend the event **Sales** Vote for issue	**Ratings** Reviews **Recommendations** Recommendations rate

The AMEC Social Media Valid Framework: Paid, Owned, Earned. *Source*: AMEC and Don Bartholomew, Ketchum.

#LRNSMPR

Learn More: Social Media Measurement

- "The Conclave: Complete Social Media Measurement Standards—June 2013": http://bit.ly/1cKw9l4
- AMEC Social Media Measurement Framework, United Kingdom's Chip My Dog Campaign: http://bit.ly/1WhkcL8
- "Defining Earned, Owned, and Paid Media": http://bit.ly/1ajx4WH
- "Five Social Media Measurement Questions I Hope (NOT) to See in 2014": http://bit.ly/1aWZOoj
- "A Digital Leader Looks at the Agency of Tomorrow": http://bit.ly/1d116Ol

Notes

[1] Bernadette Coleman, "The Real Social Media ROI Formula," *SEJ Search Engine Journal*, August 27, 2013, http://www.searchenginejournal.com/the-real-social-media-roi-formula/66047.

[2] Don Bartholomew, "About," *MetricsMan*, http://metricsman.wordpress.com/about.

[3] See the website of the International Association for Measurement and Evaluation of Communications (AMEC) at http://amecorg.com; Conclave, http://www.smmstandards.com/about/the-conclave-members.

[4] AMEC.

[5] AMEC.

[6] AMEC.

[7] AMEC.

[8] John Marston, *The Nature of Public Relations* (New York: McGraw-Hill, 1963), 161–73.

[9] Wilber Schramm, *Mass Media and National Development* (Stanford, CA: Stanford University Press, 1964).

[10] D. Wilcox et al., *THINK Public Relations* (Upper Saddle River, NJ: Pearson Education, 2013).

[11] Don Bartholomew, "The Digitization of Research and Measurement in Public Relations," *Social Media Explorer*, May 12, 2010, http://www.socialmediaexplorer.com/online-public-relations/the-digitization-of-research-and-measurement-in-public-relations.

[12] Don Bartholomew, "A New Framework for Social Media Metrics and Measurement," *MetricsMan*, June 12, 2013, http://metricsman.wordpress.com/2013/06/12/a-new-framework-for-social-media-metrics-and-measurement.

[13] D. Bartholomew and AMEC, *Unlocking Business Performance: Communications Research and Analytics in Action* (presentation delivered at the European Summit on Measurement, Madrid, Spain, June 2013), http://amecorg.com/wp-content/uploads/2013/06/Social-Media-Valid-Framework2013.pdf.

[14] Bartholomew, "A New Framework for Social Media Metrics and Measurement."

[15] Marston, *The Nature of Public Relations*, 161–73.

[16] Bartholomew and AMEC, *Unlocking Business Performance*.

THE SOCIAL MEDIA PLAN 3 PART

The Roadmap to Success
Developing a Social Media Plan

15

The development of a social media plan helps create a roadmap for companies to follow in achieving their social media–related goals. This chapter outlines how to develop a step-by-step social media plan that can be easily implemented within your organization, then considers the future of social media.

Path to Success

Research illustrates that more than 50 percent of small businesses are not regularly engaging their targeted audiences using social media.[1] Various reasons could contribute to this lack of engagement, but the development and implementation of a proper plan with specific metrics can directly address many of these oversights.

Social media plans are a series of proposed actions that produce specific results. They are akin to a marketing or communications plan but specific to a social media strategy. Companies that plan their social media efforts prevent execution of haphazard, meaningless actions that add little value to their organizational goals. Social media plans outline a specific campaign or plan for the entire year. Presented in this chapter is a hybrid model that includes elements from a traditional public relations plan. This example not only includes elements from the research, objectives, strategy, tactics, implementation, and reporting (DOSTIR) public relations planning model conventionally implemented in a public relations plan[2] but also incorporates the fundamental premise inherent in the Circular Model of SoMe for Social Communication (*S*hare, *o*ptimize, *M*anage, *e*ngage) as well as pieces from Marketo's tactical social media planning template.[3]

Strategic and Tactical Social Media Plan Template

The following hybrid model provides an easy-to-follow template that aids in the creation of a social media plan by aligning the outcomes directly with important organizational goals. Incorporating social media within a business strategy requires a large investment in planning, support, and execution. When correctly implemented and properly maintained, a social media plan becomes a tangible driver for new leads and provides a platform for customers to participate in important conversations related to the brands that are important to them.

Step 1: Research: Develop a statement that outlines what the company wants to achieve and why. Valid objectives cannot be set without a clear understanding of the situation that led to developing a social media plan.[4] Some questions to ask when writing the situation statement include Why is a plan necessary? Are we trying to overcome an issue or challenge? Is this a one-time product launch? Are we introducing new services? Are we looking to engage more genuinely on our social platforms? Is this long-term planning?

In this research stage, be sure to define the target audience. Whether the company has cornered a niche area or your products or services target the

6 steps of the ROSTIR Public Relations Planning Model

Developing a social media plan helps create a road-map for companies to follow in achieving their social media-related goals. The process has been deconstructed into concise steps that allow for proper planning and effective implementation.

Research — #1

Start with research so that you can diagnose why a strategic plan may be necessary.

Keep your audience in mind. Listen and design your strategy around their needs.

Objectives — #2

Objectives are stated in terms of program outcomes rather than inputs and must be measurable.

Objectives should target: the audience or public, specific outcomes, measurement or magnitude of the change required to reach this outcome, and the target date.

Strategy — #3

The overarching strategy should focus on how each objective will be achieved.

Tactics — #4

Tactics are the tangible aspects of the strategy.

Tactics include annual meetings, open houses, events, blogs, case studies, infographics, mobile apps, and traditional PR efforts.

Implementation — #5

Timing plays a critical role in the implementation of the overall plan.

Develop a calendar and budget with milestones and deadlines to help guide the implementation process.

Reporting — #6

Practitioners must put metrics in place to track the results of each campaign. Reporting and evaluation can take place throughout the entire process.

---

general public, social media efforts should be directed toward a specific audience. For example, Axe body spray, a brand of Unilever Global, targets males eighteen to twenty-four years old,[5] while the wildly popular British television series *Poldark* targets women aged thirty-four to forty-nine.[6] Some campaigns have multiple audiences depending on the objectives set forth in the campaign. Make sure to take the time to properly understand the demographics that you are interested in connecting with.

Step 2: Objectives: Once you have a clear situation statement, setting objectives is the next logical step. What is your strategy for the social media plan? Describe your organization's objectives for your social media plan using the SMART strategy: *s*pecific, *m*easurable, *a*ttainable, *r*elevant, and *t*imely.[7] Describe how these objectives support your organization's mission. The program outcomes will define the objectives. For example, "position company XYZ as a leader in premium athletic wear by getting people to recognize the brand name and associate it with specific product(s)." The objectives here are overarching in nature, not to be confused or intermingled with the specific objectives located in the tactics section of the social media plan.

Step 3: Strategy: Strategies are the big-picture choices made to utilize specific channels. The strategy focuses on achieving the objectives. Describe how and why various campaign components will accomplish the overall goals. Guidelines and key messages are often included in this section. The Susan G. Komen Foundation uses four key messages in its national breast cancer awareness campaign: (1) know your risk, (2) get screened, (3) know what is normal for you, and (4) make healthy choices.[8] The organization reinforces these four messages throughout its public relations campaign and social media efforts.

To this point, the format that we have followed mirrors that of a traditional public relations plan. This is where the social media plan

International Relations: Global + Local = "Glocal"

Companies crossing over into European markets need to adapt their global strategy "locally." This includes additional efforts to educate themselves on the local cultures and nuances of the markets of interest.

Tristan Elosegui, former vice president of strategy at iCrossing in Spain, states, "Each individual country has its own culture, needs, and its own way of using social networks. Firms must be aware of those specificities and adapt their strategies, country by country. Think global, act local, so as to meet the expectations of internet users."[1]

---

[1] Lisa Toner, "How to 'Glocalise' Your Social Media Presence for a European Market," HubSpot, November 20, 2013, accessed December 2, 2015, http://blog.hubspot.com/marketing/glocalise-social-media-presence-for-european-domination-ht.

---

begins to diverge from the public relations plan. In general, most of the platforms used within the social sphere are included in this plan. However, as we have previously read, not all social media channels are appropriate for every business. Tactics can be unique for each business and consumer. Companies must decide which social platforms are right for their audiences. It is okay if Instagram is not part of your plan. If a company's audience is not engaged on Instagram, then it might not be a smart use of resources to maintain an Instagram account. Knowing your audience and its members' social habits is essential to successful implementation of a social media plan.

Step 4: Tactics: Tactics have been divided into several social media areas.[9] Let us examine how each could be included within a larger social media plan. Each tactic takes into account the measurement strategies that were previously presented and the Circular Model of SoMe for Social Communication.

Social Press: Just as public relations professionals pitch traditional journalists, public relations professionals and social media strategists must pitch bloggers and other online influencers.

Time Spent: Consider how many hours per day, week, and month will be devoted to this tactic.
Objectives:
Regularly update bloggers about products and services. Conduct interviews, conferences, and networking events.
Metrics:
Posts and referrals from the social press
Engagement and conversation
Influence
Opinion and advocacy
Impact and value

Blogs:
Time Spent: Consider how many hours per day, week, and month will be devoted to this tactic.
Remember, a good rule of thumb is to post once a day (if possible) or, at a minimum, three times per week.
Create an editorial calendar for your blog to stay motivated and to provide a guideline for content.
Objectives:
Increase recognition: for example, *x* number of posts.

Increase engagement: for example, encourage comments; add social sharing buttons.

Metrics:

Engagement and conversation

Influence

Opinion and advocacy

Impact and value

Number of posts

Number of social shares—Digg, Twitter, Facebook, etc.

Audience growth—unique and return visits

New subscribers

Inbound links clicked

Social Networks:

Time Spent: Consider how many hours per day, week, and month will be devoted to each social networking site.

Facebook:

Establish a goal for the number of posts per day.

Share a mix of relevant links, engaging content, videos, and polls.

Make sure to promote upcoming events.

Create special event pages.

LinkedIn:

Establish a goal for the number of posts per day.

Create a group.

Cultivate the LinkedIn company page.

Identify other groups to follow and participate.

Encourage employee participation.

Monitor and participate in Q&A.

Google+:

Establish a goal for the number of posts per day or week.

Optimize for SEO.

Share meaningful content, videos, images, and relevant links.

Host a Google Hangout.

Create and promote upcoming events.

Pinterest:

Establish goals for the number of pins per day.

Create boards to leverage content, company culture, and a behind-the-scenes atmosphere.

Promote consumer boards that illustrate a passion for the brand.

Follow other boards such as those of businesses, thought leaders, customers, and partners.

Metrics:

Engagement and conversation

Influence

Opinion and advocacy

Impact and value

Microblogging:

Time Spent: Consider how many hours per day, week, and month will be devoted to Twitter.

Objectives:

Compile list of company Twitter users; follow them and have employees follow the company.

Compile a list of vendors, customers, users, or members; follow them, retweet when appropriate, and engage frequently.

Communicate support issues from social media to the customer service team; ensure follow-up.

Cross-promote other social networking activities and sites through Twitter, the company blog, Facebook, and any other social networking site the company uses.

Metrics:

Engagement and conversation

Influence

Opinion and advocacy

Impact and value

Bookmarking/Tagging:

Time Spent: Consider how many hours per day, week, and month will be devoted to social bookmarking and tagging.

Objectives:

Illustrate the company as a thought leader and promote conversation using

Delicious

Sphinn

reddit

Digg

StumbleUpon

FriendFeed

Participate in communities and conversations

Metrics:

Engagement and conversation

Influence

Opinion and advocacy

Impact and value

Social Apps, Voting, and Crowdsourcing:

Time Spent: Consider how many hours per day, week, and month will be devoted to social apps, voting, and crowdsourcing.

Objectives:

Add a social element to every campaign to expand reach and increase engagement.

Share videos, reviews, ratings, and polls.

Use promotions and contests to spread your message, such as refer-a-friend or flash deals.

Promote content when applicable via social crowdsourcing and voting sites.

Let consumers have a say through crowdsourced events or interactive voting.

Metrics:

Engagement and conversation

Influence

Opinion and advocacy

Impact and value

Trends over time

Blog Commenting/Q&A Sites:

Time Spent: Consider how many hours per day, week, and month will be devoted to comments on the company blog, as well as other industry blogs. Take into consideration the time necessary to participate in Q&A sessions.

Objectives:

Participate on relevant message boards, blogs, and Q&A platforms.
Provide insight and thought leadership in your comments.
Only include a link-back when relevant.
Work positive comments into your posts and then follow up.
Focus on building authentic relationships—share, optimize, monitor, engage.

Metrics:

Engagement and conversation
Influence
Opinion and advocacy
Impact and value
Brand awareness
Link-backs
Referring traffic

Live Streaming:

Time Spent: Consider how many hours per day, week, and month will be devoted to creating, posting, and managing live-streaming apps like Periscope and Meerkat.

Objectives:

Create content that can easily be streamed.
Engage with audiences through live Q&A sessions.

Metrics:

Engagement and conversation
Influence
Opinion and advocacy
Impact and value

Online Video:

Time Spent: Consider how many hours per day, week, and month will be devoted to creating, posting, and managing online videos.

Objectives:

Create a video series.
Upload videos to the company website, YouTube, Facebook, Vine, Instagram, and other video platforms.

Metrics:

Engagement and conversation
Influence
Opinion and advocacy
Impact and value

Photo Sharing:

Time Spent: Consider how many hours per day, week, and month will be devoted to creating, posting, and managing images for the company.

Objectives:

Encourage employees to share any interesting public relations– or marketing-related photos from social marketing or company events.
Take pictures at relevant company-sponsored events like trade shows, product launches, and community happenings.
Invite influencers to take photos and share them with their followers.

Utilize photo-sharing sites to highlight images that link back to blogs and core sites:

Instagram

Pinterest

Flickr

Facebook Photo Gallery

Company blog

Google+ Photo Albums

Metrics:

Engagement and conversation

Influence

Opinion and advocacy

Impact and value

Podcasting:

Time Spent: Consider how many hours per day, week, and month will be devoted to the development of podcasts.

Objectives:

Create a list of podcast directories.

Repurpose webinar content (when applicable) for the resource section; promote it through podcast directories and iTunes.

Record relevant phone conferences for use as podcasts; promote them through podcast directories.

Interview and record company thought leaders; share their insights with your community.

Metrics:

Engagement and conversation

Influence

Opinion and advocacy

Impact and value

Presentation Sharing:

Time Spent: Consider how many hours per day, week, and month will be devoted to developing content to share on sites (such as SlideShare).

Objectives:

Highlight organizational thought leaders—if someone from your company is presenting at a conference, post the presentation to SlideShare.

Determine the number of SlideShare presentations that need to be created on a monthly or quarterly basis.

Post webinars, slide decks, and infographics.

Optimize for SEO.

Generate views and leads.

Metrics:

Engagement and conversation

Influence

Opinion and advocacy

Impact and value

Step 5: Implementation, Budget, and Timeline: Every social media plan requires a budget. Companies want to know all of the expenses related to the campaigns. Budgets should take into consideration both staff time and out-of-pocket expenses. Allocate at least 10 percent of a budget to unexpected costs.

The objectives, complexity, and timing of the campaign will dictate the time-lines. Some campaigns last six weeks, while others can last six months. Campaigns can be seasonal or targeted to a specific product or event. For example, the Lay's® Do Us a Flavor™ Choose Your Chip Contest accepted entries for new potato chip flavors for four months. Once entries were sub-mitted, members of the public had the opportunity to vote on their favorite chip for an additional three months.

Step 6: Reporting and Evaluation: Reporting, also known as evaluation, con-nects directly to the stated objectives. Practitioners must put metrics in place to track the results of each campaign. Reporting and evaluation do not have to take place at the end of a campaign; truthfully, quite the opposite. Savvy practitioners evaluate the metrics throughout the process. In doing so, a practitioner will know whether or not the stated objectives, strategies, and tactics are resonating with the intended audiences. It is appropriate to mea-sure objectives at any point during the implementation phase through the conclusion of the public relations campaign.

After completing these six steps, an organization has developed a complete social media plan. This plan can be incorporated into an existing public relations plan or used as a stand-alone depending on how the plan was developed. Highlighted below are examples of how companies successfully implemented social media plans. Ben and Jerry's and Oreo have both done a wonderful job of executing their social media campaigns.

As you read each "Theory into Practice" case study, think about the six steps described in this chapter, along with elements from the Circular Model of SoMe for Social Communication. Try to identify which section the information would likely fall into within the framework of the social media plan. This will provide you with a chance to practice populating a plan as well as a resource for quick reference.

Theory into Practice

Ben and Jerry's City Churned[1]

In 2013, Ben and Jerry's implemented one of the most successful social media campaigns on record. In an effort to explore and create new flavors that represent a more local flair, 360i Digital Marketing Agency and Ben and Jerry's targeted residents of New York City, Seattle, Portland, Washington, DC, and San Francisco with the City Churned cam-paign.[2] The campaign incorporated crowdsourcing to actively engage residents in both the develop-ment of flavor ideas and voting for each city's new flavor. Tactics included a variety of social media and direct interaction with the Ben and Jerry's ice-cream truck. A City Churned microsite served as the communication hub.

Objectives

The objective of the City Churned campaign was threefold:

To cultivate a deeper relationship with fans.

To capture the flair of each city with a pint of Ben and Jerry's ice cream.

To show the company's continuing commitment to being ecofriendly, good to local business, and willing to work with fair trade.

Target Audience

Ben and Jerry's has always focused on community and wellness. The target audience for this campaign was identified to include local residents in each of the targeted cities, small business owners, social media users falling between sixteen and thirty-five years of age, and all other eco-loving citizens.

Strategies and Tactics

By creating a flavor unique to that city, Ben and Jerry's looked to empower the local residents with a sense of pride for helping personalize the flavor that best represented their city. Incorporating social media within the campaign allowed Ben and Jerry's to reach a wider audience, but it also helped mobilize residents to vote for their favorite flavors at the Ben and Jerry's ice-cream truck throughout the area.

Ben and Jerry's used multiple social media platforms in the campaign and provided residents with a number of ways to vote on their favorite flavors. Voters could use social media by checking in on Foursquare or tagging photos on Instagram. Individuals could also show up in person at a Ben and Jerry's ice-cream truck and participate in the voting process by highlighting their individual styles. To get a better handle on the flavor of each city, Ben and Jerry's also partnered with local businesses and fair trade organizations for an even better "taste" of the local culture and feel.[3]

Execution

Ben and Jerry's utilized the power of crowdsourcing to communicate with residents and encourage them to visit the ice-cream truck within each city to vote and help create the ice-cream flavor for their city.

Each city had several different ways that residents could vote and help shape the flavor. No two cities used the same means of determining their favorite ingredients. However, some methods were not conscious choices. For example, whether a Seattle resident could see Mt. Rainier or which direction a New Yorker's taxi was traveling seemed to influence particular flavor votes in specific cities.

After the voting process was complete, locals had the opportunity to try free samples of their city's new flavor; however, they did have to first locate the Ben and Jerry's ice-cream truck.

Using Flickr, Ben and Jerry's posted photos from its ice-cream truck for followers to see and share.

Results and Evaluation

The Ben and Jerry's City Churned campaign wrapped up on September 28, 2013. It reached several thousand people in each city. The campaign aimed to create a buzz for the Ben and Jerry's brand in Washington, DC, Seattle, Portland, New York City, and San Francisco. This was achieved in part by using social media and crowdsourcing as supporting platforms and activities. The city with the lowest reach was Washington, DC, with roughly five thousand residents deciding between Greek frozen yogurt and ice cream. In contrast, New York City had the highest reach, with over fifteen thousand residents taking part in voting between the same two base flavors. Ben and Jerry's Instagram channel reached over sixty thousand people in New York City and over twelve thousand in Washington, DC. When the campaign shifted to using crowdsourcing, over nine thousand Washington, DC, participants came out to cast their votes for chocolate or vanilla. Not one to be outdone, over twenty-three thousand New York City residents used turnstiles to cast their votes for coffee or chocolate. The metrics generated by the City Churned campaign confirmed that both 360i Digital Marketing Agency and Ben and Jerry's had successfully created buzz around the brand in a unique way.

1   Rosemary Sheridan et al., "A City Churned" (working paper, College of Saint Rose, 2013).
2   360i Digital Marketing Agency, http://www.360i.com/work/ben-jerrys-city-churned; see the Ben and Jerry's website at http://www.benjerry.com.
3   Christopher Heine, "Ben and Jerry's Lets Subways, Cabs, and Spoons Help Vote for Ice Creams," *Adweek*, last modified June 3, 2013, http://www.adweek.com/news/technology/ben-jerrys-lets-subways-cabs-and-spoons-help-vote-ice-creams-149965.

Theory into Practice

Oreo "Daily Twist" Campaign Case Study[1]

In 2012, Oreo enlisted the public relations firm 360i Digital Marketing to help create and execute a campaign designed to celebrate Oreo's one-hundredth anniversary, while drawing consumer attention back to the brand.[2] Specifically targeting the Millennial generation through the use of social media sites (i.e., Pinterest, Facebook, Twitter, and Tumblr), Oreo created the Daily Twist campaign, which ran from June 25 to October 2, 2012. By connecting the Oreo cookie with pop culture, the campaign aimed to make the one-hundred-year-old snack food relevant again.

Objectives

In rolling out the Daily Twist campaign, Oreo was looking to highlight the Oreo cookie as a relevant, household name, even one hundred years after it was first introduced. Oreo aimed to accomplish the following:

Use creative and timely content, "with a twist," to encourage conversation and interaction between Oreo fans and the brand.

Showcase the brand as more than just a snack food; it is a brand involved in and committed to partnering with many different interests in society (e.g., images relating to Hispanic Heritage Month, LGBT, Shin-Shin/Asian culture, Comic-Con, the Emmys, Shark Week, Bastille Day).

Bring out the "kid" in Oreo consumers and fans.

Research

Research supporting this campaign was largely demographic in nature, focusing on the Millennial generation, or Generation Y (individuals born between 1980 and 1999). A 2012 study conducted by the US Chamber of Commerce noted, "Gen Yers connect to a brand through affiliation with a cause. This is more important to Gen Y than to previous generations. A brand that shows it cares is attractive to this generation."[3]

A separate study, completed by the Pew Research Center in early 2012, highlighted statistics in support of a rise in news consumption via social media channels: "On top of the increase in social network use, the poll finds that news is also more prevalent on social networking sites. The share of users who saw news there yesterday nearly doubled from 19 to 36 percent between 2010 and 2012."[4]

Execution

360i developed a number of strong tactics in order to promote the one-hundredth birthday of the Oreo cookie.

Brand Newsroom: A team was created to identify all top and trending headlines in the news, and from these, custom Oreo images were designed.

Pinterest Board:[5] For one hundred days, Oreo posted a new image related to pop culture on the Daily Twist board. Each image would relate to an event or anniversary specific to that day or week. Oreo also integrated each Pinterest post with Facebook and Twitter.

Live Event in NYC: For the finale—the one-hundredth day of the campaign—Oreo held a live event in Times Square. To build hype for the event, Oreo utilized the Times Square "spectaculars" and created a live Brand Newsroom, encased in glass. Oreo invited the online community that it had identified using its Pinterest page and other social media channels to vote on what the final image should be. When the winner was decided, the Brand Newsroom team created a related image in real time, while fans watched the action unfold before their eyes. The winning image was "Anniversary of the 1st High-Five."

Oreo Blackout Tweet: During the 2013 Super Bowl, Oreo capitalized on the temporary blackout that occurred during the game. With the Brand Newsroom ready to go, the company created an image relating to the blackout and put it on Twitter. The image was presented using the same style as the one hundred Daily Twist images but read, "You Can Still Dunk in the Dark."

Results/Evaluation

The campaign resulted in a 280 percent increase in Oreo's Facebook shares and a 510 percent increase in its Twitter followers. Oreo's Facebook page received more than 1 million likes during the campaign, while each image posted resulted in an average of ten thousand likes per post. More importantly, the campaign garnered more than 230 earned media impressions.

According to Cindy Chen, Oreo's marketing director, since the campaign's launch, "Oreo has seen a 110% growth in fan interaction per social media post—defined as any combination of shares, likes or comments. The company averaged 7,000 per post before the 'Daily Twist' launch. After, they reached an average of 14,700."[6]

Being both tactical and strategic when creating a social media plan allows a business to successfully use social media to achieve objectives, while at the same time engaging authentically with consumers. The ability to plan ensures that the time spent on social media efforts reinforces company messaging and engagement while building brand awareness, driving traffic, and ultimately engaging consumers.

1 Rosemary Sheridan et al., "Oreo: Daily Twist" (unpublished working paper, College of Saint Rose, 2013).
2 "OREO: Daily Twist," i360, last modified 2013, accessed January 27, 2014, http://www.360i.com/work/oreo-daily-twist.
3 National Chamber Foundation, "The Millennial Generation," US Chamber of Commerce, accessed November 4, 2013, http://emerging.uschamber.com/sites/default/files/MillennialGeneration.pdf.
4 "In Changing News Landscape, Even Television Is Vulnerable," Pew Research Center for the People and the Press, accessed November 4, 2013, http://www.people-press.org/2012/09/27/in-changing-news-landscape-even-television-is-vulnerable.
5 See the Oreo Daily Twist Pinterest Board at http://www.pinterest.com/oreo/daily-twist.
6 Ann-Christine Diaz, "Oreo's 100-Day 'Daily Twist' Campaign Puts Cookie in Conversation," *Advertising Age*, September 10, 2012, accessed November 4, 2013, http://adage.com/article/digital/oreo-s-daily-twist-campaign-puts-cookie-conversation/237104.

Theory into Practice

Discover Everything That Is Pure Michigan

Year after year, the Pure Michigan campaign has won top awards for promoting Michigan's state tourism by incorporating television and radio advertising, a large social media presence, a partnership-advertising program, and public relations efforts into its campaigns. In fact, the state of Michigan's social media program ranked first in a study conducted by Gammet Interactive.[1] The comprehensive study evaluated fifty state tourism offices and their use of social media, including Facebook, Twitter, Flickr, YouTube, and others. The state of Michigan topped the list based on its active Facebook community of almost six hundred thousand fans and more than eighty thousand Twitter followers, along with its popular and active blog at PureMichiganBlog.org.

An interview with Chad Wiebesick, director of social media for Michigan Economic Development Corp. and the brains behind the Pure Michigan campaign, outlines the social media strategy approach that was followed (the interview is available at http://ginaluttrellphd.com/videos).

By using the framework provided in this chapter, can you accurately identify and populate a social media plan using tactics implemented by the state of Michigan? Consider the Circular Model of SoMe for Social Communication (*Share*, *optimize*, *Manage*, *engage*), and ask how a public relations practitioner can thrive in a world inundated with multiple social channels and new influencers.

1 "Michigan Tourism Takes Over No. 1 Spot in Social Media," CBS Detroit, 2010, http://detroit.cbslocal.com/2010/08/05/michigan-tourism-takes-over-no-1-spot-in-social-media.

The Burgeoning Horizon: A Look Forward

And so we have arrived at the end of our journey. You have been introduced to the first instances of people using social media as well as how it has evolved and is practiced today. We've covered much ground, exploring the good, the bad, and the ugly, as well as many of the finer points of social media and public relations. However, I have yet to answer the question of where the profession is headed. I'm sure you are wondering what's next, so let's peek into the future!

Over the past several years, social media has experienced explosive growth. PR practitioners are now able to create and implement viable social strategies, explore new integrated marketing communication approaches, and evaluate a variety of platforms to make content public.

What does all of this mean? It's all good news for public relations professionals and social media strategists. Fantastic news, in fact. And before we part ways, I'll share with you a few of my final thoughts and predictions for the future of social media. But remember, I'm always eager to continue our conversations. Let's chat and connect using Twitter (@ginaluttrell) and through my website (www.ginaluttrellphd. com), where you will find tidbits, case studies, new research, articles, and some video footage that didn't make it into the book. It is my hope that our relationship will grow and mature in the years to come.

On to the good stuff now!

#LRNSMPR

Learn More: Creating Social Media Plans

- "How to Build a Social-Media Strategy That Works": http://entm.ag/1NYZScE
- "7 Steps in Creating a Winning Social Media Marketing Strategy": http://bit.ly/1PFbwKq
- "A Strategic Guide to Social Media for Nonprofits": http://bit.ly/1StYDFx
- "Why Does Social Media Matter?": http://bit.ly/1PFbuIC

$upport

Commitments from C-suite executives will continue to increase in support of social media efforts. These executives not only understand the importance of social media but are also responding with bigger budgets and dedicated resources for social strategies. Reports indicate that social networking spending will reach $35.98 billion over the next two years, representing 16 percent of all digital spending globally. Decision makers clearly understand the value that social media adds to their companies and are willing to support smart initiatives.

Live-Stream and Go

All of the major social media platforms are moving toward full adoption of video in an effort to capture more real-time content that drives so much global conversation. Social media is already moment to moment by nature, but live streaming allows for more "in the now" than ever before. The obsession with live streaming and live social events will ramp up, particularly as Snapchat adds new features, Periscope and Meerkat compete, and Facebook enters the live-streaming game. Social apps will aim to put the user at an event—virtually—as much as possible. Instagram and Snapchat already support on-the-go, in-the-moment updates as opposed to after-event retrospectives and could collectively usher in a new era of immediacy in social media. As virtual reality technology becomes more mainstream, practitioners may have to forget about scheduling the company's social media posts in advance.

Click and Buy

Leading the trend of enabling mobile consumers to purchase products that they have seen in a sponsored post with a single click, Facebook and Pinterest both introduced the "buy" feature on their platforms. This allows users of these social medial channels the option of purchasing a product without ever leaving the app. One can imagine that Instagram and other social platforms will not be far behind in incorporating some form of "buy" button as part of their social campaigns.

Read and Stay

When Facebook rolls out innovative initiatives, you can bet that other social platforms will follow suit. In 2015, the company introduced Instant Articles as a new form of publishing, allowing users to locate referenced articles and play videos instantly when scrolling. Think of this feature as an in-post search engine. Other platforms such as Twitter and Instagram are trying to expand their platforms similarly, allowing users to access additional resources without ever leaving the app. This "never leave our app" trend is expected to increase over time, providing social strategists more opportunities to engage with their audiences on one platform—their own.

Publish and Share

Facebook's introduction of Instant Articles is only the start of a new publishing strategy available to consumers. Supporting publishers are allowed to publish full-length articles to Facebook users, most notably without the need for an external link. The trend of developing multiple options for business and organizational publishing will continue as social platforms continue to innovate ways to keep users in-app for as long as possible. An upcoming project being developed by Twitter, Project Lightning, provides users with a publication avenue that is dynamic in nature, yet functional and flexible at the same time.

Privacy and Trust

With another year of high-profile security breaches inundating the media, privacy concerns will continue to be important to consumers. Snapchat, for example, is wildly popular due to its ability to support users in a private, secure environment. In response to multiple privacy concerns, Facebook is also rolling out numerous privacy awareness tools for its users. Going forward, it would not be unrealistic to

THE FUTURE OF SOCIAL MEDIA

6

Start preparing... NOW!

#1 $upport

#2 Live Streaming

Executive Level Support
Executive level support for social media efforts will continue as executives now understand the value social media brings and are willing to dedicate budgeting dollars toward resources for social strategies.

Increased Live Streaming
The obsession with live-streaming and live social events will continue to ramp up. Companies need to focus on creating opportunities for human engagement between the brand and their audience.

#3 Click & Buy

#4

Click to Purchase
Shopping will become even easier. Consumers who see a product they like in a sponsored post can now simply click to purchase! Pinterest paved the way, but others are following suit.

Social Media Publishing
Publishers, like the Washington Post, are publishing full-length content directly to social platforms. Users can read articles without ever leaving the social app.

#5

#6

Increased Social Budgets
Social networking spending will reach $35.98 billion, representing 16 percent of all digital spending globally. US and Canada place a premium on social media and will increase spending by 31 percent, passing $10 billion for the first time ever.

Importance of Privacy

Users are going to demand more private and secure methods of communication and engagement on social platforms.

Conclusion
We are moving toward a social world where simply tweeting about an upcoming event isn't enough. We are entering a social sphere where users are looking for more impactful and tailored messages. This wave will transform the way we think of social, and hopefully impact the world for the better.

Sources: Social Media: How To Engage, Share, And Connect Second Edition
http://www.emarketer.com/Article/Social-Network-Ad-Spending-Hit-2368-Billion-Worldwide-2015/1012357
http://www.quicksprout.com/2015/01/05/10-marketing-predictions-you-should-prepare-for-in-2015/

consider that the most relevant social platforms will be the ones that provide users with a high level of privacy and security.

The future of public relations and social media is exciting. When I look at where our profession has come and where it's headed, I am filled with anticipation. Public relations practitioners have always been at the epicenter of building relationships with consumers, and social media has only enhanced what we already knew. Companies are searching for professionals who can combine social media understanding with tried-and-true public relations strategies. It's a good time to be in public relations—truly it is!

Notes

[1] "Constant Contact Small Business Pulse," Constant Contact, last modified December 2013, accessed January 27, 2014, http://news.constantcontact.com/sites/constantcontact.newshq.businesswire.com/files/research/file/SMBPulseReport3-26-13.pdf.

[2] R. Luttrell and L. Capizzo, *Public Relations Campaigns: An Integrated Campaigns Approach* (Thousand Oaks, CA: Sage, forthcoming).

[3] "Sample Social Media: Tactical Plan," Marketo, last modified 2013, accessed January 27, 2014, http://www.marketo.com/worksheets/social-media-tactical-plan.

[4] Glen T. Cameron and Dennis L. Wilcox, *Public Relations: Strategies and Tactics* (Boston: Pearson/Allyn and Bacon, 2009).

[5] See the Unilever Global website at http://www.unilever.com.

[6] Scott Collins, "PBS Reveals Who's Really Watching *Downton Abbey*," *Los Angeles Times*, March 28, 2012, accessed January 27, 2014, http://latimesblogs.latimes.com/showtracker/2012/03/pbs-reveals-whos-really-watching-downton-abbey-.html.

[7] Jennifer Kyrnin, "SMART Goals," About.com, 2012, http://webdesign.about.com/od/strategy/qt/smart_goals.htm.

[8] "Breast Self-Awareness Messages," Susan G. Komen Foundation, http://ww5.komen.org/BreastCancer/BreastSelfAwareness.html.

[9] "Sample Social Media: Tactical Plan."

Glossary

authenticity   Being trustworthy, genuine, and real in online interactions.

authority   A person who is a recognized expert on a particular subject.

bitly   A free URL-shortening service that provides statistics for the links that users share online. Bitly condenses long URLs, making them easier to share on social networks such as Twitter.

blog   Created from two words: "web" and "log." Blogs are maintained by individuals or businesses with regular entries of commentary, descriptions of events, and other material such as graphics and videos.

blogger   A person who blogs.

blogroll   Typically found on blogs, a list of links to other blogs or websites that the blogger commonly references or is affiliated with. Blogrolls help bloggers establish and build their blogging communities.

blogTalkRadio   A free web application that allows users to host live online radio shows.

bookmarking   Saving content that you found important or enjoyed or marking where you left off to continue reading later.

chat   Communication over the Internet.

circles   Clusters of a user's friends on Google+, meaning that you can group certain people you choose to connect with on Google+ into specific circles—such as colleagues, college connections, family, and so forth. When you want to share content with only these individuals, you include that circle in your post's sharing options.

citizen Journalism   Any type of news gathering and reporting (including writing and publishing articles, posting photographs, and creating videos about newsworthy topics) that is done by members of the larger general public rather than the mainstream media.

cloud   A network of servers that exist in data centers across the world that allow people to conduct simple activities like checking email, logging into social networking sites, and accessing applications.

CMO   Chief marketing officer.

comment   A response that provides an answer or reaction to a blog post or message on a social network. Comments are a primary form of two-way communication on the social web.

creative commons licenses   Licenses that help creators retain copyright while allowing others to copy, distribute, and make some uses of their work, at least noncommercially.

crowdsourcing   The practice of obtaining needed services, ideas, or content by soliciting contributions from a large group of people, especially from an online community, rather than from traditional avenues. Wikipedia is the most prominent example of crowdsourcing.

dashboard   A user interface that organizes and streamlines online activity so that a person can publish content, respond, monitor, update, and listen from one central place.

ebook   An electronic version of a printed book.

engagement   Participation in the online community via direct conversations.

facebook   A social networking site that connects people with friends, colleagues, family, and other people across the globe. Facebook is currently the largest social network in the world.

favorite   A means to bookmark information or to illustrate to the online community that you like what you are reading.

feed   Frequently updated content published by a website. Feeds are usually used for news and blog websites, as well as for distributing a variety of digital content, including pictures, audio, and video. Feeds can additionally be used to deliver audio content. They are commonly referred to as RSS feeds, XML feeds, syndicated content, Twitter feeds, or web feeds.

friends   Individuals you consider close enough to see your Facebook profile and engage with you.

google+   Google's social network.

hangout   A video service on Google+ that allows individuals to video chat with multiple Google+ users at one time. Users can name the chats, watch YouTube videos together, open Google Docs with colleagues, and much more.

hashtag   A word or unspaced phrase prefixed with the hash, or pound, symbol ("#"), such as #LRNSMPR or #PRStudChat. Hashtags link conversations among people with similar interests.

hootSuite   A social media management system that allows brands to streamline social media efforts and campaigns across social networks that include Twitter, Facebook, LinkedIn, WordPress, and Google+ pages. Social strategists collaboratively monitor, engage with, and measure the results of social campaigns from one secure, web-based dashboard.

infographic A representation, also known as an information graphic, of information in a graphic format designed to make the data easily understandable at a glance. People use infographics to quickly communicate a message, to simplify the presentation of large amounts of data, to see data patterns and relationships, and to monitor changes in variables over time.

instagram A photo-sharing application that lets users take photos, apply filters to their images, and share the photos instantly on the Instagram network and other social networks, including Facebook, Flickr, Twitter, Pinterest, and Foursquare.

keywords Specific words used to describe content that ultimately boosts visibility and rankings on the web.

klout A measure of social influence. Klout allows users to connect various social accounts and then provides users with a Klout score. The score is out of one hundred; the higher the score, the more influence a user has in the social world.

like An action that can be taken by a Facebook user to illustrate appreciation of content shared by others.

link-Back A notification to authors, such as bloggers, when other authors link to one of their online publications. This enables authors to keep track of who is linking, or referring, to their articles, blogs, and other online publications.

linkedIn A business-oriented social networking site.

listening Monitoring conversations and activity occurring on the web.

livecast Streaming of video or audio so that users can experience an event together via the web.

mashup The combination, visualization, and aggregation of webpages and applications that use and combine data from two or more sources.

meerkat A mobile app that enables users to broadcast live video streaming through their mobile devices.

meme An image with text above and below it (although it can also come in video and link form). A meme on the Internet is used to describe a thought, idea, joke, or concept shared online.

participation Engagement in online activity while contributing content.

periscope A video streaming/broadcasting service from Twitter.

permalink An address, or URL, for a particular post within a blog or website.

podcast A series of digital media files, either audio or video, that are released episodically and often downloaded through an RSS feed.

real-time search The method of indexing content being published online into search engine results with virtually no delay.

retweet (RT) To share another person's tweet. This is a great way to spread links exponentially. A best practice is to credit the tweet that you are retweeting. Clicking the "Retweet" button on the newsfeed page of your Twitter account will make this happen automatically. Use the RT symbol and copy and paste, simply adding "(via @username)" after the RT.

RSS feed RSS (really simple syndication) is a group of web-feed formats used to publish frequently updated content such as blogs and videos in a standardized format. Content publishers can syndicate a feed, which allows users to subscribe to the content and read it when they have time, from a location other than the original website or blog, such as a reader or mobile device.

search engine optimization (SEO) The process of improving the volume or quality of traffic to a website from search engines via unpaid or organic search traffic such as Google.

sentiment The attitude of user comments related to a brand online.

skype A free program that allows for text, audio, and video chats between users.

slideshare An online social network for sharing presentations and documents.

snapchat A mobile messaging application used to share photos, videos, text, and drawings.

social media Media designed to be disseminated through social interaction.

social media monitoring A process of monitoring and responding to interactions occurring on social media sites.

social sphere The entirety of one's connections on the web, through social media and various networks.

tag A keyword used to describe content on a blog or in social networks.

tag Cloud A visual collection of the most frequent tags produced by a user, blog, profile, page, or descriptions on webpages.

transparency Honest, open, authentic participation in social media.

tweet An update shared on Twitter.

tweetup or twitterchat Events organized on Twitter.

views Number of times content (including text, photos, and videos) is viewed by people.

Index

About the Author

Regina Luttrell, PhD, is associate professor of public relations and social media at Eastern Michigan University, where she researches, publishes about, and discusses public relations, social media, and the Millennial generation's roles in both the classroom and the workforce. Prior to entering the educational field, Luttrell spent the first half of her career in corporate public relations and marketing. Her extensive background includes strategic development and implementation of public relations and social media, advertising, marketing, and corporate communications. She has led multiple rebranding campaigns, managed high-level crisis situations, designed numerous websites, and garnered media coverage that included hits with the *New York Times*, the *CBS Evening News*, and the Associated Press. Her recent publications include "Diversity and Inclusion in the 21st Century: Guidelines for Managers," "An In-Depth Look at R.A.C.E: Creating a Public Relations Plan," "5 Questions to Ask When Writing News Releases," and *The Millennial Mindset: Unraveling Fact from Fiction*, which garnered rave reviews.